International Series in Operations Research & Management Science

Volume 271

More information about this series at http://www.springer.com/series/6161

Yu Yu • Yao Chen • Qinfen Shi

Strategy and Performance of Knowledge Flow

University-Industry Collaborative Innovation in China

 Springer

Yu Yu
College of Auditing and Evaluation
Nanjing Audit University
Nanjing, Jiangsu, China

Qinfen Shi
Suzhou University of Science
& Technology
Suzhou, Jiangsu, China

Yao Chen
College of Auditing and Evaluation
Nanjing Audit University
Nanjing, Jiangsu, China

Manning School of Business
University of Massachusetts at Lowell
Lowell, MA, USA

ISSN 0884-8289   ISSN 2214-7934   (electronic)
International Series in Operations Research & Management Science
ISBN 978-3-319-77925-6   ISBN 978-3-319-77926-3   (eBook)
https://doi.org/10.1007/978-3-319-77926-3

Library of Congress Control Number: 2018935602

Printed on acid-free paper

This Springer imprint is published by the registered company Springer International Publishing AG part of Springer Nature.
The registered company address is: Gewerbestrasse 11, 6330 Cham, Switzerland

Preface

A new round of technological revolution and industrial transformation is in the making, further sharpening international competition to stay ahead of the curve. China has entered a new phase of economic development featuring deep structural adjustments amid the ongoing driving competitive forces. Only through innovation can China sustain its strong momentum of development. Now more than ever, the powerful forces of science, technology, and innovation are needed to further enhance the domestic economy.

Amid downward economic pressure, innovation-driven development should be the core of China's new growth impetus. China should actively promote collaborative innovation and utilize the innovations of systems and mechanisms on policy projects. China must foster a collaborative innovation system to achieve sustainable growth and encourage universities, scientific research institutes, and enterprises to carry out in-depth cooperation, establish strategic alliances of collaborative innovation, promote the sharing of resources, jointly carry out major scientific research projects, make practical achievements in key realms, and popularize the innovation approach based on core-group innovation that is enabled by wider circles of collaboration. Greater support is expected to be given to companies in setting up collaborative innovation platforms with universities, research institutes, and makers.

Collaborative innovations are based on knowledge integration and knowledge sharing in order to create new knowledge. The initial processes in collaborative innovation system involve flows of knowledge. In this regard, how to accelerate the knowledge flow in the university-industry collaborative innovation nexus is the key for China to foster a system that can achieve sustainable growth.

In this book we examine the knowledge flow in the process of this particular nexus. We look at knowledge flow problems in collaborative innovation from both the micro-level and macro-level. The book consists of 11 chapters, and each one is summarized as follows.

Chapter 1 provides a comprehensive review about the classical development of university-industry collaborative innovation (UICI). Next, we summarize the development of UICI in China and address its challenges in the country. Given these challenges, we propose the main research questions from the knowledge perspective. This chapter also presents the research outline in this book.

Chapter 2 constructs the model of knowledge value chain in a university and analyzes the mechanism of university knowledge value-added in the UICI process. We measure the efficiency of university knowledge value-added in 31 provinces of China through an input-oriented data envelopment analysis (DEA) model.

Chapter 3 illustrates the cooperation mechanism of the UICI system. Considering the complex internal structure of this collaborative innovation system, we establish a network DEA model with parallel decision-making units (DMUs) to assess the performance of UICI in China.

Chapter 4 addresses an empirical study that relates Big Five Personality traits to knowledge flow performance in UICI. In addition to the main effects of personality traits, it is hypothesized that trust and justice mediate or moderate the efforts on the relationship between personality traits and knowledge flow performance. We test this relationship in a sample of researchers from Chinese universities.

Chapter 5 demonstrates that goals can significantly influence individual and team performances according to the theory of motivation. In this framework, the aim of this chapter's research is to investigate relations among team goal, motivation, personality, and knowledge sharing performance in collaborative R&D teams at Chinese universities. For this purpose, we employ a structure equation model (SEM) approach to test the hypotheses in the context of collaborative R&D teams, drawing on a sample of 243 responses from eight universities in Jiangsu, China.

Chapter 6 constructs a colored Petri net model of knowledge flow based on knowledge life cycle to study the asynchronization and concurrency of tacit and explicit knowledge flows, as well as the distribution and flowing patterns in the process of UICI. The model uses tokens with different colors to represent various types of knowledge. Furthermore, we adopt CPN Tools to analyze the boundedness and liveliness of each node in the colored Petri net.

Chapter 7 shows the mechanism of knowledge value-added in the process of UICI and employs the evolutionary game theory based on bounded rationality to explore the best evolutionary stable strategy (ESS).

Chapter 8 divides the knowledge agents into different types according to the various behaviors of knowledge agents in the process of knowledge sharing in collaborative innovation. Considering the bounded rationality of knowledge agents, we construct an agent-based model to illustrate the knowledge sharing process based on the theory of cellular automaton. NetLogo platform is employed to simulate the knowledge sharing behavior of those different types of knowledge agents in this chapter.

Chapter 9 models knowledge flow in UICI as a barter process in which agents exchange knowledge. More innovation is argued to occur, because small-world networks enable dense and clustered relationships to coexist with distant and more diverse relationships. In this sense, we numerically study the knowledge innovation and sharing process on small-world networks. The average knowledge stock level as a function of time is measured, and the corresponding variance of knowledge stock is defined and computed.

Chapter 10 applies the differential game theory to analyze the knowledge flow between enterprises and universities in UICI. The equilibrium knowledge flow strategies of these two are explored in a dynamic framework. Furthermore, we compare three different optimal knowledge flow strategies.

Chapter 11 concludes the book and suggests some topics for future research.

This book intends to provide a better understanding of the mechanism of knowledge flow in UICI from theoretical and practical research undertaken on this nexus in China. Furthermore, it will broaden our knowledge of the equilibrium strategies that are adopted by industry and universities so as to further improve the efficiency of knowledge flow in the UICI process in China. The research findings of this book provide some policy implications for policy makers to establish a collaborative and interactive innovation system.

The intended readership of the book includes advanced undergraduate and graduate students of marketing, management science, operations research, and quantitative business administration who have an interest in strategic and intertemporal decision-making. The book can also be used by students in game theory who wish to get an insight into a particular field of application – namely, dynamic competition. Moreover, the book should be valuable to researchers in marketing, management science, applied mathematics, and operations research who work, or intend to work, on dynamic competition. Generally speaking, the topics covered by the book relate to such research areas as knowledge management, collaborative innovation, and organizational behavior.

The authors would like to thank Prof. Weiwei Zhu of Nanjing University of Posts and Telecommunications for his constructive comments and suggestions that have helped to improve the quality of the book to its current standard. The authors also would like to thank Dr. Meini Han of Nanjing Audit University, and Ms. Lulu Gai, Ms. Yang Huang, Ms. Lu Gu, Ms. Yanling Qiu, Ms. Yue Wang, Ms. Xuewen Xiang, and Ms. Yufei Zhang for their contribution to the realization of this book. In addition, we would like to thank all the authors of the papers cited. Their original research has inspired us a lot and encouraged us to join this exciting research field. This research is supported by the National Natural Science Foundation of China (Grant No. 71771161, 71471091, 71771126, 71271119, and 71301080) and the Priority Academic Program Development of Jiangsu Higher Education Institutions.

Nanjing, Jiangsu, China   Yu Yu
Lowell, MA, USA   Yao Chen
Suzhou, Jiangsu, China   Qinfen Shi

Contents

About the Authors

Yu Yu is a lecturer in the College of Auditing and Evaluation, Nanjing Audit University, China. His research interests are in the areas of knowledge management, innovation management, and performance evaluation. He received his PhD in Management Science and Engineering from Hohai University in China in 2016. He has also worked as a research trainee at Desautels Faculty of Management in McGill University from September 2014 to August 2015. He has published over 20 articles in international and Chinese journals.

Yao Chen is Professor of Operations Management, Manning School of Business, University of Massachusetts at Lowell. She is also a distinguished Professor in College of Auditing and Evaluation, Nanjing Audit University, China. Her current research interests include efficiency and productivity issues of information systems, information technology's impact on operations performance, and methodology development of data envelopment analysis. Her researches are published in journals such as *European Journal of Operational Research*, *OMEGA*, *Computers and Operations Research*, *Annals of Operations Research*, *International Journal of Production Economics*, and others.

Qinfen Shi is Professor in Business School, Suzhou University of Science and Technology. Her research interests are in the areas of knowledge management and innovation management. She has published over 100 articles in Chinese journals and international journals and has more than 1000 citations. She received her PhD from Soochow University in 2006. She has served as principal investigator of five general programs of National Natural Science Foundation of China (NSFC). She is also the member of Chinese Association for Science of Science and S&T Policy.

List of Figures

List of Tables

Chapter 1
Introduction

1.1 University-Industry Collaborative Innovation

Faster technological development, shorter product life cycles, and more intense global competition have transformed the current competitive environment for most firms (Bettis and Hitt 1995). This new competitive landscape forces organizations to actively acquire knowledge since a firm's competitive advantage is now more dependent on continuous knowledge development and enhancement (Santoro and Gopalakrishnan 2000). As competitive pressures increase, firms are often placed in positions where they have neither the time nor resources to internally develop the knowledge needed to achieve competitive success through product and process innovations. Thus, knowledge acquisition from external source partners has been identified as a key competency for sustained success in the competitive marketplace. A common and frequently viable option in this situation is the acquisition of technological knowledge from outside sources.

It is commonly accepted that universities are an important source of new knowledge, especially in the areas of science and technology. First, universities train the next generation of leaders, managers, and professional and technical personnel. Second, through their research, they are engaged in the creation of codified knowledge in different forms—publications, patents, and prototypes. Third, they contribute to local and national economies through research commercialization, problem-solving, and providing public space (Poyago-Theotoky et al. 2002; Abdullateef 2000). With the rise of the knowledge economy, universities are increasingly seen as a source of knowledge, innovation, and technological progress.

A large body of literature suggests that universities and industrial firms have complementary resources and skills (Bower 1993). The notion of complementarity is therefore key to university-industry collaborative innovation (UICI). For example, while universities have access to intellectual resources and a world-class basic research infrastructure, industrial firms usually have practical expertise, financial

© Springer International Publishing AG, part of Springer Nature 2018
Y. Yu et al., *Strategy and Performance of Knowledge Flow*,
International Series in Operations Research & Management Science 271,
https://doi.org/10.1007/978-3-319-77926-3_1

resources, internship opportunities for students, and employment opportunities for graduates and students. In some developed countries with strong innovation capacities, multiple players, such as enterprises, higher-learning institutions, government agencies, and nongovernmental organizations, have joined hands to participate in the research and development drive (Santoro and Gopalakrishnan 2000).

Collaboration between universities and industries is widely recognized as one of the key factors that contribute to the improvement of innovative capabilities of companies (Dyer et al. 2004; Lundvall 1992) and the development of innovative countries (Lundvall 1992; Nelson 1993). The concept of university and industry (UI) research collaboration is not an invention of the twenty-first century but has existed since the 1800s in Europe and since the industrial revolution in the United States. These partnerships have, however, increased and intensified over the past decade and have received much public and institutional attention.

The growth of UI research collaboration is due to various factors. Two key factors are more effective and efficient knowledge transfer for the benefits of industry and more funding opportunities for the benefits of academic researchers. Furthermore, the industry partner benefits from direct access to state-of-the-art research, can potentially influence the research agenda, and can experience a positive effect on overall corporate culture as a result of the collaboration. At the same time, the university partner benefits from the opportunity to apply research results to market products, from access to good facilities and from gathering first-hand information about the state of the market. It stands to reason, therefore, that UI research collaborations will continue to grow in number, making it relatively safe to say that it is a very promising model for innovation. There are many types of university-industry links, with different objectives, scopes, and institutional arrangements, which are adapted from Perkmann and Walsh (2007) (see Table 1.1).

Collaboration may be more or less intense and may focus on training or research activities. Collaboration may be formal or informal, from formal equity partnerships, contracts, research projects, patent licensing, and so on to human capital mobility, publications, and interactions in conferences and expert groups, and among others (Hagedoorn et al. 2000). It is also useful to differentiate between short-term and long-term collaborations. Short-term collaborations generally consist of on-demand problem-solving with predefined results and tend to be articulated through contract research, consulting, and licensing. Long-term collaborations are associated with joint projects and public-private partnerships (including private-funded university institutes or chairs, joint university-industry research centers, and research consortia), often allowing firms to contract for a core set of services and to periodically recontract for specific deliverables in a flexible manner. Longer-term collaborations are more strategic and open ended, providing a multifaceted platform where firms can develop a stronger innovative capacity in the long run, building upon the capabilities, methods, and tools of universities (Koschatzky and Stahlecker 2010).

The form that university-industry collaborations take differs widely from country to country. Rahm et al. (2000) explore these similarities and differences with specific attention to the implementation of university-industry R&D collaboration in the United States, the United Kingdom, and Japan. These three countries differ vastly

Table 1.1 A typology of university-industry links, from higher to lower intensity

High (relationships)	Research partnerships	Interorganizational arrangements for pursuing collaborative R&D, including research consortia and joint projects
	Research services	Research-related activities commissioned to universities by industrial clients, including contract research, consulting, quality control, testing, certification, and prototype development
	Shared infrastructure	Use of university labs and equipment by firms, business incubators, and technology parks located within universities
Medium (mobility)	Academic entrepreneurship	Development and commercial exploitation of technologies pursued by academic inventors through a company they (partly) own (spin-off companies)
	Human resource training and transfer	Training of industry employees, internship programs, postgraduate training in industry, secondments to industry for university faculty and research staff, and adjunct faculty of industry participants
Low (transfer)	Commercialization of intellectual property (IP)	Transfer of university-generated IP (such as patents) to firms (e.g., via licensing)
	Scientific publications	Use of codified scientific knowledge within industry
	Informal interaction	Formation of social relationships (e.g., conferences, meetings, social networks)

Source: Adapted from Perkmann and Walsh (2007), Tables 2 and 3

in the way that they implement their respective R&D policies. Some of these differences stem from national culture, others from the historical evolution of the institutions that support innovation efforts, and some from the extent of available resources (both monetary and other) that can be applied to the effort. Despite their differences, Japan, the United Kingdom, and the United States serve as models of particular aspects of innovation policy: Japan for cooperative strategies as well as technological targeting; the United Kingdom for research foresight planning; and the United States for long-term investment in basic scientific research.

The United States and the United Kingdom tend to share a number of similarities, while Japan is very different. Many of the similarities and differences begin with the nature of higher education in each country, the cultural norms that dominate, as well as the economic and legal structures. The United States and United Kingdom have large research university systems that possess enormous capacity and potential, as well as growing government commitment to fostering university-industry collaboration. Japan has a far smaller university system, many cultural and legal barriers to professorial involvement with industrial R&D, and a tradition of relying on Western science to fuel its technological advance. Having said that, Japan has adopted a new policy direction that seeks to change its universities using the United States as a model.

When looking at China, the government developed its own idiosyncratic system of university/public research-industry relations that first centered on the higher education sector (including China Academy of Science (CAS)) and was secondly based on entrepreneurial action by universities as institutions rather than by individual faculty. The mid-1990s especially experienced a surge of setups of so-called university-owned technology enterprises (UOTE) or university-run enterprises. These enterprises had the double virtue of circumventing both the problem of finding a suitable industrial partner and the restrictive legislation concerning "real" spin-offs, since the vast majority of the shares was typically held by the universities. As a side effect, many universities hoped to generate extra income in times of scarce financial resources. Similar enterprises can be found at leading public research institutions such as CAS. In short, the type, extent, and success of university-industry R&D collaborations vary greatly by country.

1.2 University-Industry Collaboration in China

China suffered in the past from the legacy of its past innovation model being influenced by the former Soviet Union, which separated publicly funded research institutions and universities from product development within firms. Ever since the adoption of the opening-up policy in 1978, China has initiated a number of programs to reform its innovation system (Ma et al. 2009) as follows:

In 1992, a policy-oriented "University-Industry Alliances on Collaborative Development Engineering" was jointly initiated in China by the former State National Economic and Trade Committee (the main body of the current Ministry of Commerce and National Economic Development & Reform Committee), the Ministry of Education, and China Academy of Science (CAS).

In 2006, China announced its "Guideline for the National Medium- and Long-term Science and Technology Development Programs (2006–2020)" for the next 15 years. The focus is to emphasize the strategic role of technology innovation and to lay out a number of goals and specific measures so as to realize China's aspiration to become an innovation center by 2020.

In 2007, the Progress of Science and Technology Law was passed. Often referred to as the Chinese Bayh-Dole Act—a celebrated 1980's US patent rights law credited with accelerating US industrial innovation— this law enables the intellectual property generated by government-funded research to be commercialized by the research group that conducted the investigation.

On April 24, 2011, former President Hu Jintao gave an important speech at the conference for the 100th anniversary of the founding of Tsinghua University, indicating that China would actively promote collaborative innovation. Moreover, by depending on innovations of systems and mechanisms and policy projects, China shall encourage universities, scientific research institutes, and enterprises to carry out in-depth cooperation, establish strategic alliances of collaborative innovation, promote the sharing of resources, jointly carry out major scientific research projects, and make practical achievements in key realms.

Taking that speech as the basis, the Ministry of Education and the Ministry of Finance decided to launch "Plan 2011." "Plan 2011" is open to universities of various kinds; takes universities as major objects of its implementation; actively attracts participation by scientific research institutes, industrial enterprises, local governments, and international innovation forces; greatly encourages universities to cooperate with universities, scientific research institutes, industrial enterprises, local governments, and foreign scientific research organizations; and explores collaborative innovation ways to meet different requirements. "Plan 2011" focuses on reforms of universities' systems and mechanisms, focuses on promoting the collaborative development of universities' internal and external innovation forces, and targets the setup of collaborative modes. Since 2012, 38 national collaborative innovation centers (CICs) have been established nationwide. Those government-funded centers are designed to link science with industry for the benefit of the economy.

According to the Global Innovation Index report, which was co-released by the World Intellectual Property Organization, Cornell University, and INSEAD in August 2016, China has for the first time joined the world's top 25 most innovative economies, which are dominated by developed economies. The report shows that China's research and development expenditure as a percentage of GDP ranks second in the world after that of the United States. Though China is seen as a "follower" of science and technology and a "manufacturer" for global firms, the government hopes it can evolve into an innovative country by 2020, as noted by former President Mr. Hu Jintao: "It is necessary to strive unremittingly to build an innovation-oriented society."

China has until now achieved astounding growth in both its economy and technology over the past three decades and has aspired to be at the center of the world's technology/innovation, rather than be the world's factory. China's research and development (R&D) spending has consistently gone up despite its slowing economy, as the country seeks to foster new growth engines by boosting innovation. R&D spending hit 1.42 trillion yuan (about $208.38 billion) in 2015, up 8.9% over 2014, according to a report jointly published by the National Bureau of Statistics (NBS), the Ministry of Science and Technology, and the Ministry of Finance. R&D expenditure equaled 2.07% of GDP in 2015, up from 2.02% in 2014 and marking the third straight year above the 2% mark. Chinese companies were the largest contributor, according to the report. Enterprises, led by those in the manufacturing, computer, and telecommunications sectors, spent 1.09 trillion yuan on R&D in 2015, up 8.2% from the previous year and accounting for 76.8% of the total. R&D spending by government-affiliated research institutes expanded 10.9% to 213.65 billion yuan, taking up 15.1% of the total, while that by universities and colleges grew 11.2% to 99.86 billion yuan or 7% of the total.

1.3   Research Questions

University-industry cooperation is of strategic significance in terms of the cultivation of engineers and technicians at different levels, scientific research and knowledge innovation, industrial upgrade, and the development of the national economy.

Despite being the world's second-largest R&D spender behind the United States, China still lags behind developed countries that normally spend 3% of their GDP on R&D. Studies show that in developed countries with a technological edge, R&D investment generally accounts for more than 2% of their GDP, while science and technology contribute to more than 70% of economic growth. Those countries are also much less dependent on foreign technologies in achieving economic growth. However, R&D investment in China has reached just 2% of GDP, while science and technology contribute to less than 40% of economic growth. Furthermore, China is also more dependent on foreign technologies for economic development, and interactions and R&D activities between firms and academia are rare outside of science parks and university-run incubators (Lu and Etzkowitz 2008).

There has been a lack of integration of knowledge networks between large state-owned enterprise, foreign-owned R&D, and Chinese small- to medium-sized enterprises (SMEs) in terms of high-tech development and innovation collaboration. The overall innovation capacity of Chinese firms and the technological level of China's industries to independently innovate are low. The emerging Chinese paradox is the disparity between high R&D spending and the relatively low level of industrial innovation (Lu and Etzkowitz 2008). The Global Innovation Index 2017 states that the index of university/industry research collaboration is 55.9 for China, ranking it 29 among the 127 countries.

According to OECD reviews of innovation policy, China's national innovation system (NIS) is not fully developed and is still imperfectly integrated, with many weak linkages between actors and subsystems (e.g., regional versus national). To the outside observer, NIS appears as an "archipelago" or is made up of a very large number of "innovative islands" with limited synergies between them and, above all, limited spillovers beyond them. China should learn from these experiences and establish a collaborative and interactive innovation system that enables efficient collaboration among various players in order to achieve sustainable growth (OECD 2008). Collaborative innovations between Chinese firms and research institutions have certainly not been promoted effectively so as to optimize the diffusion and utilization of new knowledge (Lu and Etzkowitz 2008).

Amid downward economic pressure, innovation-driven development should be the core of China's new growth impetus. China should undertake various measures to make up for its deficiency in original innovation and fundamental research to enhance the nation's independent innovation capacity. China should foster a collaborative innovation system to achieve sustainable growth, and the key to achieving that goal is to establish a market-oriented innovation mechanism that centers on enterprises. In some developed countries with strong innovation capacities, multiple players, such as enterprises, higher-learning institutions, government agencies, and nongovernmental organizations, have joined hands to participate in the R&D drive. China must learn from their experiences and establish a collaborative and interactive innovation system that enables efficient collaboration among various players.

Collaborative innovations are based on knowledge integration and knowledge sharing for the creation of new knowledge. The initial processes in a collaborative innovation system are flows of knowledge (Wang 2012). In this sense, how to accelerate the knowledge flow in UICI is the key for China to foster a system to achieve sustainable growth. In this book we will examine the knowledge flow in the process of collaborative innovation, investigating knowledge flow problems in collaborative innovation at the microlevel and macro-level.

First, one is required to track and analyze the development of UICI in China. Thus, an objective evaluation of UICI efficiency (UICIE) is necessary. We propose the university knowledge value chain (UKVC) and measure the performance of university knowledge value-added with the DEA model. Moreover, collaborative innovation is a complex system with the integration of each innovation element as well as the unhindered flow of innovation resources within the system. The UICI system has a complex internal structure that consists of multiple subsystems. Network DEA will be employed to evaluate UICI's performance in China, considering such complexity from the macro-level aspect.

Second, based on the development of UICI, it is necessary to identify the factors influencing its effectiveness and performance. Knowledge flow comprises the set of processes, events, and activities through which data, information, and knowledge are transferred from one entity to another. The end results are knowledge capture, creation, retention, and application (Mu et al. 2008). Previous studies have focused on different aspects as predecessors of knowledge flow (Bell and Zaheer 2007; Sorenson et al. 2006). However, organizational knowledge creation is the process of making available and amplifying knowledge created by individuals. Collaboration between individuals is an essential part of organizational knowledge creation (von Krogh et al. 2012). Enabling knowledge creation and knowledge sharing is essential to innovation and organizational success. At the individual level, it may evoke perceptions of a conflict of interest or vulnerability (Mooradian et al. 2006). Moreover, individual behavior is typically determined by abstract personality traits (Jadin et al. 2013). Personality is the sum total of the physical, mental, emotional, and social characteristics of an individual. I. Nonaka et al. (2008) argue that knowledge as a management resource cannot be understood without understanding the interactions of the human beings who create it. This book will describe an empirical study that relates Big Five personality to knowledge flow in the process of UICI in China. Moreover, we employ the cellular automata model to stimulate the knowledge flow in UICI based on different knowledge agents' personality traits.

Third, after identifying the key factors influencing the knowledge flow in the UICI, we will explore the optimal knowledge flow strategy in the process of it to improve the effectiveness and performance of it. We initially will explore the knowledge flow strategy with bounded rationality. It is obvious that UICI is a dynamic complex system with a shortened knowledge life cycle that requires continuous knowledge flowing among different innovation elements. Thus, the optimal knowledge flow strategy should be explored in a dynamic framework. Differential game models incorporate the dynamic effect of the current state and the decisions on future states. Differential games can be considered as a fusion of game theory and optimal control theory and will be applied to solve these research questions.

1.4   Research Outline

In order to accelerate the knowledge flow in UICI, this book examines the knowledge flow in the process of collaborative innovation. The reminder of this book is structured as follows.

Chapter 2 constructs the model of knowledge value chain in universities and analyzes the mechanism of university knowledge value-added in the UICI process. We measure the efficiency of university knowledge value-added of 31 provinces in China with the input-oriented DEA model.

Chapter 3 illustrates the cooperation mechanism of universities and industries in the collaborative innovation system. Considering the complex internal structure of this system, we establish a network DEA model with parallel decision-making units to assess the performance of UICI in China.

Chapter 4 addresses an empirical study that relates Big Five personality traits to knowledge flow performance in UICI. In addition to the main effects of personality traits, we also hypothesize that trust and justice mediate or moderate the efforts on the relationship between personality traits and knowledge flow performance. We test the relationship with a sample of researchers from Chinese universities.

Chapter 5 demonstrates that goals can significantly influence individual and team performance according to the theory of motivation. In this framework, the aim of this chapter's research is to look at the relations among team goal, motivation, personality, and knowledge sharing performance in collaborative R&D teams at Chinese universities. For this purpose, we employ a structure equation model (SEM) approach to test the hypotheses in the context of collaborative R&D teams, drawing on a sample of 243 responses from eight universities in Jiangsu, China.

Chapter 6 constructs a colored Petri net model of knowledge flow based on the knowledge life cycle to study the asynchronization and concurrency of tacit and explicit knowledge flows, as well as the distribution and flowing patterns in the process of UICI. The model uses tokens with different colors to represent various types of knowledge. Furthermore, we adopt CPN Tools to analyze the boundedness and liveliness of each node in the colored Petri net.

Chapter 7 shows the mechanism of knowledge-value added in the process of UICI and employs the evolutionary game theory based on bounded rationality to explore the best evolutionary stable strategy (ESS).

Chapter 8 divides the knowledge agents into different types according to the various behaviors of knowledge agents in the process of knowledge sharing in collaborative innovation. Considering the bounded rationality of knowledge agents, we construct an agent-based model to illustrate the knowledge sharing process based on the theory of cellular automaton and employ NetLogo platform to simulate the knowledge sharing behavior of those different types of knowledge agents in this chapter.

Chapter 9 models the knowledge flow in UICI as a barter process in which agents exchange knowledge. It is argued that more innovation occurs, because small-world networks enable dense and clustered relationships to coexist with distant and more diverse relationships. In this sense, we study numerically the knowledge innovation and sharing process on small-world networks. The average knowledge stock level as a function of time is measured, and the corresponding variance of knowledge stock is also defined and computed.

Chapter 10 applies the differential game theory to analyze the knowledge flow between enterprise and university in UICI. The equilibrium knowledge flow strategies of enterprises and universities are explored in a dynamic framework. Furthermore, we compare three different optimal knowledge flow strategies.

Chapter 11 concludes the book and suggests some topics for future research.

This book provides a better understanding of the mechanism of knowledge flow in UICI from the theoretical and practical research aspects on it in China. Furthermore, it broadens our knowledge of the equilibrium strategies adopted by industries and universities in order to improve the efficiency of knowledge flow in the process of UICI in China. The research findings of this book offer some policy implications to help policy makers establish a strong collaborative and interactive innovation system.

Chapter 2
Measuring the Performance of Knowledge Value-Added in University-Industry Collaborative Innovation

2.1 Introduction

Universities play an important role as a source of fundamental knowledge and, occasionally, relevant industrial technology in modern knowledge-based economies. Universities are the main knowledge dissemination and innovation places in national innovation system (NIS). Higher education in China has played an important role in the nation's economy, science progress, and social development by bringing up a large scale of advanced talents and experts for the construction of socialist modernization. In 2015, all together there were 2560 higher education institutions (HEIs), among which 1219 were universities, 275 were independent colleges, and 1341 were higher vocational colleges. There were also 292 higher education institutions for adults. In 2015, the total number of new entrant admitted by and the total enrollment of undergraduates in regular HEIs were, respectively, 7,378,495 and 26,252,968. The total number of new entrants admitted by and the total enrollment of postgraduates in regular HEIs were, respectively, 645,055 and 1,911,406. The total number of new entrants admitted by and the total enrollment of new recruitments and the total enrollment of adult higher education institutions were 2,367,455 and 6,359,352. China spent nearly 3.9 trillion yuan ($565.6 billion) on education in 2016, an increase of 7.57% from 2015, according to preliminary statistics released by the Ministry of Education. Expenditure for higher education exceeded 1 trillion yuan, up 6.22% from 2015. Every year, universities input a great deal of knowledge and employ teachers and researchers to create new knowledge value on the original knowledge basis in order to achieve knowledge value-added through knowledge accumulation, knowledge sharing, knowledge internalization, and other knowledge-based activities. Universities also input a large number of knowledge resources to create new knowledge in order to improve the university knowledge stock. In view of this, it is important to discuss the efficiency of university knowledge value-added to find out the influence factors of this value added. It will help universities to

© Springer International Publishing AG, part of Springer Nature 2018
Y. Yu et al., *Strategy and Performance of Knowledge Flow*,
International Series in Operations Research & Management Science 271,
https://doi.org/10.1007/978-3-319-77926-3_2

optimize their allocation of knowledge resources so as to achieve highly effective knowledge value-added efficiency.

This chapter constructs the model of university knowledge value chain (UKVC) and analyzes the mechanism of university knowledge value-added. We analyze the efficiency of university knowledge value-added for 31 provinces in China with the input-oriented BCC model. The research finds that Beijing and 13 other provinces exhibit effective university knowledge value-added efficiency, and the technical efficiency of universities in Yunnan province is the highest among all. University knowledge value-added efficiency of Chongqing and 13 other provinces was ineffective. There was input redundancy or a lack of knowledge output at these universities.

This chapter is in seven parts, of which this is the first one. Section 2.2 provides a theoretical framework of university knowledge value chain. Section 2.3 describes the knowledge value-added efficiency of universities. Section 2.4 supplies the basic DEA history and models, while the data and the models are in Sect. 2.5. The results of the analysis are in Sect. 2.6, while the final section presents conclusions that can be drawn from the study.

2.2   University Knowledge Value Chain

The concept of value chain was described and popularized by Porter (1996) as a value-adding process in which an organization might engage. Based on this understanding, more researchers have continued to improve the knowledge value chain (KVC) with their own specific emphasis. Holsapple and Singh (2001) advance a knowledge chain model, which is comprised of five primary activities that an organization's knowledge processors perform when manipulating knowledge resources, plus four secondary activities that support and guide their performance. Lee and Yang (2000) introduce the knowledge value chain model as a knowledge management framework. The model consists of knowledge infrastructure, the process of knowledge management, and the interaction among those components resulting in knowledge performance. Eustace (2003) develop it as a model that integrates different perspectives from various interest groups. Carlucci et al. (2004) model KVC as a series of stages of KM. Wang and Ahmed (2005) set up a KVC that has four categories: KM processes, KM enablers, organizational capabilities, and performance. The KM value-adding processes come together to create capabilities through the infrastructural systems and procedures of the organization. KM processes are primary activities involved in the knowledge value-adding process. Cooke et al. (2006) propose a biosciences knowledge value chain (BKVC) that passes from exploration through examination to exploitation knowledge as basic research evolves to the stage of preclinical and clinical trials and then to the commercialization stage where due diligence skills and venture capital skills ultimately determine whether or not a "prospect" start-up may reach stock market listing, license its technology, or be acquired by another owner. Xu and Bernard

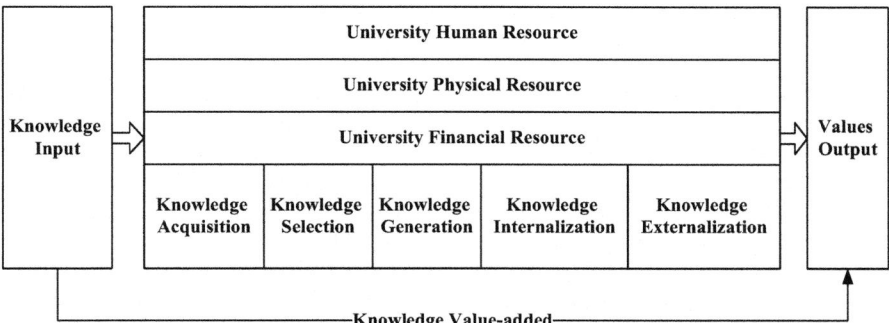

Fig. 2.1 University knowledge value chain

(2010) regard the knowledge value chain as a sequential flow of knowledge in which knowledge value increases, thus aim at proposing a model based on the knowledge value chain to measure knowledge value, and survey the mutual impact between knowledge and product.

In common with Holsapple and Singh (2001), this chapter introduces a university knowledge value chain (UKVC) model (see Fig. 2.1). It consists of three parts: university knowledge input, university knowledge activities, and university knowledge values output. The university knowledge inputs include the tacit knowledge input and the explicit knowledge input. University knowledge activities are comprised of primary activities that a university's knowledge processors perform when manipulating knowledge resources, plus three secondary activities that support and guide their performance. The primary activities in UKVC include knowledge acquisition, knowledge selection, knowledge generation, knowledge internalization, and knowledge externalization. The support activities in UKVC include university human resource input, university physical resource input, and university financial resource input. The university knowledge value outputs include published books, issued papers, applied patents, and technology transfers.

From UKVC model we can find that the university knowledge value-added process is the process of creating new knowledge. Every year universities input a large number of human, material, and financial resources into knowledge activities, such as in basic research and applied research, the applications of R&D achievements, some other scientific and technical services, and so on. Teachers and researchers at universities create new knowledge to realize knowledge value-added through the activities of knowledge acquisition, knowledge selection, knowledge generation, knowledge internalization, and knowledge externalization. The form of university knowledge value-added includes the scientific and technical achievements gained from a series of university knowledge activities.

2.3 Universities' Knowledge Value-Added Efficiency

The higher education sectors of many countries obtain at least some of their income from public funds, hence making it essential, in the interests of accountability, to measure the efficiency of the institutions that comprise these sectors. The higher education sector, however, has characteristics that make it difficult to measure efficiency: it is nonprofit; there is an absence of output and input prices, and higher education institutions (HEIs) produce multiple outputs from multiple inputs. Data envelopment analysis (DEA) has become a popular tool for measuring the efficiency of nonprofit institutions such as hospitals, schools, and universities. Its popularity in these contexts derives from the fact that it is based on a distance function approach and hence can handle multiple outputs and multiple inputs; it does not assume any specific behavioral assumptions of the firm (e.g., cost minimization or profit maximization); it makes no assumption regarding the distribution of efficiencies, and it requires no a priori information regarding the prices of either the inputs or the outputs. Avkiran (2001) uses DEA to examine the relative efficiency of Australian universities. Johnes and Yu (2008) employ DEA to examine the relative efficiency of research production at 109 Chinese regular universities in 2003 and 2004. Despite there being a plethora of studies that look at the efficiency of the higher education sectors of various countries, little work has been done on measuring the efficiency at producing any of the outputs of HEIs from the perspective of knowledge management. Guan and Wang (2004) evaluate the knowledge production efficiency of research groups in the area of information science in China. By taking the research groups as decision-making units (DMUs), the budget of the projects and size of the groups as inputs and the quantity and quality of publications produced by the groups as outputs of the model, the relative efficiencies of 21 research projects are evaluated.

This chapter adopts DEA (Charnes et al. 1978) to study the larger number of inputs and outputs that contribute to university knowledge value-added efficiency. We discuss how to optimize the allocation of knowledge resources to achieve highly effective knowledge value-added efficiency and how to maximize the university knowledge values output.

2.4 Basic Theory of Data Envelopment Analysis

This section briefly introduces the basic DEA model, which is adapted from Cooper et al. (2011). DEA is a "data-oriented" approach for evaluating the performance of a set of peer entities called decision-making units (DMUs), which convert multiple inputs into multiple outputs. The definition of a DMU is generic and flexible. Recent years have seen a great variety of applications of DEA for use in evaluating the performances of many different kinds of entities engaged in many different activities in many different contexts in many different countries. These DEA applications have used DMUs of various forms to evaluate the performance of entities, such as hospitals, US Air Force flight wings, universities, cities, courts, business firms, and others, including the performance of countries, regions, etc. Because it requires very few assumptions, DEA has also opened up possibilities for use in cases that have been resistant to other approaches, because of the complex (often unknown) nature of the relations between the multiple inputs and multiple outputs involved in DMUs.

As pointed out in Cooper et al. (2007), DEA has also been used to supply new insights into activities (and entities) that have previously been evaluated by other methods. For instance, studies of benchmarking practices with DEA have identified numerous sources of inefficiency in some of the most profitable firms—firms that had served as benchmarks by reference to this (profitability) criterion—but DEA provides a vehicle for identifying better benchmarks in many applied studies. Because of these possibilities, DEA studies on the efficiency of different legal organization forms such as "stock" vs. "mutual" insurance companies have shown that previous studies fall short in their attempts to evaluate the potentials of these different forms of organizations. Similarly, the use of DEA has suggested a reconsideration of previous studies about the efficiency with which pre- and post-merger activities have been conducted in banks that were studied by DEA.

Since DEA was first introduced in 1978 in its present form, researchers in a number of fields have quickly recognized that it is an excellent and easily used methodology for modeling operational processes for performance evaluations. This has naturally been accompanied by other developments. For instance, Zhu (2009) provides a number of DEA spreadsheet models that can be used in performance evaluation and benchmarking. DEA's empirical orientation and the absence of a need for the numerous a priori assumptions that accompany other approaches (such as standard forms of statistical regression analysis) have resulted in its use in a number of studies involving efficient frontier estimation in the governmental and nonprofit sectors, in the regulated sector, and in the private sector.

In their original research, Charnes et al. (1978) describe DEA as a "mathematical programming model applied to observational data [that] provides a new way of obtaining empirical estimates of relations - such as the production functions and/or efficient production possibility surfaces - that are cornerstones of modern economics." Formally, DEA is a methodology directed to frontiers rather than central tendencies. Instead of trying to fit a regression plane through the center of the data as in statistical regressions, one "floats," for example, a piecewise linear surface to rest on top of the observations. From this perspective, DEA proves particularly adept at uncovering relationships that would remain hidden from other methodologies. For instance, we may consider what one wants to mean by "efficiency," or more generally, what one wants to mean by saying that one DMU is more efficient than another DMU. This is accomplished in a straightforward manner by DEA without requiring explicitly formulated assumptions and variations that are required by various types of models such as linear and nonlinear regression models.

To allow for applications to a wide variety of activities, we use the term decision-making unit (DMU) to refer to any entity that is to be evaluated in terms of its abilities to convert inputs into outputs. These evaluations can involve governmental agencies, not-for-profit organizations, and business firms. The evaluation can also be directed to educational institutions, hospitals, police forces (or subdivisions thereof), or army units for which comparative evaluations of their performance are to be made.

We assume that there are n DMUs to be evaluated. Each DMU consumes varying amounts of m different inputs to produce s different outputs. Specifically, DMU$_j$ consumes amount x_{ij} of input i and produces amount y_{rj} of output r. We assume that $x_{ij} \geq 0$ and $y_{rj} \geq 0$ and further assume that each DMU has at least one positive input and one positive output value.

We now turn to the "ratio form" of DEA. In this form, as introduced by Charnes, Cooper, and Rhodes, the ratio of outputs to inputs measures the relative efficiency of the DMU$_j$ = DMU$_o$ to be evaluated relative to the ratios of all of the DMU$_j (j = 1, 2, \ldots, n)$. We can interpret the CCR construction as the reduction of the multiple-output/multiple-input situation (for each DMU) to that of a single "virtual" output and "virtual" input. For a particular DMU, the ratio of this single virtual output to single virtual input provides a measure of efficiency that is a function of the multipliers. In mathematical programming parlance, this ratio, which is to be maximized, forms the objective function for the particular DMU being evaluated, so that symbolically:

$$\max h_o(u, v) = \frac{\sum_r u_r y_{ro}}{\sum_i v_i x_{io}}, \tag{2.1}$$

where it should be noted that the variables are u_r and v_i and y_{ro} and x_{io} are the observed output and input values, respectively, of DMU$_o$, the DMU to be evaluated. Of course, without further additional constraints (developed below), (2.1) is unbounded.

A set of normalizing constraints (one for each DMU) reflects the condition that the virtual output to virtual input ratio of every DMU, including DMU$_j$ = DMU$_o$, must be less than or equal to unity. The mathematical programming problem may thus be stated as:

$$\max h_o(u, v) = \frac{\sum_r u_r y_{ro}}{\sum_i v_i x_{io}}$$
$$\text{subject to}$$
$$\frac{\sum_r u_r y_{rj}}{\sum_i v_i x_{ij}} \leq 1 \; for \; j = 1, 2, \ldots, n \tag{2.2}$$
$$u_r, v_i \geq 0, \forall i, r$$

This ratio form generalizes the engineering science definition of efficiency from a single output to a single input and does so without requiring the use of a priori chosen weights.

Remark A fully rigorous development can replace $u_r, \; v_i \; \geq \; 0$ with $\dfrac{u_r}{\sum\limits_{i=1}^{m} v_i x_{io}}, \dfrac{u_r}{\sum\limits_{i=1}^{m} v_i x_{io}} \geq \varepsilon > 0$ where ε is a non-Archimedean element smaller than any positive real number. This condition guarantees that the solutions are positive in these variables. It also leads to $\varepsilon > 0$ in (2.6) which, in turn, leads to the second-stage optimization of the slacks as in (2.10). It should be noted that (2.1) and (2.2) generalize the engineering science definition of efficiency, which deals with a single-output to a single-input ratio and requires an a priori assumption of weighting values to deal with multiple outputs and inputs.

The above ratio form yields an infinite number of solutions; if (u^*, v^*) is optimal, then $(\alpha u^*, \alpha v^*)$ is also optimal for all $\alpha > 0$ and $a > 0$. However, the transformation developed by Charnes and Cooper (1962) for linear fractional programming selects a solution [i.e., the solution (u, v) for which $\sum_{i=1}^{m} v_i x_{io} = 1$] and yields the equivalent linear programming problem in which the change of variables from (u, v) to (μ, v) is a result of the "Charnes-Cooper" transformation:

$$\max z = \sum_{r=1}^{s} u_r y_{ro}$$
$$\text{subject to}$$
$$\sum_{r=1}^{s} u_r y_{rj} - \sum_{i=1}^{m} v_i x_{ij} \leq 0 \tag{2.3}$$
$$\sum_{i=1}^{m} v_i x_{io} = 0$$
$$u_r, v_i \geq 0$$

Here, the LP dual problem is:

$$\theta^* = \min \theta$$
$$\text{subject to}$$
$$\sum_{i=1}^{m} x_{ij}\lambda_j \leq \theta x_{io} \quad i = 1, 2, \ldots, m \tag{2.4}$$
$$\sum_{r=1}^{s} y_{rj}\lambda_j \geq y_{ro} \quad r = 1, 2, \ldots, s$$
$$\lambda_j \geq 0 \quad j = 1, 2, \ldots, n$$

This last model, (2.4), is sometimes referred to as the "Farrell model," because it is the one used in Farrell (1957). In the economics portion of the DEA literature, it is said to conform to the assumption of "strong disposal," but the efficiency evaluation it makes ignores the presence of non-zero slacks. In the operations research portion of the DEA literature, this is referred to as "weak efficiency."

Possibly because he uses the literature of "activity analysis" for reference—see Koopmans—Farrell also fails to exploit the very powerful dual theorem of linear programming, which we have used to relate the preceding problems to each other. This use of activity analysis also caused computational difficulties for Farrell, because he did not take advantage of the fact that activity analysis models can be converted to a linear programming equivalent that provides immediate access to the simplex method and other methods for efficiently solving such problems. We thus now begin to bring these features of linear programming into play.

By virtue of the dual theorem of linear programming, we have $z^* = \theta^*$. Hence, either problem may be used. One can solve (2.4) to obtain an efficiency score. Because we can set $\theta = 1$ and $\lambda_k^* = 1$ with $\lambda_k^* = \lambda_o^*$ and all other $\lambda_j^* = 0$, a solution of (2.4) always exists. Moreover, this solution implies $\theta^* \le 1$. The optimal solution, θ^*, yields an efficiency score for a particular DMU. The process is repeated for each DMU$_j$, i.e., solve (2.4), with $(X_o, Y_o) = (X_k, Y_k)$, where (X_k, Y_k) represents vectors with components x_{ik}, y_{rk} and, similarly, (X_o, Y_o) has components x_{ok}, y_{ok}. DMUs for which $\theta^* < 1$ are inefficient, while DMUs for which $\theta^* = 1$ are boundary points.

Some boundary points may be "weakly efficient," because we have non-zero slacks. This may appear to be worrisome, because alternate optima may have non-zero slacks in some solutions, but not in others. However, we can avoid being worried even in such cases by invoking the following linear program in which the slacks are taken to their maximal values.

$$\max \sum_{i=1}^{m} s_i^- + \sum_{r=1}^{s} s_r^+$$

subject to

$$\sum_{i=1}^{m} x_{ij}\lambda_j + s_i^- = \theta^* x_{io} \quad i = 1, 2, \ldots, m \tag{2.5}$$

$$\sum_{r=1}^{s} y_{rj}\lambda_j - s_r^+ = y_{ro} \quad r = 1, 2, \ldots, s$$

$$\lambda_j, s_i^-, s_r^+ \ge 0 \ \forall i, j, r$$

Here, we note that the choices of s_i^- and s_r^+ do not affect the optimal θ^*, which is determined from model (2.4).

Definition 1.1 (DEA Efficiency) The performance of DMU$_o$ is fully (100%) efficient if and only if both (1) $\theta^* = 1$ and (2) all slacks $s_i^{-*} = s_r^{+*} = 0$.

Definition 1.2 (Weakly DEA Efficient) The performance of DMUo is weakly efficient if and only if both (1) $\theta^* = 1$ and (2) $s_i^{-*} \ne 0$ and/or $s_r^{+*} \ne 0$ for some i or r in some alternate optima.

We state that the preceding development amounts to solving the following problem in two steps:

$$\min \theta - \varepsilon \left(\sum_{i=1}^{m} s_i^- + \sum_{r=1}^{s} s_r^+ \right)$$

subject to

$$\sum_{i=1}^{m} x_{ij}\lambda_j + s_i^- = \theta x_{io} \quad i = 1, 2, \ldots, m \tag{2.6}$$

$$\sum_{r=1}^{s} y_{rj}\lambda_j - s_r^+ = y_{ro} \quad r = 1, 2, \ldots, s$$

$$\lambda_j, s_i^-, s_r^+ \ge 0 \ \forall i, j, r$$

Here, s_i^- and s_r^+ are slack variables used to convert the inequalities in (2.4) to equivalent equations, and $\varepsilon > 0$ is a so-called non-Archimedean element defined to be smaller than any positive real number. This is equivalent to solving (2.4) in two stages by first minimizing θ and then fixing $\theta = \theta^*$ as in (2.2), where the slacks are to be maximized without altering the previously determined value of $\theta = \theta^*$. Formally, this is equivalent to granting "preemptive priority" to the determination of θ^* in (2.3). In this manner, the fact that the non-Archimedean element ε is defined to be smaller than any positive real number is accommodated without having to specify the value of ε.

One could have alternately started with the output side and considered instead the ratio of virtual input to output. This would reorient the objective from max to min, as in (2.2), to obtain:

$$
\begin{aligned}
&\min \frac{\sum_i v_i x_{io}}{\sum_r u_r y_{ro}} \\
&\text{subject to} \\
&\frac{\sum_i v_i x_{ij}}{\sum_r u_r y_{rj}} \geq 1 \ \ for \ j = 1, 2, \ldots, n \\
&u_r, v_i \geq 0, \forall i, r
\end{aligned}
\tag{2.7}
$$

Here, $\varepsilon > 0$ is the previously defined non-Archimedean element.

The Charnes and Cooper (1962) transformation for linear fractional programming again yields model (2.8) (multiplier model) below, with the associated dual problem, (2.9) (envelopment model), as in the following pair:

$$
\begin{aligned}
&\min q = \sum_{i=1}^{m} v_i x_{io} \\
&\text{subject to} \\
&\sum_{i=1}^{m} v_i x_{ij} - \sum_{r=1}^{s} u_r y_{rj} \geq 0 \\
&\sum_{r=1}^{s} u_r y_{ro} = 0 \\
&u_r, v_i \geq \varepsilon \quad \forall r, i
\end{aligned}
\tag{2.8}
$$

$$
\begin{aligned}
&\max \varphi + \varepsilon \left(\sum_{i=1}^{m} s_i^- + \sum_{r=1}^{s} s_r^+ \right) \\
&\text{subject to} \\
&\sum_{i=1}^{m} x_{ij} \lambda_j + s_i^- = x_{io} \ \ i = 1, 2, \ldots, m \\
&\sum_{r=1}^{s} y_{rj} \lambda_j - s_r^+ = \varphi y_{ro} \ \ r = 1, 2, \ldots, s \\
&\lambda_j \geq 0 \ \ j = 1, 2, \ldots, n
\end{aligned}
\tag{2.9}
$$

See also the remark following (1.2).

We now use a model with an output-oriented objective in contrast with the input orientation in (2.6). However, as before, model (2.9) is calculated in a two-stage process. First, we calculate φ^* by ignoring the slacks. Second, we optimize the slacks by fixing φ^* in the following linear programming problem:

$$\max \sum_{i=1}^{m} s_i^- + \sum_{r=1}^{s} s_r^+$$

subject to

$$\sum_{i=1}^{m} x_{ij}\lambda_j + s_i^- = x_{io} \quad i = 1, 2, \ldots, m \qquad (2.10)$$

$$\sum_{r=1}^{s} y_{rj}\lambda_j - s_r^+ = \varphi^* y_{ro} \quad r = 1, 2, \ldots, s$$

$$\lambda_j \geq 0 \quad j = 1, 2, \ldots, n$$

We then modify the previous input-oriented definition of DEA efficiency to the following output-oriented version.

Definition 1.3 DMUo is efficient if and only if $\varphi^* = 1$ and $s_i^{-*} = s_r^{+*} = 0$ for all i and r. DMUo is weakly efficient if $\varphi^* = 1$ and (2) $s_i^{-*} \neq 0$ and/or $s_r^{+*} \neq 0$ for some i and r in some alternate optima.

Table 2.1 presents the CCR model in input- and output-oriented versions, with each in the form of a pair of dual linear programs. These are known as CCR (Abraham Charnes et al. 1978) models. If the constraint $\sum_{r=1}^{s} \lambda_j = 1$ is adjoined, then they are known as BCC (Banker et al. 1984) models. This added constraint introduces an additional variable, μ_o, into the (dual) multiplier problems. This extra variable makes it possible to effect returns to scale evaluations (increasing, constant, and decreasing). Thus, the BCC model is also referred to as the VRS (variable returns to scale) model and is distinguished from the CCR model, which is referred to as the CRS (constant returns to scale) model.

A DMU is inefficient if the efficiency score given by the optimal value for the LP problem is less than one ($\theta^* < 1$ or $z^* < 1$). If the optimal value is equal to one and if there exist positive optimal multipliers ($\mu_r > 0$, $v_i > 0$), then the DMU is efficient. Thus, all efficient points lie on the frontier. However, a DMU can be a boundary point ($\theta^* = 1$) and be inefficient. Note that the complementary slackness condition of linear programming yields a condition for efficiency that is equivalent to the above; the constraints involving X_o and Y_o must hold with equality, i.e., $X_o = X\lambda^*$ and $Y_o = Y\lambda^*$ for all optimal λ^*, where X_o and Y_o are vectors and X and Y are matrices.

An inefficient DMU can be made more efficient by projection onto the frontier. In an input orientation, one improves efficiency through a proportional reduction of inputs, whereas an output orientation requires a proportional augmentation of outputs. However, it is necessary to distinguish between a boundary point and an

Table 2.1 CCR DEA model

Input-oriented	
Envelopment model	Multiplier model
$\min \theta - \varepsilon \left(\sum_{i=1}^{m} s_i^- + \sum_{r=1}^{s} s_r^+ \right)$ subject to $\sum_{i=1}^{m} x_{ij}\lambda_j + s_i^- = \theta x_{io} \quad i = 1, 2, \ldots, m$ $\sum_{r=1}^{s} y_{rj}\lambda_j - s_r^+ = y_{ro} \quad r = 1, 2, \ldots, s$ $\lambda_j, s_i^-, s_r^+ \geq 0 \ \forall i, j, r$	$\max z = \sum_{r=1}^{s} u_r y_{ro}$ subject to $\sum_{r=1}^{s} u_r y_{rj} - \sum_{i=1}^{m} v_i x_{ij} \leq 0$ $\sum_{i=1}^{m} v_i x_{io} = 0$ $u_r, v_i \geq 0$
Output-oriented	
Envelopment model	Multiplier model
$\max \varphi + \varepsilon \left(\sum_{i=1}^{m} s_i^- + \sum_{r=1}^{s} s_r^+ \right)$ subject to $\sum_{i=1}^{m} x_{ij}\lambda_j + s_i^- = x_{io} \quad i = 1, 2, \ldots, m$ $\sum_{r=1}^{s} y_{rj}\lambda_j - s_r^+ = \varphi y_{ro} \quad r = 1, 2, \ldots, s$ $\lambda_j \geq 0 \quad j = 1, 2, \ldots, n$	$\min q = \sum_{i=1}^{m} v_i x_{io}$ subject to $\sum_{i=1}^{m} v_i x_{ij} - \sum_{r=1}^{s} u_r y_{rj} \geq 0$ $\sum_{r=1}^{s} u_r y_{ro} = 0$ $u_r, v_i \geq \varepsilon \quad \forall r, i$

efficient boundary point. Moreover, the efficiency of a boundary point can be dependent upon the model orientation.

Theorem 1.1 Let (θ^*, λ^*) be an optimal solution for the input-oriented model in (2.9). Next, $(1/\theta^*, \lambda^*/\theta^*) = (\varphi^*, \widehat{\lambda}^*)$ is optimal for the corresponding output-oriented model. Similarly, if $(\varphi^*, \widehat{\lambda}^*)$ is optimal for the output-oriented model, then $(1/\varphi^*, \widehat{\lambda}^*/\varphi^*) = (\theta^*, \lambda^*)$ is optimal for the input-oriented model. The correspondence need not be 1–1, however, due to the possible presence of alternate optima.

For an input orientation, the projection $(X_o, Y_o) \rightarrow (\theta^* X_o, Y_o)$ always yields a boundary point, but technical efficiency is achieved only if all slacks are zero in all alternate optima so that $\theta^* X_o = X\lambda^*$ and $Y_o = Y\lambda^*$ for all optimal λ^*. Similarly, the output-oriented projection $(X_o, Y_o) \rightarrow (X_o, \varphi^* Y_o)$ yields a boundary point that is efficient (technically) only if $X_o = X\lambda^*$ and $\varphi^* Y_o = Y\lambda^*$ for all optimal λ^*. In other words, the constraints are satisfied as equalities in all alternate optima for (2.4). To achieve technical efficiency, the appropriate set of constraints in the CCR model must hold with equality.

2.5   Model

In this study we construct a model of university scientific and technological resources input and knowledge value output (see Fig. 2.2) to assess the efficiency of university knowledge value-added, and choose the input-oriented BCC (Banker et al. 1984) (BCC-I) model under variable returns to scale. The BCC-I model used for analyzing the knowledge value-added efficiency of universities in Chinese provinces runs as follows.

Suppose we have a set of decision-making units (DMUs) $\{DMU_j : j = 1, 2, \cdots, n\}$. Let (x_j, y_j) denote the input and output vectors of DMU_{j_0}. The input and output of DMU_{j_0} are denoted as $\left(x_{j_0}, y_{j_0}\right)$, and the input-oriented variable returns to scale (VRS) BCC model for efficient DMU_{j_0} can be expressed as:

$$
\begin{aligned}
\min \ & \theta \\
\text{s.t.} \ & \\
& \sum_{j=1}^{n} x_j \lambda_j \leq \theta x_0 \\
& \sum_{j=1}^{n} y_j \lambda_j \geq y_0 \\
& \sum_{j=1}^{n} \lambda_j = 1 \\
& \lambda_j \geq 0
\end{aligned}
\tag{2.11}
$$

In the model, θ is the relatively comprehensive efficiency of DMU_j, reflecting the efficiency of the input-output of science and technology of a university in province j. If θ is higher, then it indicates that the efficiency of the input-output of science and technology of a university in province j is higher than that of other provinces, suggesting lower efficiency and a higher degree of waste of science and technology (S&T) resources.

Solving the expression above, we get the efficiency of the knowledge value-added of universities in each province, which is the technical efficiency (TE) under variable returns to scale. Its economic meaning stands for the actual proportion of investment in S&T resources for achieving the best efficiency of the knowledge value-added of the universities while keeping the scientific and technological output level of them unchanged.

2.5.1   Input

The inputs of a university's knowledge resources include human, material, and financial aspects. In conjunction with the relevant data availability, the quantity of university teaching and scientific research personnel in every year is selected as the input of a university's human resources. The number of university research and development institutes is selected as the physical input index. The university research and development institutes include key laboratories and engineering research centers.

Fig. 2.2 Model of university scientific and technological resources input and knowledge value output

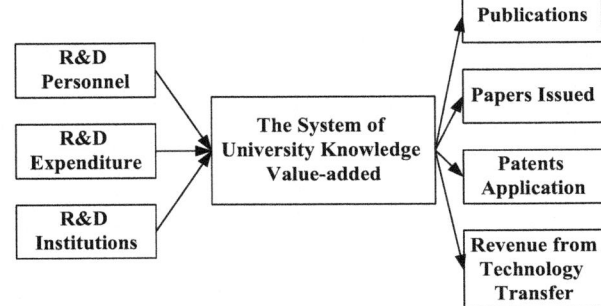

2.5.2   Output

We select the number of published books, papers, patent applications, and the income from technology transfer as the knowledge value output index.

2.6   Empirical Analysis of the Efficiency of University Knowledge Value-Added

This chapter is based on the data compilation of university technology statistics from 2009 to 2010, covering 31 provinces, autonomous regions, and municipalities. Given the fact that intellectual input-output operates with a time lag, we adopt data in 2009 for input analysis and data in 2010 for the output analysis.

2.6.1   Technical Efficiency

By implementing the DEA model mentioned above with DEAP2.1, we are able to figure out the overall efficiency, pure technology efficiency, and scale efficiency of university knowledge value-added.

Overall efficiency is equal to technology efficiency when the scale effect is not considered. The overall efficiency is relatively effective if it is no less than 1 and relatively ineffective if less than 1, which implies either input redundancy or output inadequacy, respectively. By analyzing the statistics in Table 2.2, we reach the conclusion that 14 of the 31 provinces, including Beijing, exhibit effective efficiency, while the others (17 provinces) do not. With further analysis about pure technology efficiency and scale efficiency, we can find out the reasons why those provinces' efficiencies are ineffective.

The inefficiencies in Shandong, Guangdong, and Tibet are caused by having a scale efficiency of less than 1, while their pure technology efficiencies are all equal to

Table 2.2 Comprehensive evaluation of universities' intellectual value-added DEA in each province

Province	Technical efficiency	Pure technical efficiency	Scale efficiency	Scale effect
Beijing	1	1	1	Constant
Shanghai	1	1	1	Constant
Jiangsu	1	1	1	Constant
Zhejiang	1	1	1	Constant
Anhui	1	1	1	Constant
Jiangxi	1	1	1	Constant
Henan	1	1	1	Constant
Hubei	1	1	1	Constant
Guangxi	1	1	1	Constant
Hainan	1	1	1	Constant
Yunnan	1	1	1	Constant
Shaanxi	1	1	1	Constant
Gansu	1	1	1	Constant
Xinjiang	1	1	1	Constant
Shandong	0.998	1	0.998	Decreasing
Guangdong	0.943	1	0.943	Decreasing
Tibet	0.363	1	0.363	Increasing
Hebei	0.887	0.887	1	Constant
Inner Mongolia	0.851	0.851	0.999	Constant
Jilin	0.876	0.877	0.999	Decreasing
Chongqing	0.968	0.974	0.994	Increasing
Sichuan	0.963	0.966	0.997	Increasing
Hunan	0.915	0.918	0.997	Increasing
Ningxia	0.865	0.947	0.914	Increasing
Guizhou	0.861	0.872	0.987	Increasing
Liaoning	0.859	0.86	0.999	Increasing
Fujian	0.843	0.847	0.995	Increasing
Tianjin	0.807	0.819	0.986	Increasing
Heilongjiang	0.77	0.773	0.996	Increasing
Qinhai	0.763	0.882	0.865	Increasing
Shanxi	0.738	0.747	0.988	Increasing

1, implying effective knowledge productivity efficiencies. Shandong and Guangdong show a decreasing effect of scale, and therefore they need to reduce technical investments, while Tibet should raise investments in the technical field with an increasing effect of scale. Hubei and Inner Mongolia have stable scale effects, but their pure technology effects are both less than 1, and thus they need to increase the quantity and productivity of knowledge by knowledge transfer and innovation within the universities. Universities in Jilin have neither pure technology efficiency nor scale efficiency, and they are in the stage of decreasing economies of scale. Thus, they should achieve better efficiency by reducing technical investment and raising knowledge productivity. Universities in the other provinces are neither pure technology effective nor scale effective, and they are in the phase of declining economies of scale, which makes raising technical investment and knowledge productivity an appropriate option.

2.6.2   Slack Analysis

With the optimum input and output combination calculated by DEA, we can guide administration departments in the 14 provinces to reallocate resources. Pure technology efficiencies in Table 2.2 indicate that the major reasons leading to ineffective DEA are redundant input and inadequate output. By calculating slack variables in the DEA model, we see the disadvantages of the invalid DEA and how to adjust the corresponding output in order to achieve the optimum status. Table 2.3 indicates that less technical investment and higher knowledge productivity are needed to improve conditions in the pure technology inefficient provinces.

As we can see from Table 2.3, in the technical input aspect, 12 of the 14 DEA ineffective provinces need to reduce their number of research institutions, which involves 85.7% of the total ineffective provinces. A common phenomenon found in these areas is low efficiency of university scientific research institutions, such as key labs, engineering centers, and researching centers, and therefore evaluation rules and indicator systems need to be set up when constructing those technical platforms. Detailed suggestions include technical personnel cultivation, comprehensive evaluation, and cancellation of unqualified labs.

Universities in Heilongjiang, Liaoning, Sichuan, and Tianjin invest too much in terms of research expenditure, while their knowledge outputs are so low. Hence, relevant authorities should enhance operational management in research fund expenditure and avoid aimless spending while at the same time improving efficiency.

There are too many teachers and researchers in Qinghai, Ningxia, and Inner Mongolia. Measures like performance evaluation, promotion, and demotion can be implemented to better manage technical staffs.

In terms of technical productivity, Sichuan, Heilongjiang, Tianjin, Hunan, Shanxi, and Ningxia should place emphasis on technology transfer. They should also build an internal driving mechanism for scientific achievements.

Government and enterprises, together with universities, need to establish driving mechanisms to promote cooperation among the three parties. The common goal should be to put universities' scientific achievements into practical use, or in other words, increasing the effectiveness of academic knowledge.

Universities in Hunan, Hebei, Chongqing, and Sichuan produce relatively few published books and papers, and they should pay more attention to monographs

Table 2.3 Technology input and knowledge output optimization

Provinces	Input redundancy			Output inadequacy			
	R&D institutions (unit)	R&D expenditure (1000 yuan)	R&D personnel (person)	Publication on S&T (piece)	Papers issued (piece)	Patent applications (piece)	Revenue from technology transfer (1000 yuan)
Chongqing	60	0	0	78	0	0	0
Sichuan	6	61,672	0	55	0	942	171,896
Ningxia	14	0	717	0	0	7	241
Hunan	0	0	0	262	0	569	16,051
Hebei	0	0	0	230	0	0	0
Qinghai	8	0	783	10	0	0	55
Jinlin	38	0	0	24	0	1	0
Guizhou	2	0	0	16	0	0	0
Liaoning	149	295,734	0	0	2224	0	0
Inner Mongolia	21	0	136	0	0	0	0
Fujian	37	0	0	12	0	0	0
Tianjin	32	59,087	0	0	0	0	62,316
Heilongjiang	3	306,938	0	0	0	229	66,541
Shanxi	10	0	0	0	0	0	6427

rather than just research papers. Sichuan, Hunan, and Heilongjiang suffer great deficiency in patent applications, which is disproportionate to their technical resources. Therefore, they should enhance university faculties' sense of intellectual property protection and encourage patent applications.

2.6.3   Super-Efficiency

The introduction of the DEA super-efficiency model is for the purpose of better efficiency comparison among various units. Andersen and Petersen (1993) propose a super-efficiency model that can achieve this goal. In this chapter, we introduce a model proposed by Andersen and Petersen (1993) that leads to a concept called "super-efficiency." The efficiency scores from these models are obtained by eliminating the data on the DMUo to be evaluated from the solution set. For the input model, this can result in values that regard DMUo with the status of being "super-efficient." These values are then used to rank the DMUs and thereby eliminate some (but not all) of the ties that occur for efficient DMUs.

We start with the model used by Andersen and Petersen, which takes the form of a CCR model and thereby avoids the possibility of a non-solution that is associated with the convexity constraint in the BCC model. In vector form this model is:

$$\theta^* = \min_{\theta,\,\lambda,\,s^-,\,s^+} \theta - \varepsilon e s^+$$

$$[\text{Super Radial I} - \text{C}] \quad \theta x_o = \sum_{j=1,\,\neq o}^{n} \lambda_j x_j + s^- \qquad (2.12)$$

$$y_o = \sum_{j=1,\,\neq o}^{n} \lambda_j y_j + s^+$$

Here, all components of λ, s^-, and s^+ are constrained to be nonnegative, $\varepsilon > 0$ is the usual non-Archimedean element, and e is a row vector with unity for all elements.

We refer to (2.12) as a "radial super-efficiency" model and note that the vectors x_o and y_o are omitted from the expression on the right in the constraints. The data associated with the DMUo being evaluated on the left are therefore omitted from the production possibility set. However, solutions will always exist so long as all elements are positive in the matrices X, $Y > 0$.

Based on the previous model, we reach the conclusion that universities in 14 provinces are technical effective, and we can figure out their scores as well as ranks with the software named EMS (Efficiency Measurement System) version 1.3 (see Table 2.4). The top-ranking provinces utilize technical resources more efficiently and which have higher knowledge efficiencies. For instance, the super-efficiency ratio of Jiangsu is 110.93%, which implies Jiangsu can remain knowledge effective if it invests an additional 10.93% into technical resources.

Table 2.4 Super-efficiency and ranking of universities in selected provinces

Provinces	Super-efficiency	Ranking
Yunnan	3.156	1
Henan	2.896	2
Xinjiang	2.358	3
Beijing	1.654	4
Zhejiang	1.322	5
Anhui	1.263	6
Shaanxi	1.219	7
Shanghai	1.124	8
Jiangsu	1.109	9
Hubei	1.107	10
Jiangxi	1.051	11
Hainan	1.039	12
Guangxi	1.039	13
Gansu	1.009	14

2.7   Conclusion

This chapter indicates that among universities in 31 provinces, 14 provinces (led by Yunnan) are knowledge effective, while the others are either input redundant or output inadequate. Therefore, relevant authorities should reallocate technical resources and create a better environment for innovation, utilization, and integration of scientific achievements. At the same time, universities should make full use of technical resources and establish relevant driving mechanisms for motivating scientific personnel's spirit of innovation and improving the schools' knowledge efficiency.

Chapter 3
Efficiency Evaluation of Knowledge Flow in University-Industry Collaborative Innovation in China

3.1 Introduction

Under economic globalization, innovation is increasingly more open, and the creation, innovation, and application sectors of technological knowledge need to build an open collaborative innovation. Collaborative innovation is a transdisciplinary approach for developing global synergy to improve the competitiveness of an organization through holistic, competitive, and complementary interactions between and among innovation participants in a specific environment (Swink 2006). A collaborative innovation system essentially consists of three sectors: industry, universities, and the government, with each one interacting with the other two, while at the same time playing its own role.

In April 24, 2011, President Hu Jintao made an important speech at the Tsinghua University Centennial Conference. He pointed out that China should promote collaborative innovation proactively; guide and encourage universities, research institutions, and enterprises to execute concrete cooperation using institutional innovation and policy projects; establish a collaborative innovation strategic union; promote resource sharing; carry out major research projects together; and achieve substantial results in critical areas. Collaboration innovation is a large-span integrated innovative organizational model that aims to achieve major technological innovations; it is formed by enterprises, government, knowledge production agencies (universities and others), intermediary agency, and users. University-industry linkage is an organizational model of collaborative innovation. Building UICI will help fasten the conversion of public technological achievements, push scientific research to meet the needs of industry innovation, and help advance both technology development and industry development.

Scholars have studied UICI from different aspects with a variety of methods. By analyzing a sample of Swiss companies, Arvanitis et al. (2006) find that increasing R&D investments plays a significant role in strengthening the dominant position of

© Springer International Publishing AG, part of Springer Nature 2018
Y. Yu et al., *Strategy and Performance of Knowledge Flow*,
International Series in Operations Research & Management Science 271,
https://doi.org/10.1007/978-3-319-77926-3_3

high-tech enterprises in a national innovation system. It accelerates knowledge transfers from universities and research institutions to enterprises. Leydesdorff and Etzkowitz (1996) put forward a Triple Helix model of university-industry-government. Leydesdorff and Guoping (2001) conduct research on the Chinese university-industry-government innovation system, and Inzelt (2004) analyzes the evolutionary process of the university-industry-government innovation system under transition economies.

A UICI system integrates various innovative elements and the accessibility flow of innovation resources internally. The goal is to form a multiple-subject synergistic interactive network innovation mode, where industry, universities, and research are key factors and government, financial institutions, intermediaries, innovation platforms, and nonprofit organizations play supporting roles. Through in-deep collaboration and resource integration between knowledge creation subjects and technology innovation subjects, the system produces a superposed nonlinear utility. It is a complex system that is composed of several subsystems, and there are complex internal mechanisms between the various subsystems.

A collaborative innovation system is a complex conglomerate of interacting independent parties. The network of institutional relations among universities, industries, and governmental agencies has been considered as a Triple Helix (TH). A collaborative innovation system (CIS) is based on a multi-input, multi-output transformation relation. Thus, it is an important issue to investigate the performances related to the transformation process of limited innovation resources when looking to improve collaborative innovative outputs.

Previous studies have evaluated the performance of collaborative innovation. Regarding the efficiency of UICI, Bonaccorsi and Piccaluga (1994) believe it relies on matching the degree of the features during knowledge transfer and structure (process) of the partnership. Measuring UICI efficiency cannot just focus on enterprises' expectation of the collaboration, and universities should not be passive during the evaluation process. Abraham Charnes et al. (1978) propose the DEA method to calculate the relative efficiency of the system. DEA is a method for measuring the efficiency of peer decision-making units (DMUs), and it does not need to estimate the parameters in advance. It has some advantages that cannot be underestimated when trying to avoid subjective factors and the simplification of operations, reduction of errors, etc. DEA has been applied in the efficiency evaluation of university-industry collaboration. Anderson et al. (2007) measure technology transfer efficiency of 54 American universities under UICI using the multistage DEA method. Liu (2011) analyzes the research background and significance of the performances of industry-university cooperation and discusses university-industry cooperation data in 28 provinces through DEA. Hu et al. (2010) use DEA to measure the efficiency of university-industry-research cooperation in Guangdong, putting forth some relative countermeasures and suggestions for maintaining sustained and stable innovation efficiency.

Those studies fail, however, to consider the complexity of the collaborative innovation system. The UICI system integrates all kinds of innovative resources and allows them to flow freely in the system. In order to achieve these actions, the key point is to form the network innovation model for multi-subject interaction, which takes universities, industries, and research institutions as the core factors and takes the government, financial institutions, intermediaries, innovation platforms, nonprofit organizations, and others as supplementary factors. Creating in-depth knowledge and resource cooperation and integration among knowledge creation subjects and technological innovation subjects produces nonlinear utility of multiple systems. A UICI system is a complex system, consisting of many innovative subjects. When the traditional DEA model is used to evaluate the relative effectiveness of complex systems with multiple subsystems, then the subsystems are usually regarded as a whole. Accordingly, DEA cannot fully reflect the system's efficiency and will overestimate the efficiency index.

Researchers in recent years have begun to pay attention to the technical efficiency evaluation of production systems with a complex internal structure and have built a relevant network DEA model with a network structure. Hence, this chapter focuses on the internal structure of the UICI system and builds the efficiency evaluation model of knowledge flow in UICI in China based on Network DEA. In this sense, there is a great need to study the efficiency evaluation and improvement of knowledge flow in UICI.

This study proposes a Network DEA with parallel production systems to measure UICI efficiency. The purpose of the present research is to construct a complete measurement framework characterizing the UICI system's production framework from original S&T investment to final outputs and to measure the UICI system's process-oriented technical efficiency, which is implemented in the context of China. It is hoped that this study will benefit China's collaborative innovation policy-making.

3.2 DEA and Network DEA

Data envelopment analysis (DEA), introduced by Abraham Charnes et al. (1978), is a mathematical programming approach that computes an efficiency score ranging from 0 to 1 to reflect the level of a firm's relative efficiency in transforming inputs into outputs, where "0" reflects the lowest level of efficiency and "1" represents the optimal level of efficiency in the transformation process for the firms in the sample. The boundary or frontier of a DEA model is formed by best practice firms, which represent the maximum potential output that can be achieved by the firms in the sample for a given set of inputs. Firms performing at levels inside the estimated frontier are deemed "inefficient." The efficiency of a firm is computed relative to the efficiency of other firms in the sample.

3.2.1   Basic DEA Models

The basic DEA models include both CCR and BCC.

1. Abraham Charnes et al. (1978) proposed the CCR efficiency evaluation model. The model is analyzed from the aspect of input(s). It is assumed that the production technology of each DMU is fixed returns to scale. The efficiency frontier boundary is obtained by a linear programming method, and the relative efficiency of each DEA is then calculated. The DMU falling on the boundary is efficient, and its efficiency is 1; the DMU that does not fall on the boundary is inefficient, and so its value is less than 1 and greater than 0. Suppose there are n DMUs. Each DMU uses m input indices to produce s output indices. The input and output of DMU$_j$ is (x_{ij}, y_{rj}), where $i = 1,2,...,m$; $r = 1,2,...,s$; and $j = 1,2,...,n$. We present the CCR model, evaluating the efficiency of DMU$_o$, as

$$\theta_o = \max \frac{\sum_{r=1}^{s} u_r y_{ro}}{\sum_{i=1}^{m} v_i x_{io}}$$

$$\text{s.t.} \quad \frac{\sum_{r=1}^{s} u_r y_{rj}}{\sum_{i=1}^{m} v_i x_{ij}} \leq 1 \quad \forall j \tag{3.1}$$

$$v_i, u_r \geq 0 \quad \forall i, r$$

The parameters v_i and u_r represent the ith input and the rth output of the weighted indices, respectively, while θ_o represents the efficiency value of the o^{-th} DMU. Using the Charnes-Cooper transformation, we transform the model into the following equivalent model:

$$\theta_o = \max \sum_{r=1}^{s} u_r y_{ro}$$

$$\sum_{i=1}^{m} v_i x_{io} = 1$$

$$\text{s.t.} \quad \sum_{r=1}^{s} u_r y_{rj} - \sum_{i=1}^{m} v_i x_{ij} \leq 1 \quad \forall j \tag{3.2}$$

$$v_i, u_r \geq 0 \quad \forall i, r$$

By finding the dual form of the model, we can get the CCR model in the envelopment form:

$$\min \theta$$
$$s.t. \sum_{j=1}^{n} x_{ij}\lambda_j \leq \theta x_o$$
$$\sum_{j=1}^{n} y_{rj}\lambda_j \geq y_o \tag{3.3}$$
$$\lambda_j \geq 0$$
$$\forall i, r$$

2. Banker et al. (1984) remove the hypothesis of fixed returns to scale in the CCR model and establish the BCC model with variable returns to scale. They add the convexity assumption based on the original model, which decomposes the technical efficiency into pure technical efficiency and scale efficiency. The efficiency values calculated by the CCR model are the total efficiency values in the BC2 model, while the efficiency values calculated by the BC2 model are pure technical efficiency values (PTE). As a result, the pure technical efficiency is not greater than the total efficiency. If and only if total efficiency = 1, then scale efficiency (SE) = 1 and pure technical efficiency = 1.

$$\min \theta$$
$$s.t. \sum_{j=1}^{n} x_{ij}\lambda_j \leq \theta x_o$$
$$\sum_{j=1}^{n} y_{rj}\lambda_j \geq y_o$$
$$\sum_{j=1}^{n} \lambda_j = 1 \tag{3.4}$$
$$\lambda_j \geq 0$$
$$\forall i, r$$

3. Seiford and Thrall (1990) propose an efficiency evaluation model in the case of nondecreasing economies of scale. The model supposes that all of the evaluated units are at stages of constant or increasing economies of scale. The model can be presented as

$$\min \theta$$
$$s.t. \sum_{j=1}^{n} x_{ij}\lambda_j \leq \theta x_o$$
$$\sum_{j=1}^{n} y_{rj}\lambda_j \geq y_o$$
$$\sum_{j=1}^{n} \lambda_j \geq 1 \tag{3.5}$$
$$\lambda_j \geq 0$$
$$\forall i, r$$

In addition to the three basic DEA models described above, in order to deal with different problems and evaluation environments, relevant scholars have extended the basic model and constructed a series of DEA models, such as SBM (slack-based measure) model (Tone 2001), RAM (range-adjusted measure) model (Cooper et al. 1999), etc.

3.2.2 Network DEA Model

With the DEA evaluation method more and more widely used in the real world in recent years, some shortcomings and defects in the traditional DEA method have arisen. Its direct application may lead to inaccurate calculation results and may not even offer practical significance. The traditional basic DEA model treats the DMU as a black box. The inputs through this black box are just transformed into outputs, ignoring the specific production process. With the development of society, management practices put forward higher requirements for efficiency evaluation. Thus, what is required is to find a new way to open the black box and to delve deeper into the decision-making unit to find the crux of its low efficiency.

Färe and Grosskopf (1996) present that the black box is composed of a series of subunits. There are a series of input-output activities between these subunits, and these activities have an impact on the system's overall efficiency. Färe and Grosskopf (2000) first use the network DEA method to open the DMU's black box, so as to directly analyze the internal operation mechanism. Lewis and Sexton (2004) measure the efficiency of the network structure based on the radial measure framework. Tone and Tsutsui (2009) employ the non-radial SBM method based on the slack variable to research the efficiency of network DEA. Cook et al. (2010) and Kao (2014) study the efficiency decomposition of network DEA from different perspectives. Chen et al. (2013) discuss the pitfalls in network DEA with respect to divisional efficiency and projection.

3.3 Methodology

3.3.1 Conceptual Framework

The process of university-industry-research collaborative innovation involves knowledge sharing, knowledge cooperation, and knowledge creation between various subjects of production and research, and thus it has advantage in knowledge (Wang 2012). Therefore, the performance evaluation of such innovation is essentially the performance evaluation of knowledge flows in the process of university-industry-research collaborative innovation. Guan and Zuo (2014) separate the innovation process into the knowledge production process (KPP) and the knowledge commercialization process (KCP) and evaluate the efficiency of a national

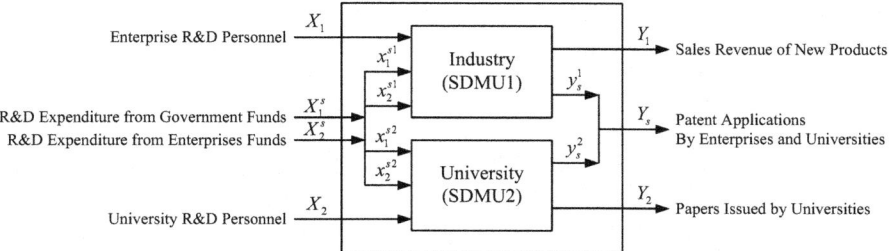

Fig. 3.1   Performance evaluation model of knowledge flow in a UICI system

innovation system from the use of the two-stage DEA model. This chapter also evaluates the efficiency of knowledge flows in UICI in China under the light of Guan and Zuo (2014).

On September 23, 2012, the Central Committee of the Communist Party of China (CPC) and the State Council issued the opinions on deepening the reform of the scientific and technological system to speed up the construction of the national innovation system in China. This targets the business of collaborative innovation. To highlight the main role of enterprise technological innovation, colleges and universities should provide more support and services for enterprise technological innovation. Therefore, to simplify the analysis and take into account data availability, and combined with the definition of the main body of the UICI system in the first chapter, this chapter considers that the main bodies in such a system mainly include two subsystems: businesses and higher education institutions. From the macro-level view, we take the provinces in China as the research objects and build an efficiency evaluation of knowledge flows in the UICI for China (see Fig. 3.1).

In the study of university-industry efficiency, the relevant literature generally uses R&D expenditure and personnel inputs as the knowledge input variables of efficiency measures, such as Guan and Chen (2012). For enterprises and universities, which are two subsystems in the knowledge flow in a UICI system, the internal expenses of R&D funds mainly come from government funds and enterprise funds. Government funds are annually invested in enterprises and universities and used to guide and support R&D activities. At the same time, companies invest a certain amount into their own R&D. On the one hand, R&D funds are used for companies' own internal R&D expenses. On the other hand, they are used as commissions for universities, because R&D activities are allocated to or under cooperation with them. Hence, this chapter takes government and corporate R&D investments as the common inputs of Sub-DMUs in the parallel structure model. Full-time R&D staff equivalent is an international indicator and is used to compare the scientific and technological inputs. It refers to the converted sum of the workload according to the actual working hours of full-time R&D staff (staff engaged in R&D activities who have accumulated working hours that account for 90% of all working hours and above throughout the year) and part-time R&D staff. This chapter takes enterprises' and universities' full-time R&D staff equivalent as independent inputs of various DMUs.

The output indices of knowledge flow of UICI generally take the sales income of a company's new products, the number of patent applications, and the number of papers published in colleges and universities as the output variables, such as Bonaccorsi and Piccaluga (1994) and Guan and Chen (2012). This chapter utilizes the sales income of an enterprise's new products as its independent output and takes the number of papers published in colleges and universities as their independent output. Both enterprises and universities are subsystems. Patent applications come from both enterprises and universities, and so they are taken as common outputs of the two.

According to the analyses above, knowledge flow in a UICI can be considered as a parallel DMU with shared inputs and outputs.

3.3.2 DEA Model with Parallel Structure

Without loss of generality, suppose that the DMU has two Sub-DMUs. Some inputs of the DMU are consumed by both Sub-DMU1 and Sub-DMU2, and some outputs of the DMU are produced by both Sub-DMU1 and Sub-DMU2. In addition, some inputs and outputs are consumed and produced separately by Sub-DMU1 and Sub-DMU2. We define the variables as follows: $X_1 = \left(x_{1j}^1, \ldots, x_{mj}^1 \right)$ represents m units of inputs consumed only by Sub-DMU1; $X_2 = \left(x_{1j}^2, \ldots, x_{hj}^2 \right)$ represents h units of inputs consumed only by Sub-DMU2; $X_s = \left(x_{1j}^s, \ldots, x_{lj}^s \right)$ represents one unit of inputs consumed by both Sub-DMU1 and Sub-DMU2; $Y_1 = \left(y_{1j}^1, \ldots, y_{sj}^1 \right)$ represents s units of outputs produced only by Sub-DMU1; $Y_2 = \left(y_{1j}^2, \ldots, y_{tj}^2 \right)$ represents t units of outputs produced only by Sub-DMU2; and $Y_s = \left(y_{1j}^s, \ldots, y_{uj}^s \right)$ represents u units of inputs produced by both Sub-DMU1 and Sub-DMU2.

Assume that the common inputs and outputs of Sub-DMU1 and Sub-DMU2 are known within the system. Use $X_{s1} = \left(x_{1j}^{s1}, \ldots, x_{lj}^{s1} \right)$, $X_{s2} = \left(x_{1j}^{s2}, \ldots, x_{lj}^{s2} \right)$, $Y_{s1} = \left(y_{1j}^{s1}, \ldots, y_{uj}^{s1} \right)$, and $Y_{s2} = \left(y_{1j}^{s2}, \ldots, y_{uj}^{s2} \right)$ to represent the common inputs and outputs shared by the subsystems Sub-DMU1 and Sub-DMU2, respectively. At the same time, $X_s = X_j^{s1} + X_j^{s2}$, and $Y_s = Y_j^{s1} + Y_j^{s2}$ (see Fig. 3.2).

According to the DEA model of a network structure proposed by Färe and Grosskopf (2000), this chapter sets up a Network DEA efficiency evaluation model with shared input and output. The efficiency of parallel production systems with shared inputs and outputs under fixed returns to scale can be expressed by the following formulae:

Fig. 3.2 Parallel system structure with shared input and output

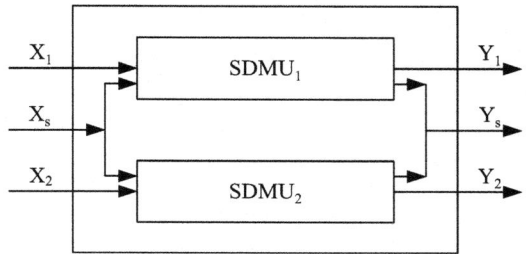

$$\overline{\theta}^*_{\mathrm{CRS}} = \min \theta$$

s.t.

$$\sum_{k=1}^{2}\sum_{j=1}^{n}\lambda_j^k y_{rj}^{sk} \geq y_{ro}^s \quad r = 1, \ldots, u$$

$$\sum_{j=1}^{n}\lambda_j^1 y_{rj}^1 \geq y_{ro}^1 \quad r = 1, \ldots, s$$

$$\sum_{j=1}^{n}\lambda_j^2 y_{rj}^2 \geq y_{ro}^2 \quad r = 1, \ldots, t$$

$$\sum_{k=1}^{2}\sum_{j=1}^{n}\lambda_j^k x_{ij}^{sk} \leq \theta x_{io}^s \quad i = 1, \ldots, l \qquad (3.6)$$

$$\sum_{j=1}^{n}\lambda_j^1 x_{ij}^1 \leq \theta x_{io}^1 \quad i = 1, \ldots, m$$

$$\sum_{j=1}^{n}\lambda_j^2 x_{ij}^2 \leq \theta x_{io}^2 \quad i = 1, \ldots, h$$

$$\sum_{j=1}^{n}\lambda_j^1 = \sum_{j=1}^{n}\lambda_j^2$$

$$\lambda_j^k \geq 0 \quad k = 1, 2; \quad j = 1, \ldots, n$$

Similarly, the efficiency evaluation model of the parallel decision-making system with variable and non-incremental returns to scale is as follows:

$$\overline{\theta}^*_{\text{VRS}} = \min \theta$$

s.t.

$$\sum_{k=1}^{2}\sum_{j=1}^{n} \lambda_j^k y_{rj}^{sk} \geq y_{ro}^s \quad r = 1, \ldots, u$$

$$\sum_{j=1}^{n} \lambda_j^1 y_{rj}^1 \geq y_{ro}^1 \quad r = 1, \ldots, s$$

$$\sum_{j=1}^{n} \lambda_j^2 y_{rj}^2 \geq y_{ro}^2 \quad r = 1, \ldots, t$$

$$\sum_{k=1}^{2}\sum_{j=1}^{n} \lambda_j^k x_{ij}^{sk} \leq \theta x_{io}^s \quad i = 1, \ldots, l \qquad (3.7)$$

$$\sum_{j=1}^{n} \lambda_j^1 x_{ij}^1 \leq \theta x_{io}^1 \quad i = 1, \ldots, m$$

$$\sum_{j=1}^{n} \lambda_j^2 x_{ij}^2 \leq \theta x_{io}^2 \quad i = 1, \ldots, h$$

$$\sum_{j=1}^{n} \lambda_j^k = 1 \quad k = 1, 2$$

$$\lambda_j^k \geq 0 \quad k = 1, 2; \ j = 1, \ldots, n$$

$$\overline{\theta}^*_{\text{NIRS}} = \min \theta$$

s.t.

$$\sum_{k=1}^{2}\sum_{j=1}^{n} \lambda_j^k y_{rj}^{sk} \geq y_{ro}^s \quad r = 1, \ldots, u$$

$$\sum_{j=1}^{n} \lambda_j^1 y_{rj}^1 \geq y_{ro}^1 \quad r = 1, \ldots, s$$

$$\sum_{j=1}^{n} \lambda_j^2 y_{rj}^2 \geq y_{ro}^2 \quad r = 1, \ldots, t$$

$$\sum_{k=1}^{2}\sum_{j=1}^{n} \lambda_j^k x_{ij}^{sk} \leq \theta x_{io}^s \quad i = 1, \ldots, l \qquad (3.8)$$

$$\sum_{j=1}^{n} \lambda_j^1 x_{ij}^1 \leq \theta x_{io}^1 \quad i = 1, \ldots, m$$

$$\sum_{j=1}^{n} \lambda_j^2 x_{ij}^2 \leq \theta x_{io}^2 \quad i = 1, \ldots, h$$

$$\sum_{j=1}^{n} \lambda_j^1 = \sum_{j=1}^{n} \lambda_j^2 \leq 1$$

$$\lambda_j^k \geq 0 \quad k = 1, 2; \ j = 1, \ldots, n$$

Definition Scale efficiency can be obtained by

$$\theta_s^* = \frac{\overline{\theta}_{\mathrm{CRS}}^*}{\overline{\theta}_{\mathrm{VRS}}^*}. \tag{3.9}$$

According to Fare and Grosskopf (1985), we note that

If $\theta_s^* = 1$, then the scale efficiency of DMU0 is constant;
If $\theta_s^* < 1$ and $\overline{\theta}_{\mathrm{CRS}}^* = \overline{\theta}_{\mathrm{NIRS}}^*$, then the scale efficiency of DMU0 is increasing; and
If $\theta_s^* < 1$ and $\overline{\theta}_{\mathrm{VRS}}^* = \overline{\theta}_{\mathrm{NIRS}}^*$, then the scale efficiency of DMU0 is decreasing.

3.3.3   Data

This study selects the data from China Science and Technology Statistical Yearbook 2013 and China Statistical Yearbook 2014. Considering that the investments from input to output need some time (Bonaccorsi and Daraio 2003; Guan and Chen 2012), we use data in 2012 as the input data (see Table 3.1) and data in 2013 as the output data (see Table 3.2). In addition, due to the lack of data for Tibet, we omit this province in our analysis. Therefore, the study's subjects in this chapter are China's 30 provinces and autonomous regions, excluding Tibet. Table 3.3 lists the descriptive statistical results of the input and output variables.

3.4   Results

We use LINGO software programming to solve models (3.3), (3.4), (3.5), (3.6), (3.7), and (3.8) and get the following results (see Table 3.4).

In Table 3.4, θ_{VRS}^* and $\overline{\theta}_{\mathrm{VRS}}^*$ are, in the case of variable economies of scale, the efficiency values of knowledge flow for UICI in various provinces under two different approaches. Here, θ_{VRS}^* is based on the black box system, which does not take into account the relationship between the subsystems in the knowledge flow-UICI system mechanism. However, $\overline{\theta}_{\mathrm{VRS}}^*$ is based on the parallel system approach. It is clear that the parallel system improves the evaluation results under the black box method. Figure 3.3 shows the distribution of efficiency values under both systems.

As can be seen from Fig. 3.3, in the black box system, 19 provinces' knowledge flows under the UICI system are effective. However, in the parallel system, only nine provinces' knowledge flows achieve effectiveness. Accordingly, we can see that the parallel DMU evaluation model is able to evaluate the efficiency of complex systems with multiple subsystems more effectively.

Table 3.1 The knowledge flow input indicators in university-industry collaborative innovation system

Province	R&D expenditure in enterprises (10,000 yuan)	Enterprise full-time equivalent of R&D personnel in enterprises (man-years)		R&D expenditure in universities (10,000 yuan)	Full-time equivalent of R&D personnel in universities (man-years)	
		Government funds	Enterprise funds		Government funds	Enterprise funds
Beijing	178,377	1,736,105	53,509.80	929,647	378,032	31,240
Tianjin	63,405	2,414,925	60,681.40	211,713	164,091	9544
Hebei	45,057	1,922,642	55,979.20	54,749	31,184	8285
Shanxi	37,926	1,021,842	31,541.60	53,683	27,029	6105
Inner Mongolia	26,413	799,778	21,508.80	27,410	5441	3972
Liaoning	244,351	2,642,180	52,063.50	157,694	196,671	16,414
Jilin	22,933	576,791	24,364.60	141,251	60,803	14,691
Heilongjiang	183,224	706,715	36,255.80	200,350	106,764	14,926
Shanghai	273,835	3,398,486	82,354.80	399,095	194,047	21,171
Jiangsu	220,523	10,366,537	342,262.40	389,912	298,122	20,880
Zhejiang	140,696	5,674,459	228,617.80	261,645	153,554	13,429
Anhui	129,592	1,927,940	73,355.70	160,890	49,669	11,867
Fujian	66,172	2,266,956	90,279.60	48,171	19,940	6326
Jiangxi	47,399	860,382	23,877.40	49,551	28,087	4978

Shandong	295,552	8,620,680	204,397.80	186,222	83,923	16,075
Henan	86,872	2,390,918	102,846.40	94,730	36,357	6565
Hubei	139,544	2,457,729	77,086.90	264,620	141,139	15,201
Hunan	92,660	2,180,258	69,784.20	162,407	65,610	13,083
Guangdong	328,683	10,298,461	424,563.20	310,962	95,379	18,426
Guangxi	33,403	666,371	20,844.70	47,513	20,000	10,204
Hainan	1767	76,150	2767.20	10,294	1157	853
Chongqing	47,467	1,112,571	31,576.80	77,481	78,857	6591
Sichuan	110,321	1,287,853	50,533.00	165,076	201,077	14,169
Guizhou	31,114	266,602	12,135.10	29,309	8609	3298
Yunnan	22,094	356,607	12,321.20	37,925	25,688	5269
Shaanxi	242,923	938,971	36,728.40	186,148	100,977	10,485
Gansu	19,933	314,807	11,445.00	39,038	27,605	3300
Qinghai	4082	80,115	2020.30	8177	536	559
Ningxia	14,994	127,106	4196.40	9801	1448	1557
Xinjiang	9255	262,978	6202.10	22,957	2963	3554

Table 3.2 The knowledge flow output indicators in a university-industry collaborative innovation system

Province	Sales revenue of new products (10,000 yuan)	Patent applications in enterprises (pieces)	Patent applications in universities (pieces)	Scientific papers issued (pieces)
Beijing	36,727,656	19,210	26,178	113,220
Tianjin	55,696,886	16,302	4442	26,869
Hebei	29,160,256	9171	1325	31,005
Shanxi	10,272,735	5083	1333	13,373
Inner Mongolia	6,285,040	2062	270	13,249
Liaoning	40,931,774	11,628	5383	51,531
Jilin	7,031,878	2520	1871	28,634
Heilongjiang	5,825,023	4282	5865	35,282
Shanghai	76,883,835	25,738	12,900	72,225
Jiangsu	197,142,112	93,518	22,721	104,738
Zhejiang	148,820,993	77,067	12,085	43,374
Anhui	43,790,809	32,909	2527	37,394
Fujian	34,400,997	18,896	2797	18,770
Jiangxi	16,829,309	4893	1003	24,040
Shandong	142,841,782	40,030	4625	50,325
Henan	47,914,474	14,400	2021	44,891
Hubei	46,544,784	16,321	5857	70,435
Hunan	57,246,324	17,424	3883	46,185
Guangdong	180,137,410	96,646	6895	63,073
Guangxi	15,866,038	4468	1084	24,716
Hainan	1,601,202	748	78	4715
Chongqing	26,961,130	12,221	3374	29,645
Sichuan	24,758,761	15,713	3981	55,792
Guizhou	3,683,200	3446	443	14,890
Yunnan	4,433,810	2793	1189	20,773
Shaanxi	10,154,791	7258	8089	49,872
Gansu	6,185,275	2440	786	16,951
Qinghai	125,430	334	15	2298
Ningxia	2,796,416	1132	78	5569
Xinjiang	3,533,318	2256	264	12,326

3.4.1   Returns to Scale Analysis

Through the definition of scale efficiency introduced in the previous section, we are able to obtain the returns to scale of the knowledge flow in UICI for each province. The results are in Table 3.5.

From Table 3.5 we can see that, in the traditional black box system, Fujian, Inner Mongolia, and Qinghai Provinces have increasing returns to scale of knowledge efficiency in UICI, while all the other provinces have nonincreasing returns to scale.

Table 3.3 Descriptive statistics

Variable	Average	Maximum	Minimum	S.D.
Full-time equivalent of R&D personnel in universities (man-years)	10,433.90	31,240	559	7114.93
Full-time equivalent of R&D personnel in enterprises (man-years)	74,870.04	424,563.2	2020.3	99,505.21
Enterprises' R&D expenditure from government funds (10,000 yuan)	105,352.3	328,683.3	1767.4	97,448.63
Enterprises' R&D expenditure from enterprise funds (10,000 yuan)	2,258,464	10,366,537	76,150.1	2,824,353
University R&D expenditure from government funds (10,000 yuan)	157,947.4	929,647.2	8177.037	183,283.4
University R&D expenditure from enterprise funds (10,000 yuan)	86,825.28	378,032.4	536.17	93,474.8
Sales revenue of new products (10,000 yuan)	42,819,448.27	197,142,112	125,430	54,103,953.23
Patent applications by enterprises (pieces)	18,696.97	96,646	334	25,900.81
Scientific papers issued by universities (pieces)	37,538.67	113,220	2298	27,265.75
Patent applications by universities (pieces)	4778.733	26,178	15	6305.101

In the parallel system, the returns to scale of knowledge flow efficiency in Jilin Province and Henan Province are constant. Twelve provinces, including Beijing, have decreasing returns to scale. Fourteen provinces, including Hebei, have increasing returns to scale. In addition, we can see that provinces that are economically developed are more likely to be classified by decreasing economies of scale, and provinces with increasing economies of scale are mainly located in the central and western economically underdeveloped regions of China.

3.4.2   Regional Differences Analysis

We now divide China's socioeconomic regions into eight major regions: northeast region (Liaoning, Jilin, Heilongjiang), northern coastal areas (Beijing, Tianjin, Hebei, Shandong), eastern coastal areas (Shanghai, Jiangsu, Zhejiang), southern coastal areas (Fujian, Guangdong, Hainan), the middle reaches of the Yellow River (Shaanxi, Shanxi, Henan, Inner Mongolia), the middle reaches of the Yangtze River (Hubei, Hunan, Jiangxi, Anhui), southwest region (Yunnan, Guizhou,

Table 3.4 Efficiency measures of different models

Province	θ^*_{CRS}	θ^*_{NIRS}	θ^*_{VRS}	$\overline{\theta}^*_{CRS}$	$\overline{\theta}^*_{NIRS}$	$\overline{\theta}^*_{VRS}$
Beijing	1.0000	1.0000	1.0000	0.5903	1.0000	1.0000
Tianjin	0.9889	1.0000	1.0000	0.9412	1.0000	1.0000
Hebei	1.0000	1.0000	1.0000	0.6656	0.6656	0.6692
Shanxi	0.4811	0.4885	0.4885	0.3089	0.3089	0.3189
Inner Mongolia	0.8052	0.8052	0.8300	0.4715	0.4715	0.4974
Liaoning	0.6486	0.7331	0.7331	0.4605	0.4605	0.4636
Jilin	1.0000	1.0000	1.0000	1.0000	1.0000	1.0000
Heilongjiang	0.5733	0.6585	0.6585	0.3869	0.3869	0.3882
Shanghai	0.8995	1.0000	1.0000	0.8232	1.0000	1.0000
Jiangsu	1.0000	1.0000	1.0000	0.8229	1.0000	1.0000
Zhejiang	1.0000	1.0000	1.0000	0.8769	0.8791	0.8791
Anhui	0.9436	0.9583	0.9583	0.6534	0.6546	0.6546
Fujian	0.8084	0.8084	0.8095	0.5968	0.5968	0.6002
Jiangxi	0.5961	0.7525	0.7525	0.5474	0.5474	0.5491
Shandong	1.0000	1.0000	1.0000	0.6453	1.0000	1.0000
Henan	1.0000	1.0000	1.0000	1.0000	1.0000	1.0000
Hubei	0.7755	1.0000	1.0000	0.6291	0.8497	0.8497
Hunan	0.8595	1.0000	1.0000	0.6651	0.6667	0.6667
Guangdong	1.0000	1.0000	1.0000	0.8773	1.0000	1.0000
Guangxi	0.8956	1.0000	1.0000	0.7016	0.7016	0.7095
Hainan	1.0000	1.0000	1.0000	0.9648	0.9648	1.0000
Chongqing	1.0000	1.0000	1.0000	0.9698	0.9903	0.9903
Sichuan	0.7254	0.9999	0.9999	0.4845	0.5530	0.5530
Guizhou	0.8308	0.9888	0.9888	0.6488	0.6488	0.6661
Yunnan	1.0000	1.0000	1.0000	0.5810	0.5810	0.6081
Shaanxi	1.0000	1.0000	1.0000	0.6860	0.6860	0.6861
Gansu	0.9041	1.0000	1.0000	0.8782	0.8782	0.8828
Qinghai	0.4748	0.4748	0.9922	0.3233	0.3233	0.8972
Ningxia	0.7523	0.7553	0.7553	0.5769	0.5769	0.6545
Xinjiang	1.0000	1.0000	1.0000	0.7036	0.7036	0.7416
Average	0.8654	0.9141	0.9322	0.6827	0.7365	0.7642

Sichuan, Chongqing, Guangxi), and northwest region (Gansu, Qinghai, Ningxia, Tibet, Xinjiang). We then compare the efficiencies of knowledge flow in UICI for these different economic regions in Table 3.6.

From Table 3.6 we see that knowledge flow efficiency is the highest in the eastern and western coastal areas. The eastern coastal areas include the Yangtze River Delta, which is economically developed in China, followed by the Bohai Rim region in the northern coastal region and the Pearl River Delta in the southern coastal areas. The three regions are already economically developed. They have scientific and technological strength and a high degree of opening up, and thus their efficiency is generally high. The northwest region is a rising star of economic development, is

Fig. 3.3 Efficiency distribution diagram for different systems

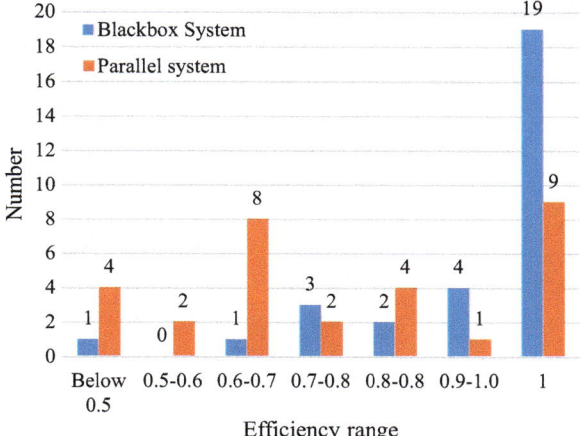

undergoing the process of UICI, and can continue to learn from the successful experiences of other regions, and thus its knowledge efficiency can also turn higher. The northeast region has the lowest efficiency, because it is China's old industrial base. The proportion of its modern service industry and high-tech industry within its GDP is low. Thus, equipment manufacturing products that support capacity and system integration capabilities need to be improved. Because its deep processing capacity of raw material industries is low and the ability of enterprise independent innovation is not strong, this region must continue to thoroughly implement a number of opinions on the comprehensive revitalization of its old industrial base to strengthen cooperation between industry, university, and research, to adhere to collaborative innovation, and to continuously improve enterprises' independent innovation capability.

3.5   Conclusions

This chapter utilizes the DEA efficiency evaluation method of the complex system with the internal structure of parallel DMUs to evaluate and analyze knowledge flow efficiency in UICI in China. The main conclusions are as follows.

First, compared with the traditional DEA efficiency evaluation model, the knowledge efficiency evaluation model in UICI in this chapter breaks through the limitation of the traditional DEA model. The limitation neglects the internal organizational structure of the system. By analyzing the efficiency of knowledge flow in the provinces' UICI, we find that the DEA model with parallel DMUs is able to effectively evaluate the efficiency of the complex system of knowledge flow in UICI with multiple subsystems, as compared to the traditional black box system.

Second, the efficiency of knowledge flow in China's overall UICI is higher. The average efficiency of each province is 0.7642, but the overall development of UICI is

Table 3.5 Results of economies of scale under different systems

Region	Province	Black box system	Parallel system
Eastern region	Beijing	CRS	DRS
	Tianjin	DRS	DRS
	Hebei	CRS	IRS
	Liaoning	DRS	IRS
	Shanghai	DRS	DRS
	Jiangsu	CRS	DRS
	Zhejiang	CRS	DRS
	Fujian	IRS	IRS
	Shandong	CRS	DRS
	Guangdong	CRS	DRS
	Hainan	CRS	IRS
Western region	Inner Mongolia	IRS	IRS
	Guangxi	DRS	IRS
	Chongqing	CRS	DRS
	Sichuan	DRS	DRS
	Guizhou	DRS	IRS
	Yunnan	CRS	IRS
	Shaanxi	CRS	IRS
	Gansu	DRS	IRS
	Qinghai	IRS	IRS
	Ningxia	DRS	IRS
	Xinjiang	CRS	IRS
Central region	Shanxi	DRS	IRS
	Jilin	CRS	CRS
	Heilongjiang	DRS	IRS
	Anhui	DRS	DRS
	Jiangxi	DRS	IRS
	Henan	CRS	CRS
	Hubei	DRS	DRS
	Hunan	DRS	DRS

Note: CRS indicates returns to scale are constant, IRS indicates returns to scale are increasing, and DRS indicates returns to scale are decreasing

not balanced. The efficiency of some provinces is very low, such as Shanxi, Liaoning, Inner Mongolia, Heilongjiang, and other provinces. Their efficiency is less than 0.5. In addition, the provinces of developed regions tend to be classified by decreasing returns to scale. Compared to those provinces, provinces with increasing returns to scale are mainly located in the economically underdeveloped areas of central and western China.

Third, from the analysis of knowledge efficiency differences in UICI of the eight economic regions, the efficiency of knowledge flow in economically developed areas is also higher, such as the provinces of the Yangtze River Delta region, the Bohai Rim region, and the Pearl River Delta region. Therefore, the central

Table 3.6 Knowledge flow efficiency in university-industry collaborative innovation in different economic regions

Regions	Eastern coastal	Northern coastal	Southern coastal	Northwest	Southwest	Middle reaches of Yangtze River	Middle reaches of Yellow River	Northeast
Rank	1	2	3	4	5	6	7	8
Average	0.9597	0.9173	0.8667	0.7940	0.7054	0.6800	0.6256	0.6173

government should establish a reasonable and fair allocation policy of science and technology resources, taking into account the regional economic development imbalance. Based on their own situation, local governments should create a good environment for innovation and reasonable arrangements for innovation scale, in order to stimulate innovation vitality.

Chapter 4
Big Five Personality Traits and Knowledge Flow in University-Industry Collaborative Innovation

4.1 Introduction

The knowledge flow along with the whole process of the collaborative innovation of industry, academia, and research essentially defines that innovation subjects gain the advantages of knowledge in the way that they acquire, transfer, apply, and get feedbacks so as to promote the sharing, transfer, and creation of knowledge. At the same time, they exert the "externalities" and "spillover effects" of it.

University researchers serve as the core factors in the process of collaborative innovation. Their final research results are directly determined by the efficiency and effect of their knowledge. Personality uniquely decides the capacity of coping with the external environment and also personal thoughts and behaviors. In psychology and behavior science, personality is used to explain or predict personal behaviors and performances. At present, the relationship between personality traits and knowledge flow has increasingly drawn the attention of researchers, who have verified a direct relationship between them (Cabrera et al. 2006; Wang and Yang 2007; Matzler et al. 2008; Jadin et al. 2013). At the same time, some researchers have pointed out that personality traits do not directly affect the flow of knowledge but implement the effect through intermediary variables (Mooradian et al. 2006; Matzler et al. 2011; Hsu et al. 2011). Although the predictive effect of personality traits on knowledge flow is beyond a doubt, the influence of personality traits on knowledge flow has no consensus in academia, and there is even a completely opposite conclusion (Teh et al. 2011).

The following questions should therefore be settled. Do the personality traits of university researchers affect the performance of knowledge flow in the process of collaborative research and innovation? Are mediator variables needed to play a role between knowledge flow performance and personality traits? The extant study shows that a change in the external environment is the main factor leading to a change in individual behavior and that the environment plays a regulatory role in the

© Springer International Publishing AG, part of Springer Nature 2018
Y. Yu et al., *Strategy and Performance of Knowledge Flow*,
International Series in Operations Research & Management Science 271,
https://doi.org/10.1007/978-3-319-77926-3_4

relationship between personality and behavior (Shalley et al. 2004). Thus, are there moderator variables to regulate the performance of knowledge flow for personality traits? The abovementioned questions have not been effectively resolved, and relevant research is also scarce.

In view of the gaps in previous research, this chapter will take the micro-perspective of scientific researchers' personal traits and form the basis of theoretical exploration through a sample survey with universities. It analyzes the influence of the personality traits of university researchers on the knowledge flow in the collaborative innovation of industry, academia, and research and then examines the mediating effect of trust among the knowledge subjects and the regulatory effect of justice on this relationship from the perspective of the social exchange theory. The results of the study not only have important theoretical implications for an in-depth study of the relationship between personality traits and knowledge flow but also have important practical significance for the reality of collaborative innovation in industry, academia, and research.

The remainder of this chapter is organized as follows. Section 4.2 gives a brief introduction about Big Five personality traits and then conducts a literature review about the effect of personality traits in Sect. 4.3. Section 4.4 discusses trust, justice, and the role of Big Five personality traits in the knowledge flow of UICI and proposes a causal model. Section 4.5 describes the details of the research design. Section 4.6 presents the results of an empirical study testing the model. The final section of the chapter draws conclusions and discusses implications.

4.2 Big Five Personality Traits[1]

Ever since Allport (1937) and Murray (1938) portray personality psychology as the scientific study of psychological individuality, personality psychologists have focused their investigations on the most important differences in social and emotional functionings that distinguish one whole person from the next. Every human life is a variation on a general evolutionary design, developing over time and in culture (McAdams and Pals 2006). Until now, personality psychologists have made significant advances in identifying many of the most socially consequential features of psychological individuality. A substantial arm of scientific literature supports the construct validity of a wide range of personality variables, from dispositional traits subsumed within the well-known Big Five taxonomy (McCrae and Costa 2008) to motives, goals, values, and the specific self-schemata featured in social-cognitive theories on personality (Mischel 2004). It is now abundantly clear that personality variables are robust predictors of behavior, especially when behavior is aggregated across different situations and over time. Moreover, personality predicts important life outcomes, such as the quality of personal relationships, adaptation to life

---

[1]This description of this section is based on Franić et al. (2014) and McAdams and Olson (2010).

challenges, occupational success, societal involvement, happiness, health, and mortality (Lodi-Smith and Roberts 2007; Ozer and Benet-Martínez 2006).

One of the most influential approaches to personality description over the past century has been the five-factor (FF) approach. Predicated on the lexical approach to personality description, as reflected in Cattell (1943b), "All aspects of human personality which are or have been of importance, interest, or utility have already become recorded in the substance of language," the FF approach is based on the idea that the identification of basic dimensions of human personality is possible via the application of factor analytic techniques to verbal descriptors of human traits.

The beginnings of the FF approach can be traced to Allport and Odbert (1936) and their selection of 4504 psychological trait terms from the Unabridged 1925 Webster's New International Dictionary. Cattell (1943a, b, 1945) augment this list in the 1940s by adding "the substance of all syndromes and types which psychologists have observed and described in the past century or so" and subsequently abbreviate it to a set of 35 variables—a factor analysis that produces 12 "primary" factors. Tupes and Christal (1992) perform a series of factor analyses on Cattell's variables and observe five recurrent orthogonal factors, which they denote as surgency/ extraversion, agreeableness, dependability, emotional stability, and culture (French 1953). Through Norman (1963) and his further addition to, and subsequent abbreviation of, Allport and Odbert's original list and the further selection of adjectives from this list by Lewis R. Goldberg (1990, 1992), a set of variables with a clearer five-factor orthogonal structure was produced. Goldberg (1981, 1982) denotes these FFs as "the Big Five." In a parallel research program and following a cluster analysis of Cattell's Sixteen Personality Factor (16PF) Questionnaire in which three factors were extracted—neuroticism, extraversion, and openness to experience—McCrae and Costa (1983) develop a 144-item, 18-facet, three-dimensional questionnaire that they term the NEO Inventory. After linking their neuroticism and extraversion factors to those from the previous lexically based research (e.g., Goldberg 1980, 1981, 1982), they fully adopt the FF approach and consequently develop measures of agreeableness and conscientiousness. The addition of these scales to the NEO Inventory results in the NEO Personality Inventory (Costa and MacCrae 1985), and the subsequent implementation of facets to measure these two new factors yields the Revised NEO Personality Inventory (NEO-PI-R; Costa and MacCrae (1992)). The NEO Five-Factor Inventory (NEO-FFI) is a shorter, 60-item version of NEO-PI-R.

The FF approach has been extraordinarily influential: numerous behavior genetics studies have assessed the heritabilities of the Big Five and more recently sought associations with measured genetic variants (de Moor et al. 2012); neural and clinical correlates of the FFs have been examined (DeYoung et al. 2010; Nigg et al. 2002); and the model has found wide practical application—for instance, in the field of personnel selection (Schmit and Ryan 1993), job satisfaction, job performance, entrepreneurial innovation, anti-production behavior, user content generation, and other practical areas. Seibert and Kraimer (2001) examine the relationship between the "Big Five" personality dimensions (neuroticism, conscientiousness, extraversion, agreeableness, and openness) and career success, showing results that extraversion is related positively to salary level, promotions, and career satisfaction and that neuroticism is related negatively to career satisfaction. Agreeableness is negatively related to career satisfaction, and openness is negatively related to salary level. Judge and Zapata (2015) develop and test an interactionist model governing the degree to which five-factor model personality traits are related to job performance. Results reveal that all five traits are more predictive of performance for jobs in which the process by which the work is done represents weak situations (e.g., work is unstructured, and employees have discretion to make decisions). Many of the traits also predict performance in job contexts that activate specific traits (e.g., extraversion better predicts performance in jobs requiring social skills, agreeableness is less positively related to performance in competitive contexts, and openness is more strongly related to performance in jobs with strong innovation/creativity requirements).

Picazo-Vela et al. (2010) examine factors that influence an individual's intention to provide an online review, based upon concepts from the Big Five personality framework. Their results show that neuroticism and conscientiousness are significant predictors of an individual's intention to provide an online review. Bui (2017) reexamines the relationship between the Big Five personality traits and job satisfaction to establish whether its findings may challenge the current literature. Hierarchical regressions were employed to investigate the impact of the Big Five traits on job satisfaction among male, female, young, middle-aged, and elderly subsamples. The results show that extraversion has no significant impact on job satisfaction in any group of employees, while up to four other traits are significantly linked to job satisfaction in the subgroups. The younger the employees are, the larger the number of traits they display that have a significant impact (both positively and negatively) on job satisfaction. That study also presents differences in this relationship between male and female employees. Its findings imply that the relationships among the Big Five traits and job satisfaction are more complex than shown in the literature. Therefore, using the dispositional approach to job satisfaction, managers should take different approaches to age and gender, because job satisfaction is likely to vary among the different aspects of the two.

In summary, the five personality traits have been widely used to explain or predict a person's behavior and performance. This chapter uses the five personality traits model as the theoretical basis of personality traits and explores the influences of scientific researchers' different personality traits on the flow of knowledge in the process of collaborative innovation in production, teaching, and research.

4.3   Literature Review

Personality traits have always been an important theme for the discussion of human behavior. Allport (1961) argues that personality is a unique form that determines an individual "adapting to the external environment" and his/her "thought and behavior." Thus, the individual's behavior will reflect his/her unique character traits, and when these features continue to appear in different situations, they are called personality traits. In psychology and behavioral science, personality traits are often used to explain or predict a person's behavior and performance. In recent years, scholars at home and abroad have carried out research on the impact of personality on knowledge flow.

4.3.1 Direct Effect of Personality Traits

Á. Cabrera et al. (2006) argue that empirical openness promotes knowledge exchange of an individual's self-reports. At the same time, the higher the degree of openness is for individual experience, the higher the curiosity is. This will stimulate the interests of seeking both advice and opinions from others. Harari et al. (2014) indicate that extraversion is the most robust determinant of knowledge transfer among the Big Five factors but that conscientiousness and openness are relevant as well. Chong et al. (2014) conduct a survey of six private colleges and six public colleges in Malaysia, finding a positive correlation between extraversion, conscientiousness, instructor support, degree of competition, technology support, and knowledge sharing patterns. There is a negative correlation between the emotional stability and knowledge sharing patterns. The study argues that teachers can contribute to the sharing of knowledge among students by organizing task groups and providing adequate support and technical support.

Matzler et al. (2008) study the impact of the three personality traits of peculiarity, accountability, and openness on knowledge sharing. Jadin et al. (2013) investigate the effects of personality traits on knowledge sharing in a virtual open content community he influence of personality on knowledge sharing in an open virtual community, based on the spillover theory and social value orientation theory, and find that trendsetting represents the most prominent trait of the three under study by increasing the likelihood of an individual's knowledge contribution to Wikipedia. Their study also suggests that authorship of Wikipedia is associated with higher levels of trendsetting and a prosocial value orientation, and this effect is moderated by individual differences in motivations to write. Teh et al. (2011) collect data from 255 university students at two Malaysian universities, finding that extraversion and neuroticism are positively related to the attitude toward knowledge sharing. Openness to experience is found to have an inverse relationship with the attitude toward knowledge sharing. Subjective norm is positively related to the attitude toward knowledge sharing. Attitude toward knowledge sharing and subjective norm are both found to be independently and significantly related to the intention to share knowledge, which significantly influences knowledge sharing behavior. Wang and Yang (2007) indicate that extraversion, agreeableness, and conscientiousness are positively related to individuals' intention to share knowledge in a high-technology laboratory.

4.3.2 Indirect Effect of Personality Traits

Hsu et al. (2011) research the relationships among the construction of team members' personality traits (five personality traits model), team progress (emotional relationships), and team results (knowledge sharing), based on the input-progress-output (IPO) model, and show that a team with a high level of conscientiousness, agreeableness, openness to experience, and extroversion has on average a high level of knowledge sharing. Agreeableness and extroversion also have effects on knowledge sharing within a team through internal emotional relationships. Matzler et al. (2011) note that agreeableness and responsibility influence knowledge sharing through affective commitment and documentation of knowledge. Their research shows that agreeableness influence affective commitment from individuals to organizations. Affective commitment and responsibility can predict the level of documentation of knowledge. Affective commitment and documentation of knowledge influence the level of knowledge sharing. Mooradian et al. (2006) analyze the influences from trust propensity and agreeableness on knowledge sharing through interpersonal trust.

4.3.3 Moderating Effect of Personality Traits

There is little research presently concerning the moderating effect of personality traits on knowledge sharing. Shim (2010) analyzes the relationship between workplace incivility and knowledge sharing intention. The results show that there is a negative correlation between workplace incivility and knowledge sharing intention, and conscientiousness has a moderating effect on the relationship. Although workplace incivility exists objectively, it is more likely that staff with a high level of conscientiousness will share knowledge than those having a low level of conscientiousness. The conclusions above indicate that the effect of personality on knowledge sharing is a much talked about theme in the aspect of knowledge sharing. Research studies have proved that effective knowledge flow benefits the completion of missions and tasks, while the human factor is the key point of knowledge sharing. Academia does not have a consensus on the effects of personality on knowledge flow, and even some completely opposite conclusions are acknowledged. Therefore, this chapter focuses on personality traits of university scientific workers and knowledge flow in UICI, with the goal of finding some issues and providing advice to promote further developments in this area.

4.4   Research Hypothesis

Personality is a unique form that decides an individual's adaptation to the external environment, thoughts, and behavior. Different personality traits of university scientific workers certainly affect the performance of knowledge flow in the progress of collaborative innovation.

4.4.1   Personality Trait

Norman (1963) constructs the five personality traits model, with a consensus later built by a series of research: the basic framework of personality consists of five factors, the so-called "Big Five," while the five personality traits model built by McCrae and Costa is the most widely accepted one. The five factors are agreeableness, consciousness, extroversion, emotional stability, and openness to experience. Neuroticism Extraversion Openness Personality Inventory-Revised (NEO-PI-R) was established from those factors above. Emotional stability means stability of individual emotions and intention of inner feelings. Extroversion means the strength and dynamic characteristics of the nervous system. Openness to experience means the openness, wisdom, and creativity of individual to experiences. Agreeableness means the orientation of humanitarianism and networking. Consciousness means the ability of self-discipline, responsibility, and motivation to make achievements. Personality is the intention of thinking-feeling-doing stability. As university scientific workers are the key point of collaborative innovation, their personality traits certainly affect the knowledge flow in its progress, thereby affecting knowledge flow performance. According to these conclusions, this research builds the following hypotheses:

H1: Personality traits of university scientific workers affect knowledge flow performance in the progress of UICI.

H1a: Agreeableness of university scientific workers positively affects knowledge flow performance in the progress of UICI.

H1b: Consciousness of university scientific workers positively affects knowledge flow performance in the progress of UICI.

H1c: Extroversion of university scientific workers positively affects knowledge flow performance in the progress of UICI.

H1d: Emotional stability of university scientific workers positively affects knowledge flow performance in the progress of UICI.

H1e: Openness to experience of university scientific workers positively affects knowledge flow performance in the progress of UICI.

4.4.2 Trust

Sabel (1993) and Rousseau et al. (1998) suppose that trust means one party is confident that the other party will not use its own vulnerability based on the positive expectations from one party to another party's behavior intention. Moorman et al. (1992) note that trust is the wish to believe trading partners and that trading partners are considered to be reliable. Vangen and Huxham (2003) state that trust is treated as a significant factor in the progress of cooperation. They highlight the significance of trust in the development of cooperation through the intensive process. Dyer and Chu (2000) present that trust is believing in partners and being willing and able to complete their duties and promises, while parties do not do harm to each other out of good expectation to the whole alliance. This research indicates that in the progress of universities participating in UICI, the trust between universities and enterprises means that each unit believes its partner will not take advantage of its own fragility, including adverse selection, moral hazard, overpricing, and other fragility, so as to achieve a positive expectation to effective cooperation. Successful UICI demands that each unit shares resources consumed in different steps of technical innovation according to each unit's advantages, mutually participating and mutually sharing risks of techniques and markets. It demands every unit to trust each other, making full use of each unit's advantages, achieving resource sharing and complementary advantages, in order to shorten the cycle and risk of innovation, achieving a win-win situation eventually.

Scholars around the world have so far done relevant studies about the mediating effect of trust on knowledge flow. Levin and Cross (2004) find that a strong relationship affects the earnings of knowledge searchers via trust. Cheng et al. (2008) research the mediating effect of trust on knowledge sharing in a supply chain. Santoro and Saparito (2003) study the mediating effect of trust on university-enterprise's joint creation of knowledge and new technology production relationships. Therefore, this essay speculates further that trust is possibly a mediating variable between the personality traits of university scientific workers and knowledge flow in UICI.

H2: Trust has a mediating effect on the relationship between personality traits of university scientific workers and knowledge flow performance in UICI.

H2a: Trust has a mediating effect on the relationship between agreeableness of university scientific workers and knowledge flow performance in UICI.

H2b: Trust has a mediating effect on the relationship between consciousness of university scientific workers and knowledge flow performance in UICI.

H2c: Trust has a mediating effect on the relationship between extroversion of university scientific workers and knowledge flow performance in UICI.

H2d: Trust has a mediating effect on the relationship between emotional stability of university scientific workers and knowledge flow performance in UICI.

H2e: Trust has a mediating effect on the relationship between openness to experiences of university scientific workers and knowledge flow performance in UICI.

4.4.3 Justice

Justice is a significant value idea in group society and the social psychology domain. Initially, the social exchange theory put forward by Homans (1958) was used to discuss distributive justice. In 1965, Adams presented the equity theory of personal concern to the input-output ratio from the perspective of social comparative psychology. Greenberg (1987) discusses whether it is fair for people to escape or avoid unfair distribution conditions that result in the dimension of content. In the dimension of program, the discussion focuses on the process of decision-making justice and people's pursuit of procedural justice. Because knowledge flow is the social exchange system in human networking, the content of procedural justice and distributive justice should be valued by managers of UICI. Therefore, this essay analyzes the effect on UICI in terms of procedural justice and distributive justice.

Distributive Justice

Distributive justice means that people will compare their input-output ratio with that of referential objects. They may feel unfair if their ratio and that of the referential objects are different. Extant research has pointed out that distributive justice significantly predicts members' working performance (Greenberg 1990; Zohar 1995; Janssen et al. 2010).

In university collaborative innovation, the acknowledgment of university scientific workers to distributive justice certainly affects the next step. Once unfairness occurs, they will refuse to devote themselves to knowledge flow business. The level of distributive justice affects the influence of personality traits of university scientific workers on knowledge flow performance in UICI. Thus, we build the hypothesis below:

H3a: The level of distributive justice in UICI has a positive effect on knowledge flow performance.

Procedural Justice

Procedural justice means the staff's cognition level on whether the organizational decision-making procedure is fair or not. Basically, the moderating and configuration of organizational resources have particular programs. Leventhal (1980) put forward seven significant program elements during organizational distribution: (1) choosing the agent to be responsible for collecting information, (2) setting the distribution decisions, (3) setting and informing related parties about the basic pay and the allocation of resources, (4) collecting and obtaining related information, (5) announcing the content of the decision-making structure, (6) providing the right to appeal for those who are discontent with the distribution results, and (7) taking protective measures to ensure program execution, while avoiding any destruction to the system. The distribution program should be equipped with a reform mechanism to amend the original one if any improper details arise.

The concept of "procedural justice" could apply to any social system. The majority of related research studies point out that the influence of procedural justice on staff not only includes the satisfaction of results but also contains the positive effect on working attitudes (organizational promises and organizational citizenship behavior). Similarly, the level of procedural justice in UICI certainly affects university scientific workers' attitudes, behavior of knowledge flow, and so on, further affecting the knowledge flow performance in UICI. Thus, we set up the following hypothesis:

H3b: The level of procedural justice in UICI positively affects knowledge flow performance.

According to the above analysis, research studies indicate that a change in the external environment is the main reason for a change in individual behavior. Environment has a moderating effect on the relationship between personality and behavior. University scientific workers with different personality traits have different cognition about distributive justice and procedural justice in UICI, which certainly results in different behavior styles. Therefore, it is reasonable to suppose that justice could be the moderating variable between university scientific workers' personality traits and knowledge flow performance in UICI. Thus, we have the next 12 hypotheses.

H4: The level of distributive justice in UICI positively regulates the influence that scientific workers' personality traits have on knowledge flow performance.

H4a: The level of distributive justice in UICI positively regulates the influence that scientific workers' agreeableness has on knowledge flow performance.

H4b: The level of distributive justice in UICI positively regulates the influence that scientific workers' consciousness has on knowledge flow performance.

H4c: The level of distributive justice in UICI positively regulates the influence that scientific workers' extroversion has on knowledge flow performance.

H4d: The level of distributive justice in UICI positively regulates the influence that scientific workers' emotional stability has on knowledge flow performance.

H4e: The level of distributive justice in UICI positively regulates the influence that scientific workers' openness to experiences has on knowledge flow performance.

H5: The level of procedural justice in UICI positively regulates the influence that scientific workers' personality traits have on knowledge flow performance.

H5a: The level of distributive justice in UICI positively regulates the influence that scientific workers' agreeableness has on knowledge flow performance.

H5b: The level of procedural justice in UICI positively regulates the influence that scientific workers' consciousness has on knowledge flow performance.

H5c: The level of procedural justice in UICI positively regulates the influence that scientific workers' extroversion has on knowledge flow performance.

H5d: The level of procedural justice in UICI positively regulates the influence that scientific workers' emotional stability has on knowledge flow performance.

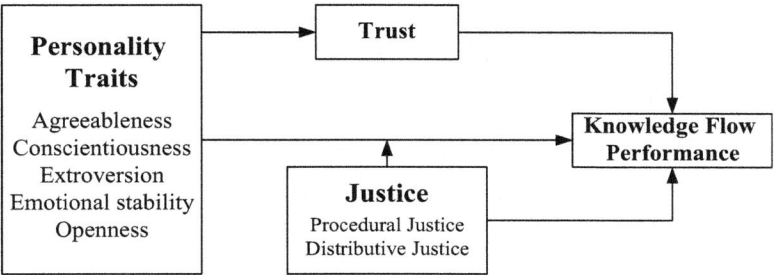

Fig. 4.1 The research framework for Big Five personality traits and knowledge flow performance

H5e: The level of procedural justice in UICI positively regulates the influence that scientific workers' openness to experiences has on knowledge flow performance.

According to the above hypotheses, this study sets up a theory framework model, shown in Fig. 4.1.

4.5 Research Design

4.5.1 Data

There are presently 3 national collaborative innovation centers and 59 provincial project construction collaborative innovation centers in Jiangsu Province. The collaborative work of innovation in Jiangsu Province is at the forefront of the country, and so this research questionnaire focused on the relevant colleges and universities in Jiangsu Province. Through the commission of the relevant university science and technology management department, the researchers who undertake or participate in the work of collaborative innovation of industry, academia, and research are the survey objects of the questionnaire.

The design of the questionnaire refers to related research around the world, and experts in the field of collaborative innovation were consulted. After the preliminary design of the questionnaire was completed, the questionnaire was published online. Relevant researchers were invited to conduct research in advance. The questionnaire was then improved according to the results of pre-research. In the formal survey, 200 questionnaires were distributed, and 105 valid questionnaires were collected. The effective questionnaire response was 52.5%. Based on the effective questionnaires, the descriptive statistical results of the survey samples are shown in Table 4.1.

Table 4.1 Descriptive statistics

Variable	Category	Number	Ratio
Gender	Male	84	80%
	Female	21	20%
Age	20–30 years old	7	6.7%
	31–40 years old	59	56.2%
	41–50 years old	28	26.7%
	51–60 years old	11	10.5%
Years working	Under 2 years	8	7.6%
	3–5 years	26	24.8%
	6–10 years	22	21.0%
	Over 10 years	49	46.7%
Title	Professor	13	12.4%
	Associate professor	64	61.0%
	Lecturer	23	21.9%

4.5.2 Measures

We employ the five-point Likert scale to evaluate the scale of the questionnaire, with 1 = very disagree to 5 = very agree.

The five personality traits of university researchers were measured by Costa and McCrae's self-assessment of the NEO five-factor personality questionnaire presented in 1992. There are 12 statements and a total of 60 questions referring to 5 categories of personality traits. Knowledge flow performance was measured using the items from Simonin (1999) and Leonard-Barton (1988). Distributive justice was adapted from Kumar et al. (1995); Colquitt (2001), and Luo (2007). We use the items from Kumar et al. (1995) and Colquitt (2001) to measure procedural justice and measure trust using the scale setup by McKnight et al. (2002).

We control the demographic characteristics that may affect the flow of knowledge in the process of collaborative innovation, including the gender, age, years working, title, degree, academic leaders, and overseas study or work experience of university researchers. Among them, gender, academic leaders, and overseas study or work experience are all categorical variables. The variable encoding rules are shown in Table 4.2.

4.6 Results

4.6.1 Reliability and Validity

In order to improve the data quality of this study, we analyze the reliability and validity of the recovered data. The reliability analysis uses Cronbach's alpha coefficients. In general, when the Cronbach's alpha value is greater than 0.6, it indicates that the questionnaire basically meets the internal consistency requirements. We explore validity analysis by exploratory factor analysis and perform KMO sample

Table 4.2   Encoding rules of control variables

Variable	Label	Value	Measure
Gender	Male	1	Nominal data
	Female	0	
Age	20–30 years old	1	Ordinal data
	31–40 years old	2	
	41–50 years old	3	
	51–60 years old	4	
Years working	Under 2 years	1	Ordinal data
	3–5 years	2	
	6–10 years	3	
	Over 10 years	4	
Title	Assistant	1	Ordinal data
	Lecturer	2	
	Associate professor	3	
	Professor	4	
Degree	Bachelor	1	Ordinal data
	Master	2	
	Doctor	3	
	Postdoctoral	4	
Academic leader	Yes	1	Nominal data
	No	0	
Overseas study or work experience	Yes	1	Nominal data
	No	0	

measurements and Bartlett tests before factor analysis. Factor analysis uses principal component analysis for Varimax rotation. In general, when the KMO value is greater than 0.5, the Bartlett test Sig value is less than 0.001, and the items of the load factor are greater than 0.5, thus indicating that the questionnaire achieves the requirements of validity. In the process of analysis, some items with poor reliability are rejected. Finally, we obtain the subject of this research variable. Reliability and validity test results are shown in Table 4.3.

4.6.2   Mediating Effect

As shown in Table 4.4, the gender, age, years working, title, degree, academic leaders, and overseas study or work experience of university researchers are introduced into the model as a control variable.

The first step, model M1, uses the knowledge flow performance as the dependent variable and then use the independent variables of the five personality traits to do the regression. The standardized coefficient of conscientiousness is 0.241, which is significant at the 0.1 level, indicating that the sense of responsibility of the university

Table 4.3 Reliability and validity test

Variable	Item	Loading coefficient	KMO	Cronbach's alpha
Openness	I am intrigued by the patterns I find in art and nature	0.740	0.710	0.646
	I often try new and foreign foods	0.766		
	Sometimes when I am reading poetry or looking at a work of art, I feel a chill or wave of excitement	0.636		
	I have a lot of intellectual curiosity	0.641		
Emotional stability	I often feel inferior to others	0.646	0.846	0.816
	When I'm under a great deal of stress, sometimes I feel like I'm going to pieces	0.635		
	I rarely feel lonely or blue	0.619		
	I often feel tense and jittery	0.651		
	Sometimes I feel completely worthless	0.565		
	I often get angry at the way people treat me	0.611		
	Too often, when things go wrong, I get discouraged and feel like giving up	0.634		
	I often feel helpless and want someone else to solve my problems	0.731		
	At times I have been so ashamed that I just wanted to hide	0.647		
Extroversion	I really enjoy talking to people	0.627	0.762	0.741
	I often feel as if I'm bursting with energy	0.725		
	I am a cheerful, high-spirited person	0.727		
	My life is fast-paced	0.702		
	I am a very active person	0.724		
Agreeableness	I often get into arguments with my family and co-workers	0.537	0.832	0.775
	Some people think I'm selfish and egotistical	0.669		
	I tend to be cynical and skeptical of others' intentions	0.748		
	Many people think of me as somewhat cold and calculating	0.727		
	If I don't like people, I let them know it	0.743		
	If necessary, I am willing to manipulate people to get what I want	0.686		

(continued)

Table 4.3 (continued)

Variable	Item	Loading coefficient	KMO	Cronbach's alpha
Conscientiousness	I'm pretty good at pacing myself so as to get things done on time	0.718	0.835	0.826
	I try to perform all the tasks assigned to me conscientiously	0.730		
	I have a clear set of goals and work toward them in an orderly fashion	0.732		
	I work hard to accomplish my goals	0.658		
	When I make a commitment, I can always be counted on to follow through	0.717		
	I am a productive person who always gets the job done	0.735		
	I strive for excellence in everything I do	0.611		
Procedural justice	There is no discrimination between us and other collaborative units	0.810	0.695	0.791
	Collaborative units sometimes change policies, because of our objections	0.844		
	The policies and plans of the collaborative units have carefully considered our objections	0.872		
Distributive justice	Our funding is fair compared to the efforts and inputs we make in the process of cooperating with collaborative units	0.904	0.805	0.926
	Our funding is fair compared to the roles and responsibilities we have in the process of cooperating with collaborative units	0.907		
	Our funding is fair compared to the amount of money that other units have received from their partnership	0.904		
	Our funding and coordination units are fair compared to the funds we have obtained from our partnership	0.905		
Trust	Collaborative units can complete the tasks entrusted to the cooperation agreement	0.889	0.739	0.875
	Collaborative units are sincere and responsible for what they agree with	0.894		
	Collaborative units treat us fairly and impartially	0.836		
	Although we do not agree with the decision of collaborative units, we believe that the will of their actions is good	0.787		

(continued)

Table 4.3 (continued)

Variable	Item	Loading coefficient	KMO	Cronbach's alpha
Knowledge flow performance	The whole process of collaborative innovation is very smooth	0.779	0.828	0.871
	The collaborative units commit funds to the lead university in full and on time	0.797		
	Cooperation achieves the desired results	0.846		
	The two sides are satisfied with the process of cooperation	0.856		
	The two sides have established long-term collaborative innovation and cooperative relations	0.707		
	Collaborative innovation has incurred corresponding innovation results	0.712		

Table 4.4 Results of the mediating effect test

		Performance of knowledge flow	Trust	Performance of knowledge flow
		M1	M2	M3
Control variable	Gender	0.047	0.021	0.034
	Age	−0.072	−0.022	−0.058
	Years working	−0.017	−0.148	0.075
	Title	−0.198	−0.111	−0.129
	Degree	0.041	−0.073	0.086
	Academic leaders	0.253	0.065	0.213
	Overseas study or work experience	0.007	0.060	−0.030
Independent variable	Agreeableness	0.045	0.099	−0.016
	Conscientiousness	0.241*	0.458***	−0.042
	Extraversion	0.109	−0.068	0.151
	Neuroticism	0.138	0.037	0.115
	Openness to experience	0.201*	0.139	0.115
Intermediate variable	Trust			0.618***
R square		0.562***	0.550***	0.762***

Note: * Sig. <0.1; *** Sig. <0.001

researchers has a significant positive impact on the knowledge flow in the process of collaborative innovation. Thus, H1b is verified. The normalization coefficient of openness is 0.201, and it is significant at the 0.1 level, which indicates that the openness trait of university researchers also has a significant positive effect on the knowledge flow. Thus, H1c is verified.

The second step, model M2, takes trust as the dependent variable and applies the five personality traits as the independent variables to do the regression. The standardized coefficient of conscientiousness is 0.458, and it is significant at the level of 0.001, which indicates that the professional personality of university researchers has a significant positive effect on the trust perception in the process of collaborative innovation. In addition, the intermediary effect needs to be further examined. The regression coefficients of other personality traits are not significant, and so there is no mediating effect.

The third step, model M3, uses knowledge flow performance as the dependent variable and uses the five personality traits and trust as the independent variables to do the regression. The normalization coefficient of trust is 0.618, which is significant at the level of 0.001. The effect of conscientiousness on knowledge flow performance is not significant. According to the test method of mediating effect from Baron and Kenny (1986), it shows that researchers' trust perception in the process of collaborative research and innovation has a complete mediating effect on the performance of knowledge flow. Therefore, H2b is confirmed.

4.6.3 Moderating Effect

The test object is for verifying the moderating effect between two variables: procedural justice and distributive justice. The gender, age, years working, title, degree, academic leaders, and overseas study or work experience of the university researchers are taken as the control variables. Five personality traits of universities' scientific researchers are set as independent variables. Knowledge flow performance is regarded as the dependent variable. Hierarchical regression analysis is then performed, based on procedural justice and distribution of justice, which are taken as moderating variables. Table 4.5 lists the results.

Model M0 is the regression model of the dependent variable for the control variables. Model M1 is the regression model of the dependent variable for the control variables and the independent variables. Models M2 and M4 are the regression models of the control variables, the independent variables, and the moderating variables to the dependent variables. Models M3 and M5 are regression models presenting the interaction effect. Models M2 and M4 find that the normalization coefficient for the impact of the distribution of justice on knowledge flow performance is 0.484 and is significant at the level of 0.001 and that the standardized coefficient referring to procedural justice is 0.481 and is significant at the 0.001 level. This shows that the distribution of equity and procedural justice in the process of collaborative innovation has a significant positive impact on knowledge flow performance. Thus, both H3a and H3b are verified.

From M3 and M5 in Table 4.5, we find that only the interaction represented in the product form between university researchers' extraversion and the distribution of justice is significant at the level of 0.1. After adding the interaction in the product form between the distributive justice and independent variables, the R square value

Table 4.5 Results of the moderating effect test

		Performance of knowledge flow					
		M0	M1	M2	M3	M4	M5
Control variable	Gender	0.169*	0.047	0.041	0.087	0.034	0.053
	Age	−0.160	−0.072	−0.219	−0.275	−0.127	−0.162
	Years working	−0.050	−0.017	0.096	0.110	0.054	0.025
	Title	−0.137	−0.198	−0.131	−0.121	−0.129	−0.062
	Degree	0.009	0.041	0.024	0.008	0.032	−0.011
	Academic leaders	0.266**	0.253	0.284	0.274	0.262	0.270
	Overseas study or work experience	−0.039	0.007	0.031	0.050	0.028	−0.004
Independent variable	Agreeableness		0.045	0.080	0.109	0.033	−0.005
	Conscientiousness		0.241*	0.054	0.077	0.269**	0.297**
	Extraversion		0.109	0.061	0.018	0.021	0.009
	Neuroticism		0.138	0.139	0.141	0.142	0.152
	Openness to experience		0.201*	0.175*	0.162	0.127	0.072
Moderating variable	Distributive justice			0.484***	0.514***	0.481***	
	Procedural justice						0.465***

Interaction						
Agreeableness × distributive justice				−0.016		
Conscientiousness × distributive justice				0.040		
Extraversion × distributive justice				0.234*		
Neuroticism × distributive justice				−0.083		
Openness to experience × distributive justice				−0.017		
Agreeableness × procedural justice						−0.230**
Conscientiousness × procedural justice						0.108
Extraversion × procedural justice						−0.061
Neuroticism × procedural justice						−0.261**
Openness to experience × procedural justice						−0.081
R square	0.120	0.315	0.481	0.546	0.521	0.563
R square change	0.120	0.195	0.165	0.066	0.206	0.042
F change	1.895*	5.245***	28.954***	2.491**	39.155***	1.653

Note PS: * Sig. <0.1; ** Sig. <0.05; *** Sig. <0.001

of the model increases, and the corresponding P value is significant at level of 0.05, which proves the validity of H4c and illustrates that the influences of distribution justice and the other four personality traits have no significant effect on knowledge flow performance in the process of collaborative innovation. Moreover, the change of the F value after increasing the justice and the independent variables is not significant. Therefore, we consider that the effect of procedural justice on the relationship between the five personality traits of university researchers and the performance of knowledge flow in the collaborative innovation does not exist.

4.7 Conclusions

This research chooses scientific researchers from Jiangsu Collaborative Innovation Center as the research objects. By analyzing the relevant literature, this chapter looks at the influencing process of university researchers' five personality traits on the performance of knowledge flow during the process of collaborative innovation of production, learning, and research. We also study the regulation effect of justice and the intermediary function of trust during the influencing process. In addition, we construct and validate a hypothesis model, concluding with several discoveries noted as follows.

First, the conscientiousness and openness to experience of university researchers have a positive effect on the performance of knowledge flow in the collaborative innovation of production, teaching, and research. The results show that the higher the degree is of conscientiousness by university researchers, the higher the degree is of openness to experience, and they are more conducive to improving knowledge flow performance in the collaborative innovation of production, teaching, and research. This is similar to the conclusion of research papers in foreign countries.

Second, mutual trust between the innovation subjects has a positive effect on the knowledge flow performance in the process of collaborative innovation. At the same time, it also plays an intermediary role between the degree of researchers' conscientiousness and knowledge flow performance. In particular, in addition to the direct effect, the degree of conscientiousness also positively influences the performance of knowledge flow through the intermediary effect of mutual trust among the various innovation subjects. In the process of examining the factors that influence the performance of knowledge flow in collaborative innovation, this chapter not only examines the microcosmic mechanism of university researchers' personality traits but also takes the macroscopic mechanism of mutual trust between the innovators into account. It thus further deepens the theoretical understanding of this problem. This research gives inspiration to managers that, by strengthening the mutual trust between universities and other innovative subjects, the researchers in colleges and universities can fully make use of the intermediate variable to make a positive effect on the performance of knowledge flow. Therefore, this result is of great significance to help managers to guide and handle the relevant innovation activities and to make a comprehensive and systematic organizational decision.

Third, procedural justice and distribution justice also have a positive effect on the performance of knowledge flow in the process of collaborative innovation. The conclusion states that managers should use procedural justice and distribution justice to improve the enterprises' commitment to synergistic units, so that the two sides can be better dedicated toward collaborative innovation. Managers should analyze the pursuit of innovation objectives, specify their preference of justice type, and pay attention to real-world practice. If so, then changing their behavior can improve the performance of knowledge flow and further enhance the ability of innovation.

Fourth, the interaction between the extroversion of researchers and the justice of the distribution has a positive effect on knowledge flow performance. This shows that the extroversion trait does not independently affect the performance of knowledge flow in the process of collaborative innovation. It needs to be combined with the distribution of justice. These two aspects have an impact on performance and illustrate that the collaborative innovation of production, teaching, and research needs a good external environment, in order to promote scientific researchers to show their own characteristics and enhance the performance of knowledge innovation.

The theoretical significance of this study is to regard the personality characteristics of university researchers as a context variable, analyze the problem of knowledge flow performance in the process of collaborative innovation, and get relevant empirical evidence. It thus breaks through the limitation of the extant knowledge flow performance research, which is only concerned about the sender's ability to send knowledge and the recipient's ability to absorb knowledge and other variables. It is of great value for future research that wants to explore the microcosmic factors of the collaborative innovation of production, teaching, and research, especially concerning the influence of the personality characteristics of the researchers on the relationship between the performance variables of knowledge flow. From the practical point of view, this chapter presents guiding significance for optimizing the composition of the innovation team. For example, in the case of a high level of knowledge flow in the collaborative innovation of production, learning, and research, the personality differences of researchers should be as great as possible in line with social norms. However, in the case of low performance level, it is not necessary to do so. Such revelations are not available from previous research studies on the improvement of performance in knowledge flow during the process of collaborative innovation of production, learning, and research, and thus this study helps fill a gap in the literature.

Chapter 5
Personality, Team Goals, Motivation, and Tacit Knowledge Sharing Performance Within a University Research Team

5.1 Introduction

As important bases to cultivate high-level innovative talents and as also two of the main forces of original innovation in basic research and high-technology field, colleges and universities continually supply fresh troops to address the issue of the national economy and to accomplish the successful transfer of technology and achievements. The research team is a group made up of researchers having complementary skills and being responsible for each other under a common research objective, research goal, and working method. In colleges and universities, the cultivation of discipline leaders, the integration of research direction, the nurturing of characteristic discipline, the promotion of overlapping discipline, the solution to important scientific problems, the acceleration of major scientific research achievements, etc. can all be achieved by forming a research team. Research teams in universities are the main conduit of knowledge dissemination and innovation in the national innovation system, as intellectual activity runs throughout the whole process. For research teams in universities with an academic organization form having the purpose of studying, tacit knowledge sharing plays a decisive role for the completion of team tasks.

Relevant scholars have studied knowledge sharing in research teams at universities from different angles. Ali et al. (2017) present the reasons for knowledge sharing reluctance among team members in a software development team. Tang and Naumann (2015) find that the interaction of teamwork's value diversity and a team's positive mood positively affects team creativity and is mediated by team knowledge sharing in Chinese R&D teams. Jafari Navimipour and Charband (2016) offer a systematic overview of the knowledge sharing mechanisms in project teams. Ghobadi (2015) provides a review on knowledge sharing drivers in software teams. Rosendaal and Bijlsma-Frankema (2015) note the indirect effects of trust variables through team identification and a direct effect of trust in team members on

© Springer International Publishing AG, part of Springer Nature 2018
Y. Yu et al., *Strategy and Performance of Knowledge Flow*,
International Series in Operations Research & Management Science 271,
https://doi.org/10.1007/978-3-319-77926-3_5

knowledge sharing, and there is no relation between work value diversity and knowledge sharing if team identification is low, while the relation takes a negative curvilinear form if team identification is high. Zhu (2016) examines the interplay between team identification and organizational identification, as well as their joint effects on knowledge sharing disparity and in-group bias. Ambos et al. (2016) state that geographical and cultural imbalances negatively affect knowledge sharing. The highest negative impact is observed in teams with geographically or culturally isolated members. Interestingly, we find no adverse effects of cultural and geographical distances (separation), which have been at the center of a large stream of research in international business.

Brenda et al. (2016) examine the interrelations of the team environment factors of trust and affiliation, the motivation factors of perceived reciprocal benefits, and the importance of enjoyment to determine how they influence knowledge sharing within loose-linked global virtual teams. Olaisen and Revang (2017) find that formal intellectual property rights are key to building up and keeping trust on the team and also for building up the right attitudes within the team. IPRs increase the innovativeness of the team and enhance incremental innovations. IPRs foster a unique knowledge sharing in a team, enabling them to work toward innovative solutions and delivering them on time. Formal IPRs foster informal trust and expertise sharing and thus also interorganizational cooperation. Confidence and knowledge sharing strengthen the possibility for future collaboration and innovations both on an individual level and on a corporate level.

Huang (2009) proposes a research model based on knowledge sharing and group cohesiveness to examine team performance in technology R&D teams. The results of that study suggest that (1) TMS positively and significantly mediates the relationship between trust and knowledge sharing and (2) group cohesiveness exerts a positive and significant effect on team performance. It also discusses the implications of knowledge sharing and group cohesiveness with team performance for technology R&D teams. Liu and Phillips (2011) examine how a transformational leadership (TFL) climate influences employees' team identity and their intentions to share knowledge and how team knowledge sharing intention subsequently influences team innovativeness. Pinjani and Palvia (2013) show that in global virtual teams, a deep level of diversity has a more significant relationship with team processes of mutual trust and knowledge sharing than a visible functional level of diversity. This relationship is moderated by the collaborative capabilities of available technology and the levels of interdependence of the task. Furthermore, knowledge sharing and mutual trust mediate the relationship between diversity levels and team effectiveness.

Ding et al. (2014) find that the relation between affect-based trust and knowledge sharing is completely mediated by team-based self-esteem and team identification. Yu et al. (2013) reveal that social capital at both levels influences an individual's explicit and tacit knowledge sharing. Furthermore, when individuals possess a moderate betweenness centrality and the full team holds moderate network density, team members' knowledge sharing can be maximized. Ghobadi and D'Ambra (2013) integrate the Coopetitive Model of Knowledge Sharing and Social

Interdependence Theory to explain the forces behind high-quality knowledge sharing in cross-functional software development teams.

Although the research on knowledge sharing at the team level has already obtained certain research results, there is a shortage of theoretical and empirical research for analyzing the effect of knowledge sharing performance from the perspective of team members' personality and goals. In this regard, this study intends to construct a framework for analyzing the influence factors of tacit knowledge sharing performance in university research teams through a summary analysis of related research. This paper discusses the relations of team members' personality, team goals, and knowledge sharing performance by means of an empirical analysis using collected data. Suggestions will be provided to promote tacit knowledge sharing in university research teams, according to the corresponding enlightenments.

5.2 Research Hypotheses

5.2.1 Personality

Personality is the product of innate biological genetic factors and acquired social influence and also the product of interaction among social practices. The result is various personalities of team members, because of different individual inheritance, different practical activities, and different tendency of subjective efforts. Personality is a kind of psychological characteristic of individual behavior, and it is the sum total of all individual responses and interaction with others. Personality factors affect the typical behavior expression of individuals in the organization, such as individual willingness of completing the task, work initiative, communication and persuasion model, interpersonal interaction, and so on, which produce an effect on individual working performance. Kwong and Cheung (2003) study Chinese managerial staff and find that some personality traits, such as responsibility ethics and loyalty to the group, are associated with the individual, thus providing a good prediction for the working dedication dimension in the relationship performance. Tett and Burnett (2003) consider that there is no direct function relationship between personality traits and working performance and there are other factors that can be a mediation or a moderator. Lewis R. Goldberg (1992) believes that personality traits bring effects on working performance through the incentive effect. Maslow (1987) makes a detailed analysis of the relationship between personality and motivation. In this sense, we offer the following hypothesis.

H1: Team members' personality has a positive effect on the motivation of tacit knowledge sharing and produces a positive impact on knowledge sharing performance through the tacit knowledge sharing motivation.

5.2.2 Team Goals

One of the most established theories of motivation is that of goal setting (Latham and Locke 2007), which demonstrates that goals can significantly influence individual and team performances (O'leary-kelly et al. 1994; Kleingeld et al. 2011). Peter F. Drucker (2006) initiates the concept of "management by objective," which is beneficial to unifying the thoughts and actions of the whole team to the same goal and ideal and is one of the effective methods to improve work efficiency and to achieve rapid development. Management by objective is the process of defining specific objectives within an organization that management can convey to organization members and then deciding on how to achieve each objective in sequence. This process allows managers to take work that needs to be done one step at a time to allow for a calm yet productive work environment. This process also helps organization members to see their accomplishments as they achieve each objective, thus reinforcing a positive work environment and a sense of achievement.

Locke et al. (1990) consider that external stimulations (e.g., rewards, feedback, monitoring, etc.) affect performance by targets. Goals can lead individual activity to target-related behavior, which makes people adjust their degree of effort according to the size of the objective, while at the same time influencing the persistence of individual behavior. Individuals will work harder to achieve a goal while they have it, and a goal not only guides the direction of the individual efforts but also increases the degree of individual efforts, which extend the period of this effort to reduce the sense of monotony and boredom during work and study. Since all team members have specific and clear goals, they will exhibit self-control and self-management consciously in the implementation process of team goals, and thus everybody's initiative, enthusiasm, and potential will be fully tapped. More people will engage in that kind of high target value and high implementation possibility behavior rather than that with a low target value and low implementation possibility. Hence, effective, reasonable, and clear team goals will motivate team members toward tacit knowledge sharing. In this regard, we have the following hypothesis.

H2: Team goals have positive effects on the motivation of tacit knowledge sharing among team members.

5.2.3 Tacit Knowledge Sharing Motivation

Motivation is an intrinsic function to cause individual activity, maintain this activity, and then promote it toward a goal. Everything people do is brought about by some certain motivations. Tacit knowledge transfer motivation is the will of teachers' knowledge transfer, with tacit knowledge as a source of their core competence of teachers and teachers as rational economic people, whose tacit knowledge sharing motivation directly affects the effect of knowledge sharing. As the provider of tacit knowledge, the knowledge transfer motivation of college and university teachers comes from their deep self-demand. Maslow's hierarchy of needs theory points out that after the human low-level needs of survival, safety, physiological, and so on are satisfied, people will then pursue high-level demands of communication and belonging, respect, honor, interest, self-realization, and so on. Likewise, for teachers in colleges and universities, they will pursue high-level demands when their low-level needs, such as the basic necessities of life and safety, are satisfied, thereby producing their motivation. The construction of a research team should start from tacit knowledge sharing among team members. It is the motivation of team members' knowledge sharing and their expectations of knowledge sharing results that usually affect the knowledge sharing performance benchmark directly and subsequently affect the process of sharing behavior among them.

Gagné (2009) presents a model of knowledge sharing motivation based on a combination of the theory of planned behavior (TPB) and self-determination theory (SDT). Kalling (2003) suggests that firm-internal knowledge transfer programs are exercises requiring a great deal of recipient motivation. Teigland and Wasko (2009) find that intrinsic motivations strongly correlate to creativity and efficiency in knowledge-intensive work. Hau et al. (2013) reveal that organizational rewards have a negative effect on employees' tacit knowledge sharing intentions, but a positive influence on their explicit knowledge sharing intentions. The analysis results confirm that reciprocity, enjoyment, and social capital contribute significantly to enhancing employees' tacit and explicit knowledge sharing intentions. Hung et al. (2011) investigate the effects of intrinsic motivation (altruism) and extrinsic motivation (economic reward, reputation feedback, and reciprocity) on knowledge sharing (number of ideas generated, idea usefulness, idea creativity, and meeting satisfaction) in a group meeting. Minbaeva (2008) explores how certain HRM practices influence extrinsic and intrinsic motivations of knowledge receivers. Wei et al. (2010) explore how an individual's intrinsic motivation derived from social norms and personal norms and extrinsic motivation derived from reward and punishment help the person make concerted efforts to shape the ultimate intention to knowledge sharing. Considering those previous studies, we have the following hypothesis.

H3: Tacit knowledge sharing motivation of team members has positive effects on knowledge sharing performance.

According to the hypothesis, we build the tacit knowledge sharing performance influencing model, exhibited in Fig. 5.1.

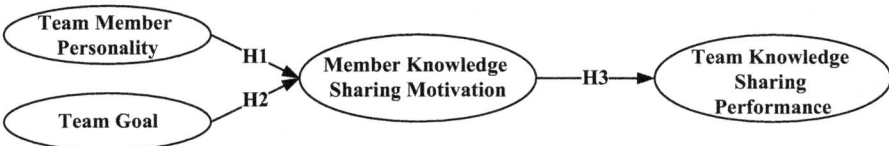

Fig. 5.1 Tacit knowledge sharing performance influencing model in university research teams

5.3 Research Design

5.3.1 Data Collection and Sample Characteristics

We employ the method of random sampling and conduct in-depth investigations on the current situation about tacit knowledge sharing performance at eight universities in Jiangsu Province. The questionnaire is developed in the form of the Likert seven-point system, which increases in order from 1 to 7, among which 1 stands for "strongly disagree" and 7 stands for "strongly agree." Before the formal investigation, we first try a small-scale survey and do proper corrections of the questionnaire according to the survey results. There are 300 questionnaires in the formal investigation, and we receive back 243 effective questionnaires for an effective recovery rate of 81%. This paper is based on the effective questionnaires, and the description of the sample results is shown in Table 5.1.

5.3.2 Variable Measurement

For measuring knowledge sharing motivation, this paper uses Maslow's needs hierarchy theory to design the scale. For measuring team members' personalities, we design the corresponding scale according to the personality description from Robbins and Judge (2014). On the basis of the psychological structure analysis of target behavior from Kleingeld et al. (2011) and Leavitt and Bahrami (1989), we design the scales to measure team goals. We also construct the scale of knowledge sharing performance based on Quigley et al. (2007) and Srivastava et al. (2006). The measurement item variables are shown in Table 5.2.

5.4 Result

5.4.1 Reliability and Validity Analysis

In order to improve the data quality in this study, this paper conducts reliability and validity analyses of the recovery data. We use Cronbach's alpha coefficient to analyze the reliability. Typically, a Cronbach's alpha of 0.7 is regarded as the benchmark of reliability analysis, which means all the items are identified as having internal consistency if Cronbach's alpha exceeds 0.7. We adopt exploratory factor analysis on validity, while we conduct the KMO sample measurement and the Bartlett sphere test before that. Factor analysis is based on principal component analysis (PCA) for doing Varimax rotation. Generally speaking, when the value of KMO is above 0.5, Bartlett stats $\leq \alpha$, and the loading coefficients of various items are all 0.50, we can incorporate the testing items of the same variable into a factor

Table 5.1 Descriptive statistics of samples

		Number	Ratio (%)
Age	20–30	54	22.2
	31–40	92	37.9
	41–50	70	28.8
	51–60	15	6.2
	Above 61	3	1.2
Gender	Male	149	61.3
	Female	92	37.9
Years working	Under 2 years	45	18.5
	3–5 years	49	20.2
	6–10 years	40	16.5
	Over 10 years	100	41.2
Positional titles	Professor	66	27.2
	Associate professor	74	30.5
	Assistant professor	49	20.2
	Teaching assistant	30	12.3
	Others	14	5.8
Educational background	PhD	101	41.6
	Master degree	75	30.9
	BA	46	18.9
	Others	8	3.3
Degree	Postdoctoral	23	9.5
	Doctor	77	31.7
	Master	77	31.7
	Scholar	45	18.5
	Others	6	2.5
Academic leader	Yes	60	24.7
	No	183	75.3
Overseas study and working experience	Yes	57	23.5
	No	186	76.5

through factor analysis. Table 5.3 lists the inspection results of reliability and validity of this study.

According to the results of the reliability and validity measurements of the questionnaire in the table, the KMO value of tacit knowledge transfer motivation is 0.673, and the Bartlett sphere test chi-square value is 559.263, which are significant at 0.0000. It shows that the sample data are suitable for factor analysis, by extracting two common factors during exploratory factor analysis with characteristic values of 2.828 and 1.132, respectively, and with an accumulative total variance explained at a rate of 79.207%, among which common factor F1 includes DJ_1 and DJ_2, and common factor F2 includes DJ_3, DJ_4, and DJ_5. The corresponding Cronbach's alpha values are 0.873 and 0.799, respectively. Common factor F1 consists of physiological needs and security needs in the performance of humans'

Table 5.2 Measurement items of tacit knowledge sharing performance in university research teams

Variable	Index	Item
Tacit knowledge sharing motivation	DJ_1	Tacit knowledge is shared with others in order to meet physiological needs
	DJ_2	Tacit knowledge is shared with others in order to meet safety needs
	DJ_3	Tacit knowledge is shared with others in order to meet association needs
	DJ_4	Tacit knowledge is shared with others in order to meet respect needs
	DJ_5	Tacit knowledge is shared with others in order to meet self-fulfillment needs
Team members' personalities	RG_1	Team members have strong self-esteem
	RG_2	Team members have innovative spirit
	RG_3	Team members have competitive spirit
	RG_4	Team members have time urgency
Team goals	MB_1	Specific team goals
	MB_2	The consistency of personal goals and team goals
	MB_3	The rationality of team goal setting
Tacit knowledge sharing performance	JX_1	Increase the number of research achievements from team members
	JX_2	Improve the quality of research achievements from team members
	JX_3	Save the research time of team members
	JX_4	Reduce the research cost of team members

basic life safeguard; therefore, it is named after life motivation of tacit knowledge sharing. Common factor F2 consists of communication needs, respect needs, and self-actualization needs with the performance caused by humans' social attributes, and that is why it is named after social motivation of tacit knowledge sharing. Cronbach's alpha values of the other index are all above 0.7, and the KMO values are all over 0.5 with only one common factor, indicating that the reliability and validity of the questionnaire are ensured.

5.4.2 Path Analysis

According to the reliability test on the previous section, we separate the knowledge sharing motivation into two levels of social motivation and life motivation, and then we adjust the original model, shown in Fig. 5.2.

In line with the survey, we use the structural equation model (SEM) and software AMOS7.0 to conducting fitting analysis of the proposed hypothesis. The variable fitting indices are shown in Table 5.4.

Table 5.3 Results of reliability and validity measurements of the questionnaire

Variable	Item	Mean	STDEV	KMO	Factor	Factor loading
Tacit knowledge sharing motivation	DJ_1	2.61	1.636	.673	F1	.913
	DJ_2	2.88	1.637			.922
	DJ_3	4.12	1.748		F2	.768
	DJ_4	4.35	1.757			.871
	DJ_5	4.93	1.736			.815
Team members' personalities	RG_1	4.06	1.484	.716	F1	.586
	RG_2	5.22	1.471			.728
	RG_3	4.62	1.668			.844
	RG_4	4.66	1.562			.778
Team goals	MB_1	5.24	1.438	.701	F1	.856
	MB_2	5.51	1.312			.911
	MB_3	5.32	1.365			.853
Tacit knowledge sharing performance	JX_1	5.36	1.388	.827	F1	.859
	JX_2	5.60	1.243			.894
	JX_3	5.58	1.235			.867
	JX_4	5.56	1.304			.857

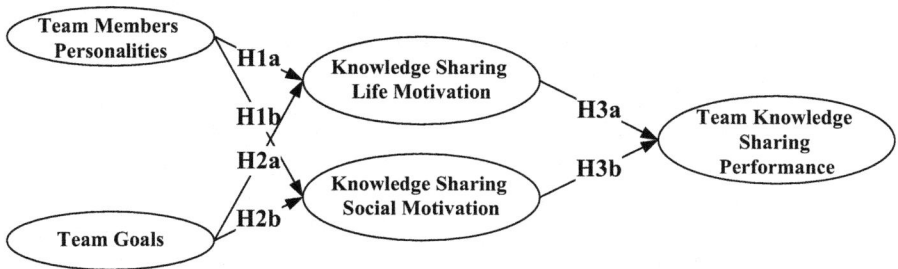

Fig. 5.2 Adjusted tacit knowledge sharing performance influencing model in university research teams

Table 5.4 Fitting index of the model

CMIN	DF	CMIN/DF	RMSEA	GFI	CFI
463.76	97	4.78	.12	.80	.82

From the perspective of the related fitting index evaluation result, the model's absolute goodness-of-fit index (GFI) is 0.80, or close to 1, and the comparative fit index (CFI) is 0.82, or close to 1. All the indicators have reached the acceptable range, thus explaining that the structure equation model fits better. Model parameter estimates are shown in Table 5.5. In the structural equation model, we make an analysis of the path relationship among the variables and get the model parameter estimates (shown in Table 5.5).

Table 5.5 Model parameter estimates

Hypothesis	Path			Standardized coefficients	Significant level p
H1a	Life motivation	<---	Member personality	.97	0.00
H1b	Social motivation	<---	Member personality	.52	0.00
H2a	Life motivation	<---	Team goals	−.46	0.00
H2b	Social motivation	<---	Team goals	.17	.14
H3a	Knowledge sharing performance	<---	Life motivation	−.08	.09
H3b	Knowledge sharing performance	<---	Social motivation	.31	0.00

As can be seen from the results in Table 5.5, the hypotheses that pass the test in this study are as follows. H1: Team members' personalities can arouse tacit knowledge sharing motivation; the higher the quality the personality has, the stronger the knowledge sharing motivation is, including life motivation and social motivation of tacit knowledge sharing, whose standardized coefficients are 0.97 and 052, respectively, with a p value having a significance level smaller than 0.001. H3b: The social motivation of team members' tacit knowledge sharing has a positive influence on tacit knowledge sharing performance, with its standardized coefficient of 0.35, while the p value has a significance level of less than 0.001.

Hypothesis H2b does not pass the significance test. Team goals have positive effects on tacit knowledge sharing motivation, and its standardized coefficient is 0.17, while the p value has a significance level equal to 0.14, which is over 0.05. That is why this hypothesis does not pass the test.

We also fail to verify H2a and H3a. H2a: In theory, team goals can stimulate members' tacit knowledge sharing motivation; the clearer and more reasonable the team goals are, the stronger the members' tacit knowledge sharing motivation is. However, the standardized coefficient of this hypothesis is −0.46, showing a negative relationship. H3a: Life motivation can improve tacit knowledge sharing performance; the stronger the motivation is, the higher the performance is of tacit knowledge sharing. However, the standardized coefficient of this hypothesis is −0.08, showing a negative relationship. We believe that tacit knowledge sharing emphasizes more on human intercommunication, because of the ambiguity and dynamics of tacit knowledge. Sharing tacit knowledge is caused by human social attributes, and life motivation is about guaranteeing basic life demands. That is why there is no effect on knowledge performance from members' knowledge sharing life motivation. Likewise, team goals have no impacts on life motivation. We can see that the key motivation is social motivation caused by human social attributes, rather than life motivation, which affect tacit knowledge sharing performance in university research teams.

5.5 Conclusion

In this study, we analyze the relationships among team goal, team members' personalities, tacit knowledge sharing motivation, and tacit knowledge sharing performance of eight universities in Jiangsu Province, through the use of confirmatory factor analysis, variance analysis, and structural equation model analysis. We also study the demographic characteristics of tacit knowledge sharing. The hypotheses in this paper have some empirical support, and their conclusions and findings are as follows.

1. Team members' personalities have direct positive influences on tacit knowledge sharing motivation and have indirect effects on tacit knowledge sharing performance. According to the questionnaires, team members' personalities consist of self-respect, innovation spirit, competitive spirit, and time urgency. That is why team leaders should strengthen the development of members' good personalities.
2. Team goals have indirect positive effects on tacit knowledge sharing performance. Management by objective should be strengthened and managing efficiency should be improved. When managing team goals, clarity and rationality of team goals should be paid attention to. Only reasonable and clear team goals can encourage members to achieve team goals, promote active communication between each member, make them learn and share knowledge, and increase the team's stock of knowledge.

This study is an empirical exploratory research. The research results enrich team characteristics, team goals, and the theory of tacit knowledge sharing performance, thus providing a new framework for subsequent research and also offering management recommendations in order to achieve effective knowledge sharing within the team. However, there are still some limitations in this study as follows.

1. Although this research is mainly based on the team as a sample, it lacks data on team characteristics (such as team size, etc.) and the relations among knowledge sharing efficiency (such as an analysis of the regulation of the team size effect).
2. This study is restricted by cost, time, and other limitations. This is why it did not use common personality inventory to measure the personalities of team members, and the conclusion is only about the relationship between one type of personality and knowledge sharing performance.
3. We failed to do an analysis of the differences between groups on different types of university research teams, because of the regional limits of Jiangsu Province. The abovementioned research limitations will become further research directions in the future.

Chapter 6
Colored Petri Net Model of Knowledge Flow Based on Knowledge Life Cycle

6.1 Introduction

Knowledge has become the most precious property of any commercial or academic institution. Knowledge management plays the key role in upgrading the competitiveness of a team. Knowledge management concerns innovating, spreading, sharing, and using knowledge. Research on knowledge management targets the management aspects, including organizational learning, personal management, culture, etc. (Drucker 1998), and the technical aspect includes models, support tools, and environments (Zhuge 2002a, b). Knowledge is power, but knowledge is not just statically stored. It evolves through being shared and developed by roles, people, and various resources within the cyber-physical-socio environment. Knowledge flow is the passing of knowledge between people or through machinery. It has three crucial attributes: direction (sender and receiver), carrier (medium), and content (shareable). Good knowledge flow enables intelligent participants (people, roles, and devices) to cooperate effectively (Zhuge 2004). The literature has investigated multiple types of flows, e.g., material flow (Brunner and Rechberger 2004), energy flow (Odum 1968), message flow (Nierstrasz 1985), control flow (Heintze 1995), etc., and the rules they follow in respective domains.

Petri nets are widely studied (Reisig 1985) and successfully applied in different discrete event dynamic systems, e.g., DiCesare et al. (1993) and Silva and Teruel (1997); they are characterized by parallelism and synchronization. The strong mathematical foundation of Petri nets and the availability of a wide range of supporting tools have made them popular among academic researchers. Petri net-based modeling and analysis of workflow and workflow systems make up an active research area in academia (Salimifard and Wright 2001; van der Aalst 1998). Unfortunately, the knowledge flow based on Petri net has not been paid enough attention. To our best knowledge, this is still a major gap in the literature. To fill such a gap, the main objective of this work is to develop a quantitative approach using

© Springer International Publishing AG, part of Springer Nature 2018
Y. Yu et al., *Strategy and Performance of Knowledge Flow*,
International Series in Operations Research & Management Science 271,
https://doi.org/10.1007/978-3-319-77926-3_6

CPNs to model knowledge flow. We show how the use of CPNs can help illustrate the knowledge flow process within and between organizations and testify its rationality through a case study.

This chapter is organized as follows. Section 6.2 introduces the brief knowledge life cycle and knowledge flow based on KLC. Section 6.3 discusses CPNs and their application to knowledge flow in organizations. Section 6.4 presents an exemplificative case study; a Petri net model is used to testify the rationality of knowledge flow in organizations. A Petri net simulation analysis is then carried out. Section 6.5 provides results and describes the case tracking.

6.2 Knowledge Flow in Organizations

6.2.1 Knowledge Life Cycle

Knowledge life cycle (KLC) is the time interval of knowledge that begins from it being vaguely observed, then studied, subsequently transferred and applied, and then eventually gone. Researchers have described different knowledge life cycles. Some models are characterized by a few general phases (Birkinshaw and Sheehan 2002; Bernard and Tichkiewitch 2008). The model includes four phases as follows.

1. Knowledge acquisition. There are two channels for an organization to acquire knowledge: (1) employees within the organization passively receive information from the outside and (2) employees within the organization discover new knowledge actively through experiments, observations, summarizations, analyses, and thinking.
2. Knowledge integration. An organization transforms its unprocessed new knowledge through codification, storage, transferring, sharing, integration, and extraction to a mature state, which is more user-friendly. The major knowledge flows in this phase are internalization, externalization, and socialization.
3. Knowledge usage. Employees within the organization apply such processed knowledge from the growth phase to practice and then commercialize it into goods/services, which an enterprise could gain profit.
4. Knowledge decline. This is the phase when knowledge vanishes. An organization actively or passively forgets the knowledge when the value of maintaining such knowledge is lower than its costs. The main knowledge flows in this phase include leakage, oblivion, and spillover.

6.2.2 Knowledge Flow Based on KLC

Considering the mainstream definitions of knowledge flow, this chapter defines it as the process of knowledge acquisition, storage, transfer and sharing, application, and creation within and among organizations, so as to enhance its efficiency and

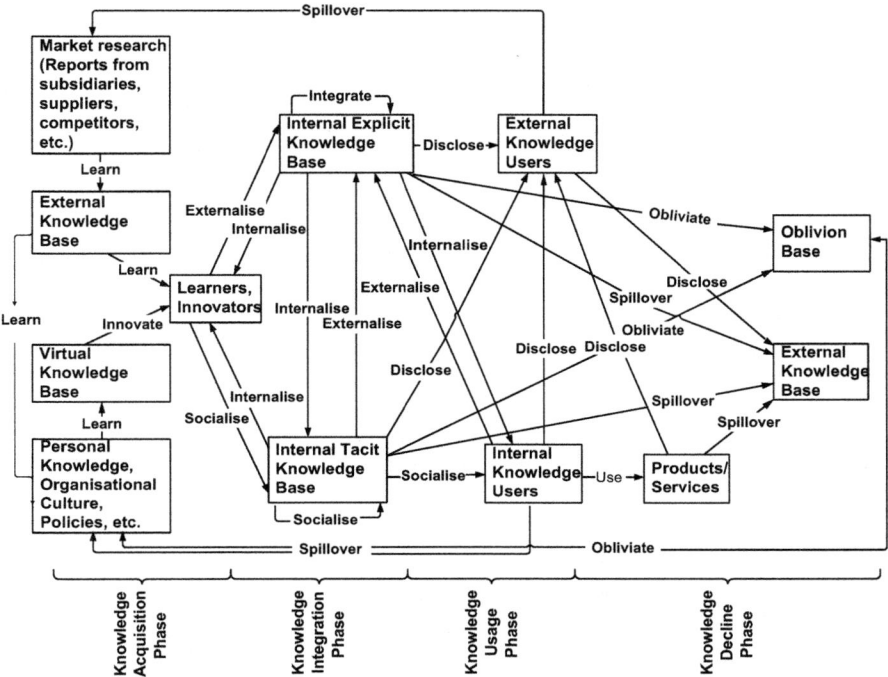

Fig. 6.1 Organizational knowledge flow model

velocity. The following organizational knowledge flow model is built based on such a logical sequence. Figure 6.1 illustrates an organizational knowledge flow model based on the knowledge life cycle.

Knowledge flow within an organization is an acquisition, integration, usage, and declining process, which is often realized through knowledge internalization, externalization, and socialization. Interorganizational knowledge flow is the knowledge interaction process among diverse organizations and is usually in the form of knowledge leakage and spillover.

6.3   CPNs in Knowledge Flow

6.3.1   An Introduction to Petri Nets

A Petri net (PN) is both a graphical and an analytical modeling tool. It was developed by Carl Adam Petri in 1962 in his Ph.D. thesis at Bonn University, Germany, as a special class of generalized graphs or nets. The chief attraction of this tool is the way in which the basic aspects of a variety of systems are identified, both conceptually and mathematically through graphical representation and eventually supported by formal programming languages. As a graphical tool, PNs can be used as a visual communication aid similar to flowcharts, block diagrams, and networks. In addition, tokens are used in these nets to simulate the dynamic activities of systems. As a mathematical tool, it allows setting up algebraic equations for formally analyzing the mathematical models governing the systems' behavior, which is similar to other approaches to formal analysis, e.g., occurrence nets and reachability trees.

PNs are characterized by their capability to describe and analyze asynchronous systems with concurrent and parallel activities. Using PNs to model such systems is simple and straightforward, making them a valuable technique for analyzing complex real-time systems with concurrent activities. They are capable of modeling material and information flow phenomena and detecting the existence of deadlock states and inconsistency and are well suited for the study of discrete event systems (DES).

Petri nets are a solid and well-defined graphic technique for the specification, analysis, and design of discrete event systems. Simple PNs have been successfully applied to a large number of real-world problems in many domains. However, some disadvantages have restricted their application for large, complex systems. For this reason, many extensions of the Petri net formalisms were proposed. These extensions are known as high-level Petri nets (timed, stochastic, etc.), with CPNs chief among them. CPN (colored Petri net) has both graphic expressions and rigid mathematical definitions, and so it can be visualized, yet it is not fuzzy, uncertain, or contradictory. CPN is extended from the classical Petri net, which is more suitable for complex systems. It puts color on tokens (objects with different attributes) and distinguishes types of attributes by different colors, so that complex systems can be designed, depicted, simulated, and testified (Jensen 1994).

A colored Petri net is a structure CPN $= (P, T, F, M, C)$ whereby:

1. Place (P), which is represented by a circle $\bigcirc$, depicts the possible state of a system.
2. Transition (T), which is represented by a square $\square$, depicts the events/conditions that would change the state of the system.
3. Arc (F), which is represented by an arrow $\rightarrow$, links Places with Transitions, while the direction of the arrow can be utilized to depict the relation between state and event; the Arc expression describes the change of state when the Transition is fired.
4. Token (M), which is represented by a dot $\cdot$, and its dynamic changes depict different states of the system; M0 is the initial state of the Petri net. Compared to general Petri nets, like Place/Transition nets, each token in the advanced CPN carries a unique type of value.
5. Color (C) maps different types of tokens to different color sets. The dynamics of the Petri net is regulated by its firing rule: if all the inputting Places before a Transition are not empty, then such a Transition can be fired. Therefore, firing the transition requires all its inputting Places to contain sufficient tokens, and their token values must meet the requirement of Arc expressions.

The mathematical definition of a CPN is as follows.

A basic Petri net, $N = (P, T, F)$, must meet the following conditions:

1. $P \cup T \neq \varnothing$
2. $P \cap T = \varnothing$
3. $F \subseteq (P \times T) \cup (T \times P)$
4. $\text{dom}(F) \cup \text{cod}(F) = P \cup T$

Here, the domain of definition of F is $\text{dom}(F) = \{x \in P \cup T | \exists y \in P \cup T : (x, y) \in F\}$.

The domain of the value of F is $\text{cod}(F) = \{x \in P \cup T | \exists y \in P \cup T : (y, x) \in F\}$.

Expanding the above triples into a simple quintuple of CPN with k colors results in $\sum = (P, T; F, W, M)$.

Here, $(P, T; F)$ is a basic Petri net, and $\text{W}:F \rightarrow \{0, 1, 2, \cdots, k\}$, $\text{M}: P \rightarrow \{0, 1, 2, \cdots, k\}$.

A k-dimensional vector represents a CPN with k colors, and the k-dimensional vector in each Place represents the number of tokens of different colors in that Place. In other words, each component is a color, while the component value is the number of tokens in each color.

6.3.2 Modeling the Organizational Knowledge Flow: CPN Tool

Complicated knowledge flow systems are usually relatively large, and even knowledge spillover and knowledge explosion are not rare. Knowledge flow modeling based on colored Petri net (CPN) uses different colored tokens to represent different types of knowledge, solving the complexity issue when modeling is based on the classical Petri net. This chapter proposes an organizational knowledge flow model based on CPN, and the implication of each element in CPN is as follows when corresponding to organizational knowledge flow.

1. Place represents the knowledge node, i.e., the senders or receivers of knowledge, such as employees or the knowledge base (KB).
2. Transition represents knowledge flow, which is the condition that can cause changes in knowledge distribution, such as knowledge acquisition, codification, storage, transferring, sharing, integration, extraction, oblivion, and leakage.
3. Arc represents the relation between knowledge node and knowledge flow, whose direction and weight can be further regulated by an Arc expression.
4. Token represents the distribution patterns of the number as well as the types of knowledge.
5. Token color represents different types of knowledge; for instance, explicit and tacit knowledge can be depicted by tokens in different color sets.

According to the rules set above, an organizational knowledge flow model based on CPN can be constructed (see Fig. 6.2).

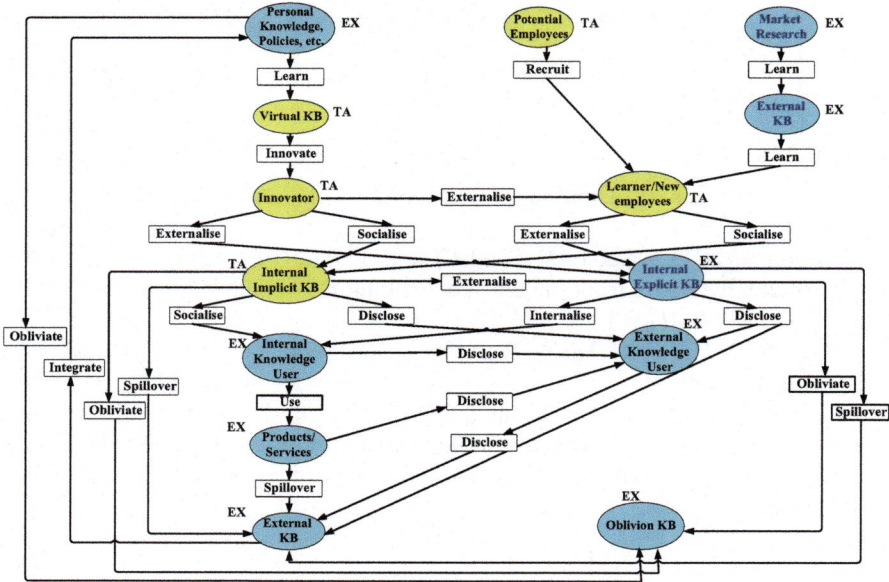

Fig. 6.2 Organizational knowledge flow model based on CPN

6.4   Case Study

To further testify the rationality of the model established, this part conducts an empirical analysis to study the characteristics of knowledge flow. The chapter selects university, or, specifically, the University of Cambridge, as the research object, because the university is the place where knowledge is highly densified and moves frequently. The chapter also studies telecommunications knowledge, in particular, telecommunications switching, because it is an area that has developed so quickly that such knowledge has already been systemized. Lastly, simulation software CPN Tools is used to examine the rationality of the model established.

6.4.1   Data Collection

This chapter searches for publications with the topic "telecommunications switching" from the years 1990 to 2013 in the database of "Web of Science," finding 2230 pieces of articles. The chapter further imports information of these 2230 pieces of articles categorized according to the institutions that the author of each article belongs to into the CPN Tools software, in order for the simulation of the model to operate.

6.4.2   CPN Simulation

In order to implement the model and perform the simulations, we select the software package CPN Tools, which is a tool for editing, simulating, and analyzing colored Petri nets (http://cpntools.org/). The tool features incremental syntax checking and code generation, which take place while a net is being constructed. A fast simulator efficiently handles untimed and timed nets. Full and partial state spaces can be generated and analyzed, and a standard state space report contains information, such as boundedness properties and liveness properties.

This study carries out a Petri net simulation analysis. The declaration of a token and its variations is as follows:

```
val n = 2;
colset EX = index ex with 1..n;
colset TA = index ta with 1..n;
var e: EX;
var t: TA;
fun explicit(ta(i)) = ex(i);
fun tacit(ex(i)) = ta(i);
```

In the above declaration, "n" is constant, and in this circumstance, n equals 2. Moreover, "colset EX" represents the color set of explicit knowledge, while "colset TA" is the color set of tacit knowledge. The two variants "e" and "t" belong to the color set of explicit knowledge and tacit knowledge, respectively. The function "explicit ()" implies transferring tacit knowledge to explicit knowledge, while the function "tacit ()" implies transferring explicit knowledge to tacit knowledge. The simulation interface of the adapted organizational knowledge flow model of telecommunications switching based on CPN Tools is depicted in Fig. 6.3. The implication of each element in Fig. 6.3 is listed below (Table 6.1).

6.5   Results and Discussion

6.5.1   Results from the Case Study

After running the simulation for 1000 steps, the results are illustrated in Table 6.2.

Table 6.2 demonstrates that the state space of the model has 1667 knowledge nodes and 9534 arcs, while the Scc Graph has 134 knowledge nodes and 3056 arcs. The significant differences of the two statistics results are normal.

Tables 6.3 and 6.4 describe the lower and upper limits of tokens that each Place contains, respectively. The output indicates that all the Places in the model have limits, and this is consistent with the reality that people can only acquire limited knowledge in a limited amount of time and space. The second and the third parts show the detailed number of tokens and their types. Taking Place 9 (P9) as an

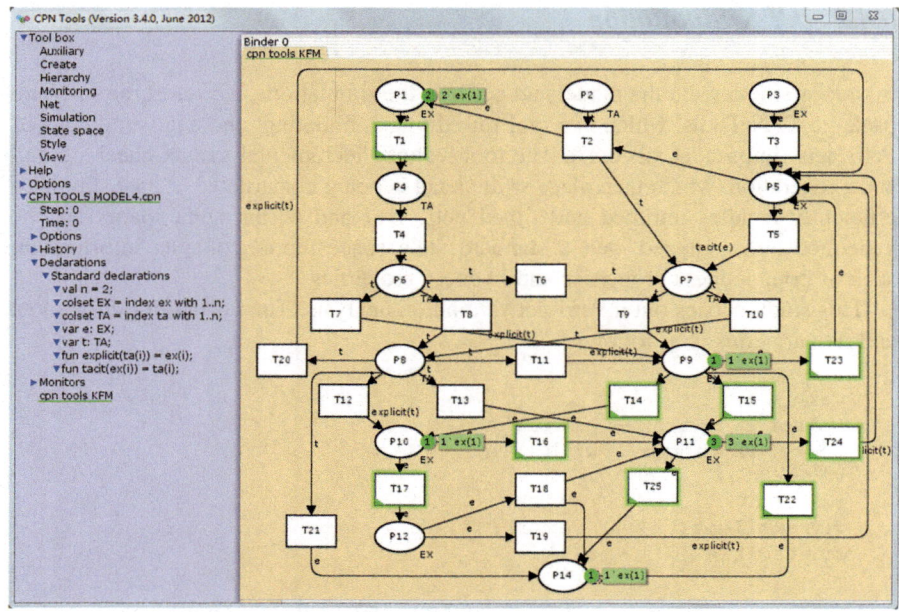

Fig. 6.3 CPN Tools interface and its parameter settings of the case study

Table 6.1 Implication of places and transitions

Place	Implication	Transition	Implication
P1	Personal knowledge, academic environment, etc.	T1, T3	Study/integrate
P2	Scholars to be recruited	T2	Recruit
P3	Research trends of other organizations	T4	Innovate
P4	Virtual knowledge base	T5	Study
P5	External knowledge base	T6, T7, T9, T11	Externalize
P6	Innovators	T8, T10, T12	Socialize
P7	New scholars	T13, T15, T16, T18	Disclose
P8	Implicit knowledge base within Cambridge	T14	Internalize
P9	Explicit knowledge base within Cambridge	T17	Use
P10	Knowledge user within Cambridge	T19, T20, T23, T24	Spillover
P11	Knowledge user outside of Cambridge	T21, T22	Obliviate
P12	Products/services		
P13	Oblivion knowledge base		

Table 6.2 Statistics analysis

	Nodes	Arcs	Secs	Status
State space	1667	9534	1	Full
Scc graph	134	3056	0	

Table 6.3 Boundedness analysis

Place	Upper	Lower
P10	3	Empty
P1	1	Empty
P11	3	Empty
P12	3	Empty
P14	3	Empty
P2	1	Empty
P3	1	Empty
P4	1	Empty
P5	3	Empty
P6	1	Empty
P7	3	Empty
P8	3	Empty
P9	3	Empty

Table 6.4 Best upper multi-set bounds of each place

Place	Token
P1	1`ta(1)
P11	2`ta(1)++1`ta(2)
P12	2`ta(1)++1`ta(2)
P14	2`ta(1)++1`ta(2)
P2	1`ta(2)
P3	1`ex(1)
P4	1`ta(1)
P5	2`ex(1)++1`ex(2)
P6	1`ta(1)
P7	2`ta(1)++1`ta(2)
P8	2`ta(1)++1`ta(2)
P9	2`ex(1)++1`ex(2)

example, the explicit knowledge base within Cambridge contains three tokens at most, i.e., two tokens of the ex(1) type and one token of the ex(2) type, which imply that the explicit knowledge acquired from all sources has been absorbed, internalized, and stored, and such knowledge has not been disclosed to competitors by any means; P9 contains at least 0 tokens, and such a situation might occur when an organization has just started to establish its explicit knowledge base; this implies no explicit knowledge has been transferred to P9 yet; however, another reason might be that the knowledge in P9 has already been disclosed to a competitor. The number of tokens as well as their types in other Places can be explained by parity of reasoning.

The Liveness Analysis Report (see Table 6.5) shows that the adapted knowledge flow model of the case study has one dead marking and zero dead transition. The only dead marking is home marking. Home marking is the marking that all other reachable markings can reach, while dead marking implies it does not contain legitimate elements that can be enabled. Node 1627 is home marking as well as dead marking, implying that it is always possible to terminate knowledge flow with a

Table 6.5 Liveness analysis

Dead markings	1627
Dead transition instances	None
Live transition instances	All

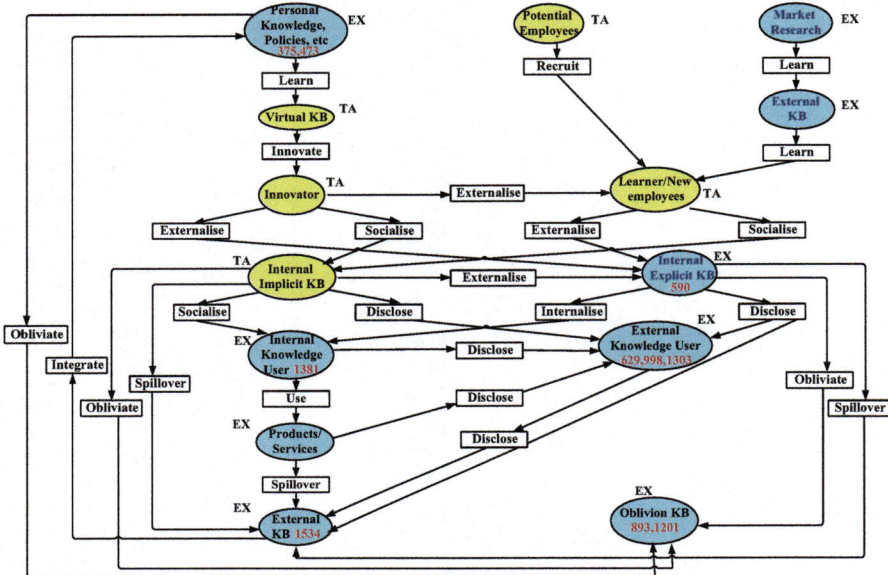

Fig. 6.4 A tracking example of knowledge flow

correct result. Dead transition is a transition in which no reachable markings can fire; therefore, no dead transition ensures all transitions are fired at least once, or in other words, all activities have been executed. Hence, the organizational knowledge flow model is rationally analyzed from its statistics, boundedness, and liveness.

6.5.2 Case Tracking

This section tracks the publications of the University of Cambridge as well as other enterprises or research institutions from 1910 to 2013 and also tracks their citation relations, in order to illustrate the knowledge flow process with real-life examples.

For the convenience of description, this section first codifies the 2230 pieces of articles according to their years published. This can help testify the correctness of citation relations qualitatively; that is, the serial number of an article must be smaller than the ones that cite it.

Figure 6.4 illustrates the citation relations of telecommunications switching knowledge among the University of Cambridge and other institutions. The brief

Fig. 6.5 The citation relations of telecommunications knowledge focusing on the University of Cambridge

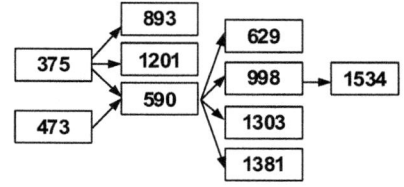

Table 6.6 The detailed information

Serial number	Title	Author(s)	Institution
375	Telecommunications applications of ferroelectric liquid crystal smart pixels	Mears R. J., Crossland W. A., Dames M. P., Collington J. R., Parker M. C., et al.	University of Cambridge
473	Dynamic holographic spectral equalization for WDM	Parker M. C., Cohen A. D., Mears R. J.	University of Cambridge
590	Dynamic digital holographic wave-length filtering	Parker M. C., Cohen A. D., Mears R. J.	University of Cambridge
629	Recent advances in arrayed wave-guide gratings and their application in optical networks	Parker M. C., Walker S. D.	Fujitsu
893	Optical routing with liquid crystal arrays	Wilkinson T. D., Crossland W. A.	University of Cambridge
998	Applications of liquid crystal spatial light modulators in optical communications	Ahderom S., Raisi M., Lo K., Alameh K. E., Mavaddat R.	Edith Cowan University
1201	Liquid crystal-based optical space switches for DWDM network	Gravey, P., et al.	Télécom Bretagne
1303	Engineering liquid crystals for opti-mal uses in optical communication systems	De La Tocnaye J. L. D.	Télécom Bretagne
1381	Liquid crystal-based continuous phase retarder: from optically neu-tral to a quarter wave plate in 200 microseconds	Broughton B. J., Clarke M. J., Betts R. A., Bricheno T., Coles H. J.	University of Cambridge
1534	VLSI circuits and systems for micro-photonic applications-art	Lachowicz S., Rassau A., Kim C., Lee S. M.	Edith Cowan University

summary of relevant articles and their citation relations is shown in Fig. 6.5, while Table 6.6 displays the detailed information of such articles.

In this example, the knowledge flow of telecommunications switching starts from articles 375 and 473, both of which are written by scholars from the University of Cambridge. However, the two articles have not been cited by any other publications within the local knowledge base, and therefore 375 and 473 belong to the "personal knowledge and academic environment" Place. The inherent knowledge of the two articles further flows through two paths. The first path is that article 590 written by scholars at the University of Cambridge cited both of them in 1998, and the authors have slightly changed, which proves that the knowledge of articles 375 and 473 has already entered the "virtual knowledge base" after being studied. The innovator, i.e., the author of article 590, innovates such knowledge and externalizes it into the "explicit knowledge base within Cambridge." The other path is that articles 375 and 473 are cited by articles 893 and 1201, respectively, while articles 893 and 1201 have not been cited by any other publications in the local database so far; therefore, they belong to the oblivion knowledge base.

The knowledge carried by article 590 keeps flowing through two paths. The first one is that it was internalized and was utilized by scholars at the University of Cambridge, i.e., the author of article 1381. The other path is that the knowledge of article 590 was disclosed to other organizations, with the evidence that the authors of articles 629, 998, and 1303 are from Fujitsu Japan, Edith Cowan University Australia, and Télécom Bretagne France, respectively.

Various channels for knowledge disclosure exist in real life. For instance, Parker M. C., the leading author of both articles 590 and 629, switches his affiliation from the University of Cambridge to Fujitsu Japan, which implies knowledge flow among different organizations through personnel turnover. At the same time, the knowledge user from other organizations (the author of article 998) further discloses such knowledge into the "external knowledge base" and was cited by the author of article 1534, thus completing the knowledge flow process of the case study.

The citation relations of telecommunications switching knowledge among various organizations within the local database can be similarly analyzed as above. It essentially depicts the knowledge flow process and can delineate commonalities of the organizational knowledge flow pattern. Another conclusion drawn from analyzing the 2230 pieces of articles is that the number of articles written by multiple authors is gradually increasing, denoting that knowledge sharing is becoming more prominent.

6.6 Conclusion

The chapter studies the knowledge flow model within and among organizations based on CPN, running a simulation to verify the rationality of the model established both qualitatively and quantitatively. The chapter first builds an organizational knowledge flow model based on CPN and uses the fitness of CPN to describe the asynchronous concurrent processes. Second, with up-to-date data from the Web of Science database, the chapter runs a simulation through CPN Tools, which is a professional simulation software tailored for CPN, and verifies the rationality of the model established through three reports generated by CPN Tools: statistics, boundedness, and liveness. Third and lastly, the chapter tracks as well as analyzes publications in the field of telecommunications switching, focusing on the University of Cambridge and the citation relations, so that the knowledge flow process can be demonstrated in a straightforward manner.

Chapter 7
Evolutionary Game Model of Knowledge Transfer in University-Industry Collaborative Innovation

7.1 Introduction

It is frequently noted that innovation has become a strategic source for creating firms' sustainable competitive advantages. Therefore, continuously generating new knowledge to enable such innovation has become a key agenda for policy makers as well as business organizations (Nonaka 1994; Grant 1996). Knowledge is viewed as a competitive advantage and a source of power for those who possess it at the right place and at the right time, while the process of knowledge transfer between organizations is essentially the game between two different knowledge agents. In the context of certain social environments, knowledge transfer is a process of transferring knowledge from a knowledge source to a knowledge receptor and from an organization that has high knowledge stock to an organization that has low knowledge stock. The successful transfer of knowledge is closely related to the willingness of the knowledge provider to transfer such knowledge and the willingness of the knowledge recipient to accept such knowledge.

Knowledge transfer between organizations is a process whereby various knowledge transfer agents game with each other. Game theory has been applied to the issues of knowledge sharing. Statistical data show that an individual's perceived payoff from sharing knowledge in a group can be characterized by a multi-person game (Samieh and Wahba 2007). Firms that have a higher degree of knowledge sharing exhibit better business performance and a higher level of innovation versus firms that do not (Shih et al. 2006). Cai and Kock (2009) study the strategic interaction between players as they decide whether and how much to collaborate with each other. They show that the social punishment should be large enough to enforce full cooperation in symmetric discrete-strategy e-collaboration games. Richard and Wayne (2009) examine the result of interactions among individuals in an organization with different preferences regarding knowledge sharing, arguing that organizations should actively encourage knowledge sharing. For knowledge sharing

© Springer International Publishing AG, part of Springer Nature 2018
Y. Yu et al., *Strategy and Performance of Knowledge Flow*,
International Series in Operations Research & Management Science 271,
https://doi.org/10.1007/978-3-319-77926-3_7

behavior to be engendered and sustained effectively among participants accessing a common knowledge base, Alton (2003) points out that the participation rate has to exceed a minimum threshold.

Samaddar and Kadiyala (2006) use the game-theoretic framework to model the collaboration for knowledge creation as a Stackelberg leader-follower game. They identify the importance of maintaining an optimal ratio between the leader's and follower's marginal gains for the formation and continuation of the collaboration. Bandyopadhyay and Pathak (2007) model the interaction between two employees serving in different firms, who have to share their knowledge to work effectively as a team. The result shows that top management should enforce cooperation between the employees so that better payoffs can be achieved when the degree of complementarity of knowledge between the employees is high enough. Koessler (2004) provides a model for the study of direct, public, and strategic knowledge sharing in Bayesian games. Y.-M. Li and Jhang-Li (2010) apply game theory to analyze the incentives of knowledge sharing activities in various types of communities of practice (COPs), characterized by individual profiles and decision structures. Cress and Martin (2006) analyze knowledge exchange with shared databases based on a game-theoretical perspective.

The above knowledge transfer game models do not describe the complex knowledge flow phenomena resulting from the knowledge agent's bounded rationality since they do not consider this factor. In fact, since each knowledge agent has his/her bounded rationality that has a significant influence on his/her knowledge sharing behavior, this factor should explicitly be considered in the knowledge transfer models.

The term "bounded rationality" refers to the fact that most people are only partly rational in their daily decision-making. This contrasts with the dominant early-twentieth-century economic theory that assumed decision-making is the fully rational process of finding an optimal choice given the available information. Simon (1955) first suggests that we use heuristics to make our decisions rather than a strict rigid rule of optimization.

Under the condition of bounded rationality, both sides of the knowledge agent often do not know what consequences their behavior will have. However, based on previous experience and information about realistic situations, knowledge providers decide whether to transfer the knowledge for achieving the value of knowledge, and knowledge recipients decide whether to accept knowledge to promote the innovation value of knowledge and organizational value. Therefore, at the beginning of knowledge transfer, both providers and recipients will not or cannot adopt the optimal strategy under perfect rational conditions. Through continuous learning and adjustment of the results rather than selecting the best strategy at one time, a better strategy may be found. Even if the optimal strategy is chosen, a further deviation may also occur.

Evolutionary game theory is a different approach to the classic analysis of games. Instead of directly calculating properties of a game, the populations of players using different strategies are simulated, and a process similar to natural selection is used to determine how the population evolves. Varying degrees of complexity are required to represent populations in multi-agent games with differing strategy spaces. Nowadays, the evolutionary game theory has been widely used in low carbon (Zhao et al. 2016), supply chain (Sikhar et al. 2012), rumor diffusion (Li et al. 2015), and other fields.

This chapter quantifies related force influential factors of knowledge transfer between organizations, establishing a subjective revenue function of knowledge transfer and constructing the intersubjective game matrix of knowledge transfer between organizations. At the same time, based on the bounded rationality of the knowledge transfer subject, this chapter uses the evolutionary game theory to study the knowledge transfer game and analyze the influences on the knowledge transfer motive force resulting from changes of force influential factors. The evolutionary strategy of a knowledge transfer agent is put forward, in order to establish a game simulation model for the following simulation analysis.

Our chapter is organized as follows. In the next section, we give a brief introduction about the evolutionary game theory. Section 7.3 builds an evolutionary game model to analyze the interaction between the two knowledge agents under bounded rationality. Section 7.4 examines the evolutionarily stable strategies (ESS) and draws implications from them, while Section 7.5 concludes the chapter.

7.2 Evolutionary Game Theory

Evolutionary game theory (EGT) originated in the work of biologists Smith and Price (1973). Taylor and Jonker (1978) and Selten (1983), among others, play an important role in applying the developed evolutionary biological concepts to boundedly rational human behavior and in establishing the connection with dynamic systems and with game-theoretic concepts such as Nash equilibrium. Here, we give a brief description about the evolutionary game theory, which is employed by Vincent (1985).

The evolutionary game involves the survival characteristics of strategies as measured by the fraction of the population of players who are using them. The foundation of the game involves the strategy set, the fraction of players using each strategy, and a transition relationship that dictates how the fraction of players using a given strategy changes from generation to generation. In particular, the evolutionary game considered herein contains the following elements.

(i) An endless series of generations starting at generation $t = 0$ and continuing for $t = 1, 2, \ldots$.

(ii) A number of distinct strategy vectors u^0, u^1, ..., u^r, where each vector $u^i = \left(u_1^i, \ldots, u_m^i\right)^T$ has the same dimension m and is drawn from the same constraint set U_i defined by

$$U_i = \{u^i \in E^m | g(u^i) = 0 \text{ and } h(u^i) \geq 0\}, \quad i = 0, \ldots, r, \tag{7.1}$$

where $g(\bullet) : E^m \to E^n$ and $h(\bullet) : E^m \to E^q$ are C^1-functions of u^i. The notations $=$ and $\geq$ apply to each component of $g(u^i)$ and $h(u^i)$, respectively.

If there are no equality or inequality constraints, then $U_i = E^m$. In order to refer to all the strategies, then we let

$$u = \left[(u^0)^T, \ldots, (u^r)^T \right]^T.$$

The notation $()^T$ denotes the transpose of $()$.

(iii) A population of players $N(t)$. Let $N_i(t)$ be the non-zero number of players from this population using a strategy u^i at generation t. Let

$$p_i(t) = N_i(t)/N(t) \text{ and } p(t) = [p_0(t), \ldots, p_r(t)]^T.$$

Clearly, the vector p at any time t must lie in the set P defined by

$$P = \{p \in E^r | p_0 + \cdots + p_r = 1 \text{ and } p_i > 0, i = 0, 1, \ldots, r\}. \tag{7.2}$$

(iv) A set of positive C^1-functions $H_i[u, p(t)]$, $i = 0, 1, \ldots, r$, which gives the ratio of the number of players using strategy u^i in generation $t + 1$ to the number of players using strategy u^i in generation t. The number of players $N(t)$ is generally large, and the number of strategies is generally small, $0 < r < < N(t)$. The functions $H_i(\bullet)$ are called the average individual fitness for players using strategy u^i.

To start the game, one can fix $N(0)$ and r and then let a random process choose $u^i \in U_i$, $i = 0, 1, \ldots, r$, where $p(0) \in P$. The game proceeds from generation to generation by calculating the fraction of players using a given strategy in the next generation. This calculation is obtained from (iv). By definition, we have

$$N_i(t + 1) = N_i(t)H_i[u, p(t)]. \tag{7.3}$$

Thus, we have

$$N(t + 1) = \sum_{i=0}^{r} N_i(t)H_i[u, p(t)] \tag{7.4}$$

Dividing Eq. (7.3) by the total number of players at $t + 1$ and using Eq. (7.4) and the definition of $p_i(t)$ yield

$$p_i(t + 1) = p_i(t)H_i[u, p(t)]/\bar{H}, \tag{7.5}$$

where

$$\bar{H} = \sum_{i=0}^{r} p_i(t) H_i[u, p(t)] \tag{7.6}$$

is the average fitness of all the players. Equation (7.5) determines the percentage of players using a given strategy from one generation to the next.

The following definition is formulated to incorporate Maynard Smith's ESS concept. Recall that there are $r + 1$ distinct strategy vectors $u^0, u^1, \ldots, u^r$ and that

$$p_i(0) > 0, i = 0, 1, \ldots, r.$$

Definition 7.1 A strategy u^0 is a local ESS if there exists an e in the interval $0 < \varepsilon < 1$ such that Eq. (7.5) yields an infinite monotone increasing sequence for $p_0(t)$, when $t = 0, 1, \ldots$, whose limit is 1 as $t \to \infty$ for all distinct $u^i \in U_i, i = 1, \ldots, r$, and for all $p \in P$, with $1 - \varepsilon < p_0(0) < 1$. If u^0 is a local ESS for $\varepsilon = 1$, then it is also a global ESS.

Note that the above definition with $\varepsilon \to 0$ satisfies the ESS concept stated previously. If u^0 is a global ESS, then this strategy is invasion proof for all starting conditions for mutant (different) strategies. In other words, a global ESS that begins as a mutant strategy will always invade a population.

It follows from the above definition that if u^0 is a local ESS, then $p = (1, 0, \ldots, 0)$ is a stable equilibrium point for Eq. (7.5). Furthermore, there can be no other equilibrium points for p with p_0 in the interval $1 - \varepsilon < p_0 < 1$, provided u^0 is a local ESS. In what follows, the argument t remains implicit but is dropped from the notation.

The above definition can show that a necessary and sufficient condition for u^0 to be a local ESS is that there exists ε in the interval $0 < \varepsilon < 1$ such that for all distinct $u^i \in U_i, i = 1, \ldots, r$ and for all non-zero $p \in P$ with $1 - \varepsilon < p_0 < 1$

$$H_0(u, p) > \bar{H}(u, p). \tag{7.7}$$

All strategies are assumed to be distinct. However, in order to guarantee that we cannot have two different payoffs corresponding to the same strategy, it is assumed that $H_i = H_0$ whenever $u^i = u^0$. This assumption, along with (7.7), yields the following theorem.

Theorem 7.1 If $u^0 \in U_0$ is a local ESS, then there exists ε, $0 < \varepsilon < 1$, such that, for all p_0 in the interval $1 - \varepsilon < p_0 < 1$, the difference $\bar{H}(u, p) - H_0(u, p)$ must take on a proper local maximum with respect to the strategies $u^0 \in U_0$ at u $u^i = u^0$, $i = 1, \ldots, r$.

In an evolutionary setting, the fitness functions would hold a close relationship to one another. Such a relationship is introduced here in the context of a balanced game.

Definition 7.2 An evolutionary game is said to be balanced if there exists a generating function

$$G(u, u^i, p) \tag{7.8}$$

such that:

(i) The average fitness functions are given by

$$H_i(u, p) \equiv G(u, u^i, p), i = 0, \ldots, r. \tag{7.9}$$

(ii) Whenever u^i and every vector in u is replaced by a common strategy vector s, then the generating function (7.8) becomes a function of s only.

A balanced evolutionary game may be formulated out of the two-strategy ($r = 1$), two-player matrix game. A payoff matrix is defined by

$$E(u^0, u^1) = (u^0)^T A u^1, \tag{7.10}$$

where A is an $m \times m$ matrix with real elements. The function $E(u^0, u^1)$ is the payoff to an individual player using strategy u^0 against a single opponent player using strategy u^1. The mixed version of this game assumes that the strategy components are the probabilities that a given pure strategy is chosen, and thus we have

$$U_i = \left\{ u^i \in E^m \middle| u_1^i + \cdots u_m^i = 1 \text{ and } u_j^i \geq 0, j = 1, \ldots, m \right\}. \tag{7.11}$$

All of the players use either u^0 or u^1. The average individual fitness for a player is the average expected payoff a given player would receive after many interactions with all the other players in the population (i.e., there are many interactions in a given generation):

$$H_0 = p_0 E(u^0, u^0) + p_1 E(u^0, u^1), \tag{7.12}$$

$$H_1 = p_0 E(u^1, u^0) + p_1 E(u^1, u^1). \tag{7.13}$$

Both conditions (i) and (ii) of Definition 7.1 are satisfied by the generating function

$$G = p_0 E(u^i, u^0) + p_1 E(u^i, u^1), i = 0, 1, \tag{7.14}$$

which yields both Eqs. (7.12) and (7.13). Hence, this game is balanced.

7.3 Research Design

In order to solve the problem, this chapter conducts a game analysis on the knowledge transfer between two knowledge agents. In the game process of knowledge transfer between organizations, $\pi_i(i = 1, 2)$ indicates the initial profit that the organization does not choose to share knowledge. In addition, knowledge transfer between organizations makes the value of knowledge itself more multiplied, so as to gain benefits of direct and newly created value (see Fig. 7.1).

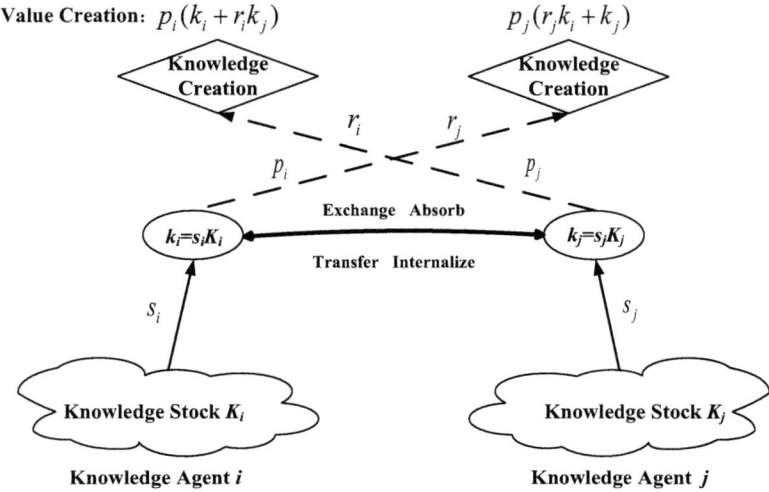

Value Creation: $p_i(k_i + r_i k_j)$ $\qquad\qquad$ $p_j(r_j k_i + k_j)$

Fig. 7.1 Framework of knowledge transfer

7.3.1 Direct Profit of Knowledge Transfer

The direct profit of knowledge transfer between organizations refers to the benefit from the knowledge provided by the other party when the organization chooses the knowledge transfer strategy. It is affected by three factors as follows.

(1). The knowledge stock of the knowledge agent. $K_i (i = 1, 2)$ is used to express the knowledge stock.

(2). The capacity of the knowledge agent to send knowledge. $s_i (i = 1, 2)$ is used to describe the capacity of the knowledge agent to send knowledge. Under the general situation, the stronger the sending capacity of the knowledge agent is, the more knowledge resources are shared by the knowledge agents. The amount of knowledge stock transferred by knowledge agents is

$$k_i = s_i K_i (i = 1, 2) \qquad (7.15)$$

(3). The absorptive capacity of the knowledge agent. $r_i (i = 1, 2)$ is used to indicate the knowledge learning and absorptive capacity of the organization.

Based on the abovementioned three factors, the direct profits of knowledge sharing between organizations can be indicated as $r_i s_j K_j (i, j = 1, 2)$.

7.3.2 Indirect Profit of Knowledge Transfer

When the organization chooses the knowledge transfer strategy, the knowledge flow, knowledge transfer, and knowledge absorptive will lead to the creation of new knowledge. Here, p_i is used to indicate the knowledge internalization innovation capacity of the knowledge agent. This chapter considers that the knowledge innovation of the organization is affected by the shared knowledge stock i in the process of knowledge transfer, and it is also affected by the knowledge stock k_j, which is shared by the other agent j and absorbed by i in the process of knowledge exchanging and sharing. Assuming that the knowledge acquired by the organization through knowledge transfer and the original knowledge are homogeneous and have the same utility, we can then express the value of knowledge innovation in the process of knowledge transfer by $p_i(k_i + r_i k_j)(i, j = 1, 2)$.

7.3.3 Cost of Knowledge Transfer

Because the knowledge has inherent implication, complexity, exclusiveness, usefulness, and other attributes, knowledge transfer cost exists in the process of knowledge transfer. Here, $c_i(i = 1, 2)$ indicates the cost coefficient of knowledge transfer, and so the transfer cost of an organization in the process of knowledge transfer is $c_i k_i(i = 1, 2)$. Above all, we can get the game payoff matrix of knowledge transfer (Table 7.1) as follows.

7.3.4 Model Structure

From the perspective of individuals' bounded rationality, the evolutionary game theory chooses groups as the research objects. It is assumed that an individual is not a behavior optimizer in reality and individual decisions are achieved by imitation, learning, mutation, and other dynamic processes between individuals. Under this assumption, the factors that influence the behaviors of individuals are incorporated into the game model, and dynamic analysis is employed to obtain the evolutionary stable equilibrium which can predict the group behavior of individuals. The evolutionary game theory emphasizes the limited rationality of economic decision-makers

Table 7.1 Payoff matrix of knowledge transfer between organizations

Knowledge agent 1	Knowledge agent 2	
	Transfer	Not transfer
Transfer	$\pi_1 + r_1 k_2 + p_1(k_1 + r_1 k_2) - c_1 k_1,$ $\pi_2 + r_2 k_1 + p_2(r_2 k_1 + k_2) - c_2 k_2$	$\pi_1 - c_1 k_1, \pi_2 + r_2 k_1$
Not transfer	$\pi_1 + r_1 k_2, \pi_2 - c_2 k_2$	π_1, π_2

and emphasizes the unity of individual rationality and collective rationality based on the design and optimization of rules, mechanisms, and systems. Therefore, the evolutionary game theory can be used to solve the problem of sharing strategy selection in the process of knowledge sharing.

In the initial state of the game, we assume that the ratio of the "transfer" strategy in knowledge agent 1 is x, and so the ratio of the "no transfer" strategy is $1 - x$; the ratio of the "transfer" strategy in knowledge agent 2 is y, and so the ratio of "no transfer" is $1 - y$.

In this way, the expected returns of the two strategies of "transfer" u_{1s} and "no transfer" u_{1n} in knowledge agent 1 and the group average profit $\overline{u_1}$ are, respectively:

$$u_{1s} = y(\pi_1 + r_1 k_2 + p_1(k_1 + r_1 k_2) - c_1 k_1) + (1 - y)(\pi_1 - c_1 k_1) \tag{7.16}$$

$$u_{1n} = y\pi_1 + (1 - y)\pi_1 \tag{7.17}$$

$$\overline{u_1} = xu_{1s} + (1 - x)u_{1n} \tag{7.18}$$

Similarly, the expected returns of the two strategies of "transfer" u_{2s} and "no transfer" u_{2n} in knowledge agent 2 and the group average profit $\overline{u_2}$ are, respectively:

$$u_{2s} = x(\pi_2 + r_2 k_1 + p_2(r_2 k_1 + k_2) - c_2 k_2) + (1 - x)(\pi_2 - c_2 k_2) \tag{7.19}$$

$$u_{2n} = x\pi_2 + (1 - x)\pi_2 \tag{7.20}$$

$$\overline{u_2} = yu_{2s} + (1 - y)u_{2n} \tag{7.21}$$

According to the multi-group dynamic replication theory of the evolutionary game, we can get the dynamic replicator equation:

$$F(x) = \frac{dx}{dt} = x\left(u_{1s} - \overline{u_1}\right) = x(1 - x)(yr_1 k_2 + yp_1(k_1 + r_1 k_2) - c_1 k_1) \tag{7.22}$$

$$G(y) = \frac{dy}{dt} = y\left(u_{2s} - \overline{u_2}\right) = y(1 - y)(xr_2 k_1 + xp_2(r_2 k_1 + k_2) - c_2 k_2) \tag{7.23}$$

According to the dynamic replicator equation $F(x)$ of the knowledge agent 1, we find that if $y^* = \frac{c_1 k_1}{r_1 k_2 + p_1(k_1 + r_1 k_2)}$, then $F(x)$ is identically equal to 0, which means that all states in the range of 0–1 are stable regarding x. If $y^* \neq \frac{c_1 k_1}{r_1 k_2 + p_1(k_1 + r_1 k_2)}$, then we note $F(x) = 0$ and that we can get $x = 0$ and $x = 1$ as two stable strategies of the dynamic equation.

According to the nature of the evolutionary stable strategy, a steady state that must be robust to a small perturbation can be called an evolutionary stable strategy. In other words, if a strategy x is the evolutionary stable strategy x^*, it must match the following conditions: (1) it has achieved balanced and (2) it can restore to x^* by dynamic replication if some individuals select another strategy which is deviated from x^* by accidental mistake. Mathematically, it is necessary for $F(x) = \frac{dx}{dt}$ to be more than 0 when the disturbance occurs in order to make x less than x^*, and when

Fig. 7.2 Phase diagram of the evolutionary game

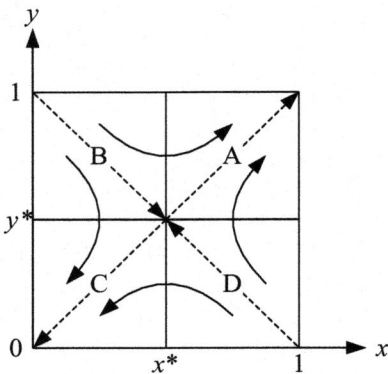

the disturbance occurs to make x above x^*, $F(x) = \frac{dx}{dt}$ must be less than 0. In other words, the derivative $\frac{dF(x)}{dx}$ at the steady state must be less than zero.

If $y > \frac{c_1 k_1}{r_1 k_2 + p_1 (k_1 + r_1 k_2)}$, $\left.\frac{dF(x)}{dx}\right|_{x=0} > 0$, and $\left.\frac{dF(x)}{dx}\right|_{x=1} < 0$, then $x = 1$ is the evolutionary stable strategy; that is, knowledge agent 1 tends to choose a "transfer" strategy.

If $y < \frac{c_1 k_1}{r_1 k_2 + p_1 (k_1 + r_1 k_2)}$, $\left.\frac{dF(x)}{dx}\right|_{x=0} < 0$, and $\left.\frac{dF(x)}{dx}\right|_{x=1} > 0$, then $x = 0$ is the evolutionary stable strategy; that is, knowledge agent 1 tends to choose a "no transfer" strategy.

For the dynamic replication equation of knowledge agent 2, if $x^* = \frac{c_2 k_2}{r_2 k_1 + p_2 (r_2 k_1 + k_2)}$, then $G(y)$ is identically equal to 0, which means that all states regarding y in the range 0–1 are stable.

If $x > \frac{c_2 k_2}{r_2 k_1 + p_2 (r_2 k_1 + k_2)}$, $\left.\frac{dG(y)}{dy}\right|_{y=0} > 0$, and $\left.\frac{dG(y)}{dy}\right|_{y=1} < 0$, then $y = 1$ is the evolutionary stable strategy; that is, knowledge agent 2 tends to choose a "transfer" knowledge strategy.

If $x < \frac{c_2 k_2}{r_2 k_1 + p_2 (r_2 k_1 + k_2)}$, $\left.\frac{dG(y)}{dy}\right|_{y=0} < 0$, and $\left.\frac{dG(y)}{dy}\right|_{y=1} > 0$, then $y = 0$ is the evolutionary stable strategy; that is, knowledge agent 2 tends to choose a "no transfer" knowledge strategy.

According to the above analysis, we can get the dynamic phase diagram of the evolutionary game (shown in Fig. 7.2). The arrow in the figure indicates the convergence direction of the evolutionary game.

Assume that the game participants in the initial state using two strategies have the same probability of any point in the interval [0, 1]. In the replicator dynamic evolutionary game, when the initial situation (x_0, y_0) falls in region A, which means $x > x^*$, $y > y^*$, then the game converges to the evolutionary stable strategy $x = 1$, $y = 1$; that is, knowledge agents share knowledge with each other. When the initial situation (x_0, y_0) falls in region C, it will converge to the evolutionary stable strategy $x = 0$, $y = 0$; that is, knowledge agents do not transfer knowledge.

7.4 Evolutionary Stable Strategy of Knowledge Transfer

According to the above evolutionary game analysis, in order to achieve the evolutionary game's stable equilibrium strategy of $x^* = 1$, $y^* = 1$ through the replicator dynamics, the probability that the initial state (x_0, y_0) falls in region A of the graph should be as large as possible. We find that a smaller value of (x^*, y^*) means a smaller value of $x^* = \frac{c_2 k_2}{r_2 k_1 + p_2 (r_2 k_1 + k_2)}$ and $y^* = \frac{c_1 k_1}{r_1 k_2 + p_1 (k_1 + r_1 k_2)}$, and the larger region A is. At the same time, when the initial state probability (x_0, y_0) of falling in region A is larger, the greater is the probability that knowledge agents choose the evolutionary strategy.

Based on the above analysis, we find that the evolutionary stable strategy of the organization in the process of knowledge transfer is influenced by the parameters in the model. The following section, respectively, discusses the effects of several parameter changes on interorganizational knowledge transfer evolutionary game models and possible control methods.

7.4.1 Cost of Knowledge Transfer

Because knowledge has its inherent attributes such as implication, complexity, exclusivity, usefulness, and so on, it is more obscure, complex, proprietary, and difficult to encode. The more exclusive it is, the more difficult to learn it. Thus, in the process of knowledge transfer, the organization faces the problem regarding the costs of knowledge transfer. The manpower, material, and financial resources consumed in the process of knowledge transfer constitute the cost of knowledge transfer and mainly include the delivery costs of the sender in the process of presenting and imparting knowledge to the others, the acceptance costs incurred by the recipient in finding the source of knowledge and learning the knowledge, and the management cost of the relevant social organization due to the management of knowledge transfer and knowledge base. The delivery cost and acceptance costs are associated with not only the content and nature of knowledge itself but also with the experience, capacity, and knowledge accumulation of the sender and the recipient and even closely with the social environment and social system. The organization is for the purpose of maximizing interests. In the process of knowledge transfer, knowledge transfer costs are the key factors affecting the knowledge transfer decision, and so when the knowledge transfer cost c_i is low, the willingness of the organization for knowledge transfer will be stronger, and it is more likely to choose an evolution stable strategy to transfer knowledge.

7.4.2 Knowledge Absorptive Capacity

The value of knowledge transfer is that knowledge absorbers can use knowledge to achieve the added value of knowledge, and not just knowledge alone. However, due to the different knowledge structures and knowledge reserves of different knowledge agents, there are often differences in the capacity to copy, absorb, and apply new knowledge. The absorptive capacity of knowledge affects not only the final result of knowledge transfer but also directly influences the transfer willingness of both sides. Cohen and Levinthal (1990) define knowledge absorptive capacity as the capacity under which enterprises recognize the value of external new knowledge, and through the integration and application of enterprise knowledge, to achieve commercial results. It is thought that knowledge absorptive capacity is a basic learning process essential to the cultivation of an enterprise's innovation capacity. Since the enhancement of knowledge absorptive capacity is based on the previous learning experience of its own absorptive capacity, it has a cumulation and path dependence, which is often determined by the organization's capacity to share knowledge and communicate internally. Therefore, the level of an organization's knowledge absorptive capacity will affect the enthusiasm of mutual knowledge transfer, thus impacting the efficiency of knowledge transfer. Therefore, the knowledge absorptive capacity of the knowledge agent is the key factor of knowledge transfer decision. The bigger the organization's absorptive capacity r_i is, the greater the returns $r_i k_j$ are that are gained from the knowledge transfer; at the same time, the smaller the values of x^* and y^* are, the more knowledge transfer agents are inclined to choose knowledge transfer, and game behavior will converge to the equilibrium point (knowledge transfer, knowledge transfer).

7.4.3 Knowledge Sending Capacity

Because knowledge itself is implicit, complex, and systematic, the transfer of knowledge is not an easy thing. Simonin (1999) argues that the implicitness, complexity, and specificity of knowledge will lead to a causal ambiguity of knowledge, bringing about causal ambiguity between knowledge action and result and hindering knowledge transfer and communication. If the knowledge provider has a good expression, description, and communication capacity of knowledge, then it can make a reasonable, effective expression and elaboration of knowledge and adopt the corresponding transfer mechanism for the different scenarios of the transferred knowledge. One can also effectively improve the performance of knowledge transfer. Therefore, knowledge providers not only have valuable knowledge but are also able to transfer the knowledge to the knowledge receiver in a way that the knowledge receiver is easy to understand and absorb. Replacing $k_i = s_i K_i (i = 1, 2)$ into x^* and y^*, we get

$$x^*(s_1) = \frac{c_2 s_2 K_2}{r_2 s_1 K_1 + p_2(s_1 K_1 + s_2 K_2)} \tag{7.24}$$

$$y^*(s_2) = \frac{c_1 s_1 K_1}{r_1 s_2 K_2 + p_1(s_1 K_1 + s_2 K_2)} \tag{7.25}$$

We can see that x^* and y^* are decreasing functions regarding s_i. Thus, the greater a knowledge agent's capacity to send is, the smaller the values x^* and y^* are. Therefore, the evolutionary stable strategy (ESS) of knowledge agents tends to choose knowledge transfer between each other.

7.4.4   Knowledge Innovation Capacity

Knowledge innovation mainly refers to knowledge agents in the process of knowledge transfer, through knowledge exchange, knowledge transfer, knowledge absorptive, and internalization, having access to new knowledge and, based on the original knowledge continue innovation of knowledge, thereby increasing their knowledge stock in order to obtain a sustainable competitive advantage. Knowledge innovation is the driving force for the sustainable development period of the organization. If the organization is to sustainably develop, it must carry out continuous knowledge innovation. When it comes to the selection of a knowledge transfer strategy, the greater the knowledge internalization innovation coefficient p_i is between organizations in the process of a knowledge transfer strategy game, the greater the benefits $p_i(k_i + k_j)$ are that knowledge innovation brings, while at the same time x^* and y^* are decreasing functions regarding p_i; therefore, the stronger the knowledge internalization innovation capacity is, the more conducive it is to the selection of a knowledge transfer strategy for organizations. In addition, the knowledge internalization innovation coefficient p_i is also related to the organization's innovation environment and mechanism design.

7.4.5   Knowledge Potential Difference

The transfer of knowledge is done from the source of the knowledge to the receptor of the knowledge, showing the direction of knowledge flow. The distribution of knowledge between knowledge agents is always asymmetric, and there are knowledge difference and knowledge potential difference, which are the source powers of the knowledge resources transfer. The knowledge potential difference reflects the potential difference of knowledge stock of the knowledge transfer agent, communicating the difference between the academic background and degree of mastery of the knowledge accumulated by agents and leading to the occurrence of active and passive knowledge communications. The distribution of knowledge among agents is always asymmetric, and knowledge asymmetry is the basis of the transfer of knowledge. It is precisely because of the existence of knowledge asymmetry that the transfer of knowledge resources is necessary and possible. Knowledge flows from a knowledge agent with high knowledge potential difference to an agent with low knowledge potential difference. This chapter argues that the difference of knowledge agents in knowledge content is the difference in the quantity, quality, and structure of knowledge. In addition, all kinds of social activities in the knowledge economy need multiple knowledge resources. Knowledge receptors are at the low end of the knowledge stock, continuing to seek knowledge to make up for the difference with the same level of agents, thus promoting the transfer of knowledge.

$$x^*(K_1/K_2) = \frac{c_2 s_2}{(r_2 s_1 + p_2 s_1)K_1/K_2 + p_2 s_2} \tag{7.26}$$

$$y^*(K_2/K_1) = \frac{c_1 s_1}{(r_1 s_2 + p_1 s_2)K_2/K_1 + p_1 s_1} \tag{7.27}$$

We note similarly that x^* and y^* are decreasing functions of knowledge potential difference K_i/K_j. Thus, when there is knowledge potential difference between the knowledge agents, the knowledge agent will tend to transfer the knowledge to compensate for this knowledge potential difference and to improve each other's knowledge stock. However, when the knowledge potential difference between both knowledge agents K_i/K_j exceeds a certain threshold, the "knowledge gap" leads to a lack of knowledge transfer motivation and willingness between knowledge agents, thus affecting their transfer strategies.

7.5 Conclusion

Based on the bounded rationality of knowledge transfer, the game model of knowledge transfer between organizations is built, and the evolutionary game theory is used to analyze the knowledge transfer between organizations. This chapter analyzes the influences on the evolutionary stable strategy from changes in parameters such as knowledge transfer cost, knowledge sending capacity, knowledge absorptive capacity, knowledge innovation capacity, and knowledge potential difference between knowledge agents during the process of knowledge transfer. Thus, it discusses the influencing factors of the evolutionary strategy selection of a knowledge agent. Through analysis of studies, this chapter finds that by changing the relevant parameters, the knowledge transfer evolutionary game can indeed achieve the optimal evolutionary stable strategy.

Chapter 8
Cellular Automaton and Tacit Knowledge Sharing

8.1 Introduction

With the advent of the knowledge economy era, knowledge has become the major source for an organization to gain its core competence, and the full absorption and utilization of knowledge resources outside the organization are the key to increasing productivity and gaining a competitive advantage. An organization's knowledge stocks determine its core competitiveness directly. Polanyi (2015) divides knowledge into two types, explicit knowledge and tacit knowledge, while Allee (1997) analogizes tacit knowledge and explicit knowledge to oceans and icebergs, respectively. In a traditional economic society, people only give credit to the role of explicit knowledge and focus on the management and utilization of themselves in their daily work. As a matter of fact, explicit knowledge is merely the "iceberg" above the water. With the advent of the knowledge economic society, people have started to draw attention to the enormous tacit knowledge under the water. Polanyi (2015) points out that in modern industries, knowledge is hard to describe as an indispensable part of technologies, thus making the sharing of tacit knowledge hard to codify as an essential component of knowledge sharing. The formation of tacit knowledge is a long-term accumulation process of personal experience, insights, and deep comprehension, which are extremely difficult to imitate and steal; therefore, tacit knowledge is the basis and source for an organization to build up its core competitiveness. Knowledge possesses abstractness and externality, which makes it possible to share, i.e., knowledge's externalities allow it to be shared at a low cost, and the more it is shared, the more valuable it becomes; on the other hand, such qualities of knowledge serve also as the obstacles to knowledge sharing. More specifically, the high cost, high risk, and uncertainty of income distributions of the knowledge innovation processes determine knowledge owners' monopolistic attitudes toward knowledge out of their own selfishness and needs for competition, which deter the dissemination and spreading of knowledge.

© Springer International Publishing AG, part of Springer Nature 2018   109
Y. Yu et al., *Strategy and Performance of Knowledge Flow*,
International Series in Operations Research & Management Science 271,
https://doi.org/10.1007/978-3-319-77926-3_8

Knowledge sharing and organizational knowledge are premised on social exchange and social capital (Casimir et al. 2012). The social exchange theory argues that knowledge sharing occurs due to a reciprocation of favors received, such as job security, status, balance of power, and maintenance of future relationships (Cabrera and Cabrera 2005). Knowledge sharing as a form of social exchange is moderated by the social value orientation of the individual (Cyr and Choo 2010). As social exchange, we treat knowledge sharing like an exchange of a valuable resource between two parties that is expected to incur costs borne by the knowledge owner and to bestow benefits to the recipient. An individual's propensity to share knowledge would then depend on a consideration of these costs and benefits. In knowledge sharing exchanges, the costs of sharing consist of the effort and time required to make the knowledge available to another person, as well as the potential loss of relative advantage or power. Personal benefits include the obligation by others to reciprocate, a heightening of self-esteem, increased self-efficacy, increased personal identification with co-workers, respect from others, a better reputation, and enjoyment in helping others.

Based on prior research, this chapter therefore sets up a cellular automaton model to simulate the tacit knowledge sharing process among different entities in knowledge-based organizations. It also analyzes the evolvement of tacit knowledge entities' sharing behaviors and strategies under the condition of bounded rationality, which provides theoretical support for the enhancement of tacit knowledge in knowledge-based organizations.

The rest of this paper is organized as follows. The next section presents the basic theory of cellular automaton. Next, we analyze the bounded rationality of tacit knowledge entities. Section 5.4 builds the rule system of behavioral change of knowledge agents and interactions among knowledge agents. Subsequently, the results of a simulation are analyzed. Finally, discussion and conclusions are presented.

8.2 Basic Theory of Cellular Automaton

This section presents the basic theory of cellular automaton, which is adapted from Kari (2005, 2012). A cellular automaton (CA) is a discrete dynamical system that consists of an infinite array of cells. Each cell has a state from a finite state set. The cells change their states according to a local update rule that provides the new state based on the old states of the cell and its neighbors. All states use the same update rule, and the updating happens simultaneously at all cells. The updating is repeated over and over again at discrete time steps, leading to a time evolution of the system.

CA is among the oldest models of natural computing, dating back over half a century. The first CA studies by John von Neumann in the late 1940s were biologically motivated and related to self-replication in universal systems. Since then, CA has gained popularity as discrete models of physical systems. This is not surprising, considering that CA possesses several fundamental properties of the physical world:

massively parallel, homogeneous, and all of its interactions are local. Other important physical constraints such as reversibility and conservation laws can be added as needed by properly choosing the local update rule.

CA has also been studied extensively as a model of computation. Computational universality is common in CA, and even an amazingly simple CA is capable of performing arbitrary computation tasks. Because CA has the advantage of parallelism, while obeying natural constraints such as locality and uniformity, it provides a framework for investigating realistic computation in massively parallel systems. Wolfram (1984) studies the rules of a simplified one-dimension CA and further classifies those rules into four categories: stable, cyclical, chaos, and complex types. Currently, CA also has been applied to many fields, such as disease spreading (Fuentes and Kuperman 1999), innovation dissemination (Bhargava et al. 1993), and traffic flow (Wolf 1999), and all of them have achieved desirable results.

This chapter only considers synchronous CA, where the underlying topology is an infinite rectangular grid. The cells are hence the squares of an infinite d-dimensional checker board, addressed by $\mathbb{Z}^d$. This is called a d-dimensional CA. The one-, two-, and three-dimensional cases are the most common.

A d-dimensional CA consists of a finite or infinite d-dimensional grid of cells, each of which can take on a value from a finite, typically small, set of integers. The value of each cell at time step t is a function of the values of a small local neighborhood of cells at time $t - 1$. The cells update their states simultaneously according to a given local rule.

8.2.1 Basic Definitions

The states of the automaton come from a finite state set S. At any given time, the configuration of the automaton is a mapping $c : \mathbb{Z}^d \to S$ that specifies the states of all cells. The set $S^{\mathbb{Z}^d}$ of all configurations is denoted by $C = (d, S)$, or briefly C, when d and S are known from the context. Constant functions are called homogeneous configurations.

The cells change their states synchronously at discrete time steps. The next state of each cell depends on the current states of the neighboring cells according to an update rule. All cells use the same rule, and the rule is applied to all cells at the same time. The neighboring cells may be the nearest cells surrounding the cell, but more general neighborhoods can be specified by giving the relative offsets of the neighbors. Let $N = (\vec{x}_1, \vec{x}_2, \ldots, \vec{x}_n)$ be a vector of n distinct elements of $\mathbb{Z}^d$. The neighbors of a cell at location $\vec{x} \in \mathbb{Z}^d$ are the n cells at locations

$$\vec{x} + \vec{x}_i \text{ for } i = 1, 2, \ldots, n.$$

The local rule is a function $f : S^n \to S$, where n is the size of the neighborhood. State $f(a_1, a_2, \ldots, a_n)$ is the state of a cell whose n neighbors were at states $a_1, a_2, \ldots, a_n$ one time step before. This update rule then determines the global dynamics of the

CA: configuration c becomes in one time step the configuration e, where for all $\vec{x} \in \mathbb{Z}^d$

$$e(\vec{x}) = f\big(c(\vec{x} + \vec{x}_1), c(\vec{x} + \vec{x}_2), \dots, c(\vec{x} + \vec{x}_n)\big) \tag{8.1}$$

We say that $e = G(c)$ and call $G : C \to C$ the global transition function of the CA.

In summary, CA is a dynamical system that is homogeneous and discrete in both time and space, which are updated locally in space. A d-dimensional CA is specified by a triple (S, N, f) where S is the state set, $N \in \left(S^{\mathbb{Z}^d}\right)^n$ is the neighborhood vector, and $f : S^n \to S$ is the local update rule. We usually identify a CA with its global transition function G and talk about CA function G or simply CA G. In algorithmic questions, G is, however, always specified using the three finite items S, N, and f.

8.2.2 Neighborhoods

Neighborhoods commonly used in CA are the von Neumann neighborhood N_{vN} and the Moore neighborhood N_{M}. The von Neumann neighborhood contains relative offsets $\vec{y}$ that satisfy $\|\vec{y}\|_1 \leq 1$, where

$$\|(y_1, y_2, \dots, y_d)\|_1 = |y_1| + |y_2| + \dots + |y_d| \tag{8.2}$$

is the Manhattan norm. This means that a cell in location $\vec{x}$ has $2d + 1$ neighbors: the cell itself and the cells at locations $\vec{x} \pm \vec{e}_i$, where $\vec{e}_i = (0, \dots, 0, 1, 0, \dots, 0)$ is the i_{th} coordinate unit vector. The Moore neighborhood contains all vectors $\vec{y} = (y_1, y_2, \dots, y_d)$, where each y_i is -1, 0, or 1; that is, all $\vec{y} \in \mathbb{Z}^d$ such that $\|\vec{y}\|_\infty \leq 1$ where

$$\|(y_1, y_2, \dots, y_d)\|_\infty = \max\{|y_1|, |y_2|, \dots, |y_d|\} \tag{8.3}$$

is the max norm. Every cell has 3^d Moore neighbors. Figure 8.1 shows the von Neumann and Moore neighborhoods in the case $d = 2$.

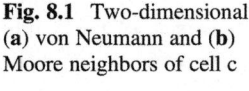

Fig. 8.1 Two-dimensional
(a) von Neumann and **(b)**
Moore neighbors of cell c

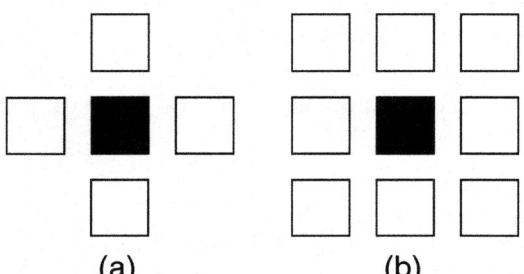

(a)   (b)

Cellular state   It is the values of an examined cell's attributes in certain respects; one CA usually has only one state variable, and there are a finite number of possible values; however, the number is often set according to real situations in practical applications.

State evolution rule   It is the mapping from a cell and its neighbor at one moment to its state at the next moment.

8.3   Bounded Rationality of Tacit Knowledge Agents

Classical economics is based on the hypothesis of "perfect rationality," which requires agents attain the optimal object out of all the choices, i.e., they must possess the capability for a decision to maximize their personal interests in certain and uncertain situations. Moreover, they are required to make perfect decisions and predictions under the interactive game environment. It is essential that not only each person owns perfect rationality but also each person believes the counterparts own it, too; that is, "each individual owns perfect rationality" is common knowledge. In real life, perfect rationality is not true. Simon (1955) asserts that a person in real life is an "economic man," whose rationality is bounded in-between perfect rationality and irrationality, rather than a "perfectly rational economic man." With the constraints of information, knowledge, cognition, systems, ethics, as well as complexity and uncertainty of social environments, decision-makers are unable to achieve perfect rationality. Generally, the basic principle of bounded rationality implies people's restricted capability to process information. Therefore, individuals are unable to behave under a fully rational mode; that is, they cannot always act in a way that maximizes their utility and are not capable of arbitrarily complex deductions toward the end. They will not always be capable of thinking through all possible outcomes and choosing that course of action which will result in the best possible outcome. People try to act in accordance with rationality, but for the limitation of rationality itself, they can only act within the boundary of bounded rationality.

Tacit knowledge sharing is a two-way process. Under certain circumstances, tacit knowledge owners communicate and share their knowledge reciprocally; they learn and internalize others' tacit knowledge in order to increase their own knowledge storages; at the same time, they combine it with their own knowledge and make knowledge innovations. The bounded rationality in the tacit knowledge sharing process implies that two sides of knowledge sharing often cannot predict what their behavior will lead to under the condition of bounded rationality, and they tend to make decisions of whether to share their tacit knowledge or not based on previous experience and current situations. Therefore, the two sides of tacit knowledge sharing cannot and will not adopt the optimal strategy under the condition of perfect rationality at the beginning, and they search for a relatively good strategy

Table 8.1 Decision characteristics of tacit knowledge entities

Types	Major characteristics	Rational choice in the sharing process
Altruists	Knowledge sharing is equal and mutually beneficial Tacit knowledge sharing can increase common knowledge The degree of sharing is positively related to two sharing parties' common benefits	Share all the tacit knowledge to maximize two parties' common incremental knowledge
Egoists	Knowledge sharing can be self-interested Tacit knowledge sharing can increase common knowledge One party's contribution in the tacit knowledge sharing process is positively related to the other party's benefits and negatively related to its own benefits	Absorb as much tacit knowledge in the sharing process as possible to maximize personal incremental knowledge under the constraints of minimizing the other party's incremental knowledge

after constant gambling and adjustments, rather than a one-time dominant strategy. Even if they choose the optimal strategy, they may depart from it again.

In this sense, knowledge entities can be divided into egoists and altruists based on the various behaviors of tacit knowledge entities out of bounded rationality in the knowledge sharing process. "Egoists" refer to individuals who are unwilling to share their knowledge or who are willing to "take a free ride" to accept others' knowledge without contributing their own. The aforementioned paradox lowers the utilization efficiency of knowledge. Related research studies have shown that real-world individuals own bounded rationality—a state in-between perfect rationality and irrationality.

To simplify the analysis, altruists are defined as tacit knowledge entities that are willing to share all of their tacit knowledge, while egoists are those who are utterly unwilling to contribute their knowledge. The two types represent two opposite attitudes in the process of knowledge sharing, and the bases of their rational decisions are listed below (Table 8.1).

8.4 Research Design

For tacit knowledge owners with bounded rationality, they have to adjust their original strategy every time a neighbor takes actions. We assume that a knowledge entity's movement in the next round is based on the benefits of five individuals (he himself and the four neighbors surrounding him) in the previous round. This specific knowledge entity will compare the sums of total payoffs of altruists and egoists respectively, and he will copy the action type of knowledge owners that has higher payoffs in the coming round.

Based on the aforementioned requirements of establishing cellular automaton models, the knowledge dissemination model of knowledge-based organizations is defined as follows.

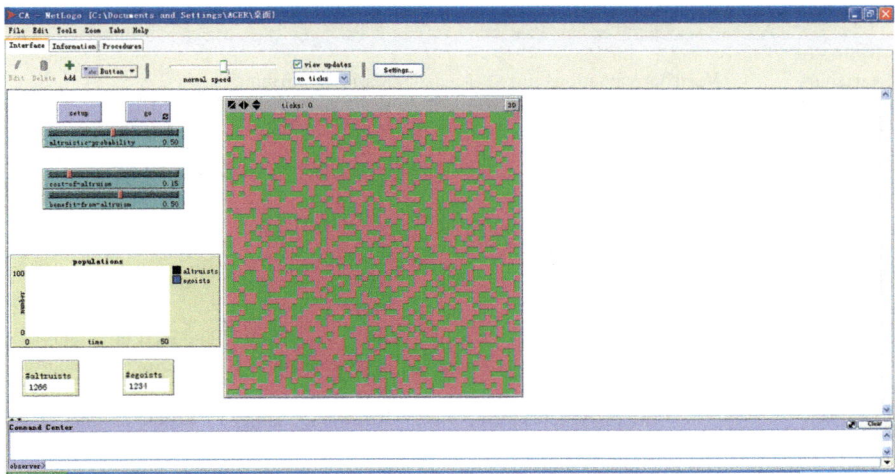

Fig. 8.2   Initial interface of the cellular automaton simulation

(a) Cells represent tacit knowledge entities and are presented by square grids.
(b) Cellular spaces represent knowledge-based organizations or teams, like universities and knowledge-based enterprises, and are presented by square board grids.
(c) von Neumann neighborhood is assumed here, i.e., each knowledge entity interacts with its neighbors up, down, left, and right.
(d) The cellular state is either 1 or 0, and 1 represents the state when knowledge owners who are willing to share their tacit knowledge (becoming altruists) have already been disseminated, while 0 denotes the state when knowledge owners who are willing to share their tacit knowledge have not yet been disseminated (becoming egoists).

As for the state evolution rule, we program the CA model using "NetLogo," an integration platform for multi-agent simulations, which is especially suited for simulations of complex systems evolving with time. First introduced by Wilensky (1999), the Northwestern University's Center for Connected Learning and Computer-Based Modeling was in charge of subsequent developments. The initial interface of the simulation program is shown in Fig. 8.2, and the related variables are defined in Table 8.2.

The initial state of knowledge sharing benefits, "benefit-from-altruism," is set at 0.5, and the knowledge sharing cost, "cost-of-altruism," is 0.2. In other words, if an altruist pays two units every time he contributes knowledge, then his neighbors will get five units of benefits from him. For instance, suppose an altruist is surrounded by three egoists and one altruist. The detailed knowledge sharing process of the five individuals is then shown as follows.

Table 8.2 Specifications of simulation variables

Names of variables	Variable valuations	Variable attributes
Altruistic-probability	Users define it through sliders, which range from 0 to 1	Proportion of altruists
Benefit-out	0 denotes egoists 1 denotes altruists	Types of knowledge entities
Benefit-from-altruism	Users define it through sliders, which range from 0 to 1	Knowledge entity i's knowledge sharing benefits
Cost-of-altruism	Users define it through sliders, which range from 0 to 1	Knowledge entity i's knowledge sharing costs
Altruism-benefit	Benefit-from-altruism * (benefit-out + sum [benefit-out] of neighbors 4)/5	Knowledge entity i and its four neighbors' average benefits in the knowledge sharing process
Fitness	(1 + altruism-benefit) for egoists [(1 − cost-of-altruism) + altruism-benefit] for altruists	Knowledge entity i's benefits in the knowledge sharing process
Neighbor-fitness	NULL	Benefits to neighbors of knowledge entity i in the knowledge sharing process
Ego-fitness	NULL	Knowledge entity i and its four neighbors' egoistic benefits
Alt-fitness	NULL	Knowledge entity i and its four neighbors' altruistic benefits
Fitness-sum	Alt-fitness + ego-fitness	Knowledge entity i and its four neighbors' total benefits in the knowledge sharing process
Ego-weight	Ego-fitness/fitness-sum	The share of knowledge entity i and its four neighbors' egoistic benefits to the total benefits
Alt-weight	Alt-fitness/fitness-sum	The share of knowledge entity i and its four neighbors' altruistic benefits to the total benefits

The average of knowledge entities' benefits:

$$\text{altruism-benefit} = 0.5 \times (1 + 1)/5 = 0.2;$$

Each egoist's benefits:

$$\text{fitness} = 1 + \text{altruism-benefit} = 1 + 0.2 = 1.2;$$

Each altruist's benefits:

$$\text{fitness} = (1\text{-cost-of-altruism}) + \text{altruism-benefit} = 1 + 0.2 - 0.2 = 1;$$

Egoists' total benefits:

$$\text{ego-fitness} = 1.2 \times 3 = 3.6;$$

Altruists' total benefits:

$$\text{alt-fitness} = 1 \times 2 = 2;$$

Total benefits of sharing:

$$\text{fitness-sum} = \text{alt-fitness} + \text{ego-fitness} = 1.2 \times 3 + 1 \times 2 = 5.6;$$

Whereby the:
Weight of altruists' benefits to all:

$$\text{alt-weight} = \text{alt-fitness}/\text{fitness-sum} = 1 \times 2/5.6 = 0.36;$$

Weight of egoists' benefits to all:

$$\text{ego-weight} = \text{ego-fitness}/\text{fitness-sum} = 1.2 \times 3/5.6 = 0.64.$$

From the previous analysis, we may conclude that the weights of benefits that altruists get in this round are less than those that egoists get. Therefore, this specific entity will choose to become an egoist in the following round; i.e., they do not share knowledge in the next round.

8.5 Results

We assume that the numbers of altruists and egoists are the same initially, making up 50% each. The cost of knowledge sharing is set at 0.1, while the benefit is 0.5. After running the simulation program, we get the results shown in Fig. 8.3, which suggest that after about 5940 rounds of interactions, all the knowledge entities become altruists—that is, they choose the strategy to share knowledge. The graph shows that the numbers of egoists and altruists vibrate constantly, and knowledge entities have to adjust their strategies based on their knowledge sharing benefits in the previous round. After 5940 rounds of simulations, the entire system reaches equilibrium, and all the knowledge entities choose to share their tacit knowledge.

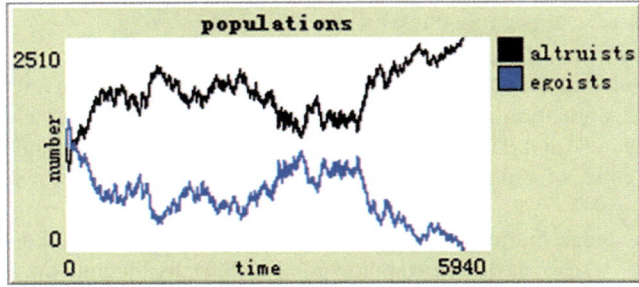

Fig. 8.3 Knowledge sharing cost, 0.1; knowledge sharing benefit, 0.5

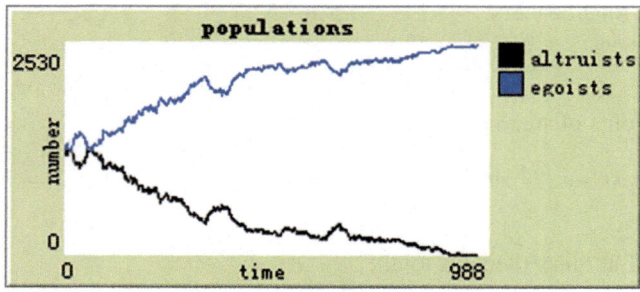

Fig. 8.4 Knowledge sharing cost, 0.1; knowledge sharing benefit, 0.45

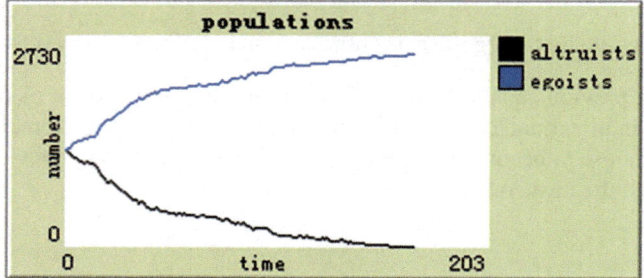

Fig. 8.5 Knowledge sharing cost, 0.15; knowledge sharing benefit, 0.5

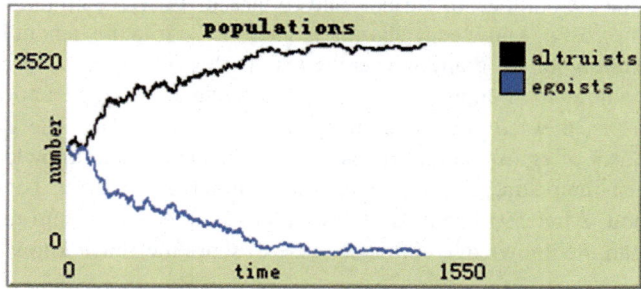

Fig. 8.6 Knowledge sharing cost, 0.1; knowledge sharing benefit, 0.55

By manipulating the benefits and costs of knowledge sharing, we are able to reach the following simulation results. After reducing the benefits of knowledge sharing (shown in Fig. 8.4) and raising the cost of knowledge sharing (shown in Fig. 8.5), by the time the entire organizational system becomes stable, all the knowledge entities turn into egoists.

If the knowledge sharing benefits increase (shown in Fig. 8.6) and the knowledge sharing costs decrease as described (shown in Fig. 8.7), by the time the entire system turns stable, all the knowledge entities choose to share their tacit knowledge.

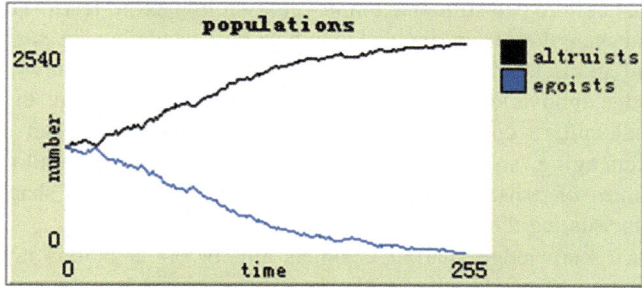

Fig. 8.7 Knowledge sharing cost, 0.05; knowledge sharing benefit, 0.5

Based on the simulation results, we hold that knowledge sharing costs and benefits do influence a knowledge entity's knowledge sharing strategies. The lower the knowledge sharing cost is, the higher its knowledge sharing benefit becomes, thus making knowledge entities willing to share their tacit knowledge. Therefore, the corresponding mechanisms should be established among organizations to lower the knowledge sharing costs and increase knowledge sharing benefits and at the same time to enhance the knowledge sharing among various organizations.

8.6 Conclusions and Policy Implications

Through the previous analysis, we find that the key parameters influencing knowledge entities' behaviors are knowledge sharing costs and benefits. Therefore, organizations can adopt the following strategies to promote tacit knowledge sharing among themselves.

Organizations should continue to reduce their knowledge sharing costs in order to increase knowledge sharing benefits. Organizations' knowledge sharing costs include the costs of knowledge senders' exhibitions, the sending costs to others during the knowledge sharing process, and the receiving costs when learning. Therefore, organizations should enhance their capacities to send and receive knowledge, so as to lower the sending and receiving costs. At the same time, they should provide more incentives for knowledge sharing, which can increase the knowledge sharing entities' benefits and their willingness to share, thus promoting more efficient knowledge management within the organization.

Excellent learning culture within the organization should be established in order to strengthen its learning capacities and improve the efficiency of knowledge sharing when costs are reduced. Organizational culture is a common value taken on by all members over a long time period. Openness, trust, cooperation, and the priority of knowledge and learning will push individuals to mutually learn together, and the sharing of knowledge among separate entities will thus be realized. A positive organizational culture can stimulate employers' willingness to learn. They will start to absorb and share their tacit knowledge, which will accelerate the establishment of a mature and stable learning mechanism; high-efficiency tacit knowledge sharing and knowledge innovation are eventually achieved. Therefore, in the process of organizational culture construction, a healthy atmosphere that can promote the learning, exchanging, sharing, and innovating of knowledge should be created. Concrete values of conscious cooperation, communication, and sharing are also essential at facilitating the sharing of tacit knowledge.

Proper tacit knowledge sharing channels among organizations must be built. While tacit knowledge is implied and complicated, it is often shared in the mode of P2P (person to person), thus making proper sharing channels a great way to reduce tacit knowledge sharing costs among organizations. A strongly constructed sharing channel can promote communication and mutual trust between two sides, thus helping to assimilate both sides organizationally and culturally. As a result, risks and knowledge sharing costs during the knowledge sharing process decrease to a great extent, leading to a big efficiency boost in tacit knowledge sharing.

Chapter 9
Small-World Network and Knowledge Sharing

9.1 Introduction

Knowledge sharing is a two-way communication process, and the compact degree and frequency of knowledge exchange are both different due to the individual cognitive background of organization members. The mutual learning and communication among members can promote continuous sharing and enhance the organization's overall knowledge level by sharing and expanding more benefits of the knowledge receiver. During communication and understanding, a knowledge dialogue is accrued, and there is a complex interactive relationship between individuals or populations, thus forming a relative network.

A network is a system that contains a lot of interactions among individuals, including complex systems with many basic units in nature. Knowledge sharing between organization members depends on the network among individuals. Milgram (1967) proposes the small-world phenomenon or "six degrees of separation." He finds that people can contact each other through "friends of friends" and that one has a relationship with anyone in the world that is separated at most by six persons. Small-world networks are defined as those networks possessing high clustering and short path lengths compared to a randomly constructed network (Watts and Strogatz 1998). A large number of studies about realistic relation networks have denoted that large-scale networks exhibit the small-world effect—that is to say, the small-world effect has universality. Therefore, considering the small-world effect of an embedding network makes it more suitable to research the knowledge sharing of members and to reflect upon the real affecting factors.

Using a small-world network to study the application of knowledge management has become an important methodology and offers practical significance as well. Metcalfe (2005) argues that small-world, self-organization phenomena illustrate a useful vision for designing a knowledge sharing vision that is appropriate for a complex environment. Cowan and Jonard (2004) find that the performance of the

© Springer International Publishing AG, part of Springer Nature 2018
Y. Yu et al., *Strategy and Performance of Knowledge Flow*,
International Series in Operations Research & Management Science 271,
https://doi.org/10.1007/978-3-319-77926-3_9

system exhibits clear "small-world" properties, in that the steady-state level of average knowledge is maximal when the structure is a small world (i.e., when most connections are local, but roughly 10% of them are long distance), and that the variance of knowledge levels among agents is maximal in the small-world region, whereas the coefficient of variation is minimal. Savolainen (2009) compares and contrasts small-world and information grounds as contexts of everyday information seeking and sharing. Carayol and Roux (2009) introduce a spatialized variation of the connections model to describe the strategic formation of links by agents who balance the benefits of forming links resulting from imperfect knowledge flows against their costs, which increase with geographic distance. Lin and Li (2010) numerically study the knowledge innovation and diffusion process on four representative network models: regular networks, small-world networks, random networks, and scale-free networks. Shi and Guan (2016) extend the idea of a small-world network to heterogeneous network positions of actors by capturing the variation of how closely a given actor is connected to others in the same network and how clustered that actor's neighbors are. This allows them to test the effects of a small-world network in the context of nanotechnology patenting in China.

According to the discussion above, our research focuses on the organizational characteristics of a small-world network structure within which organization members are exactly rooted. In addition, we construct a knowledge sharing model based on a small-world property by analyzing the characteristic of a small-world network and a knowledge sharing network. The simulation of different indicators of a network can enhance deeply our understanding of the process of knowledge sharing. With a consideration of knowledge sharing, knowledge learning, and knowledge innovation, this chapter puts forward a calculation method about knowledge level when they undertake knowledge sharing. We employ the Watts and Strogatz (WS) - small-world network model for simulation analysis, studying the impact to knowledge sharing trends from four indicators: the average shortest path network $L(p)$, clustering coefficient $C(p)$, a random reconnection probability P, and the degree of distribution K. Through comparative analysis, we find that high clustering coefficients and the short path can increase the exchange of knowledge associated with the node and enhance sharing efficiency when there is a proper degree of freedom for the degree of knowledge difference.

9.2 Basic Theory of Small-World Network[1]

The small-world phenomenon—the principle whereby most of us are linked by short chains of acquaintances—was first investigated as a question in sociology and is a feature of a wide range of networks arising in nature and technology. An experimental study of this phenomenon reveals that it has two fundamental components:

---

[1]The description in this section is an adaption of Newman (2000).

first, such short chains are ubiquitous; second, individuals operating with purely local information are very adept at finding these chains (Kleinberg 2000). The idea of a small-world network is typically attributed to the landmark work of Milgram (1967), who speculates that a small world is a network with surprisingly few degrees of separation between actors, despite the fact that actors tend to have cliquish groups of friends.

Small-world networks correspond to a class of networks in which links among actors are highly clustered, in the sense that on average one actor's connections are also likely to be connected to each other, while the average number of intermediaries needed to connect any two actors across the network, which is the average path length, remains relatively short. The unique combination of high clustering and short path lengths in the same network, along with a growing acknowledgment that small worlds appear frequently in diverse types of man-made, biological, ecological, and technological systems, suggests that small worlds offer an especially potent organizing mechanism for increasing performance in many different types of systems (Uzzi et al. 2007).

The simplest model of a small world is the random graph. Suppose there is some number N of people in the world, and on average they each have z acquaintances. This means that there are $\frac{1}{2}Nz$ connections between people in the entire population. The number z is called the coordination number of the network.

We can set up a very simple model of a social network by taking N dots ("nodes" or "vertices") and drawing $\frac{1}{2}Nz$ lines ("edges") between randomly chosen pairs to represent these connections. Such a network is called a random graph. It is easy to see that a random graph shows the small-world effect.

If person A on such a graph has z neighbors and each of A's neighbors also has z neighbors, then A has about z^2 second neighbors. Extending this argument, A also has z^3 third neighbors, z^4 fourth neighbors, and so on. Most people have between one hundred and one thousand acquaintances, and so z^4 is already between about 10^8 and 10^{12}, which is comparable with the population of the world. In general, the number D of degrees of separation, which we need to consider in order to reach all N people in the network (also called the diameter of the graph), is given by setting $z^D = N$, which implies that $D = \log N / \log z$. This logarithmic increase in the number of degrees of separation with the size of the network is typical of the small-world effect. Since $\log N$ increases only slowly with N, it allows the number of degrees of separation to be quite small even in very large systems.

There is a significant problem with the random graph as a model of social networks, however. The problem is that people's circles of acquaintances tend to overlap to a great extent. Some or all of your friend's friends are also likely to be your friends; or to put it another way, two of your friends are likely to be friends with one another. This means that in a real social network, it is not true to say that person A has z^2 second neighbors, since many of those friends of friends are also themselves friends of person A. This property is called the clustering of networks.

A random graph unfortunately does not show clustering. In a random graph, the probability that two of person A's friends will be friends with one another is no greater than the probability that two randomly chosen people will be friends with one another. On the other hand, clustering has been shown to exist in a number of real-world networks. One can define a clustering coefficient C that is the average fraction of pairs of neighbors of a node, which are also neighbors of each other (Watts and Strogatz 1998; Keeling 1999). In a fully connected network, in which everyone knows everyone else, $C = 1$; in a random graph, $C = z/N$, which is very small for a large network. In real-world networks, it has been found that while C is significantly less than 1, it is much greater than $O(N^{-1})$.

There is also another problem with random graphs as models of social networks. In a random graph, since each edge is present or not with a probability independent of all other edges, the number of edges around any given vertex—also called the degree of the vertex—has a Poisson distribution; it is for this reason that the properties of the random graph can be completely specified by the average coordination number z, since a Poisson distribution is completely specified by its mean. In some graphs, however, the distribution of vertex degrees is very far from Poissonian. This trend is most striking in data from the Internet (Albert et al. 1999). If one plots the distribution of the number of edges (or "hyperlinks") emerging from websites, then the resulting histogram has a clear power-law tail, whereas a Poisson distribution has an exponential tail. Some other networks, such as the networks of movie actors, show a similar behavior but with an exponential cutoff in the power law, while others like true social networks and neural networks appear to have exponential or Gaussian degree distributions (Amaral et al. 2000).

As the literature argues, random graphs show a small-world effect, possessing average vertex-to-vertex distances that increase only logarithmically with the total number N of vertices, but they do not show clustering—the property that two neighbors of a vertex will often also be neighbors of one another. Watts and Strogatz (1998), however, propose an alternative model for the small world, which perhaps fits better with our everyday intuitions about the nature of social networks. They build a model that is, in essence, a low-dimensional regular lattice, say a one-dimensional lattice, but which has some degree of randomness in it, like a random graph, to produce the small-world effect. As one of the most widely studied models of social networks, it shows both clustering and small-world properties. It has roughly a constant vertex degree, making it a reasonable model of true social networks, but it is probably not a good model of, for instance, the Internet.

The construction algorithm of Watts and Strogatz (1998) for small-world networks is the following. The initial network is a one-dimensional lattice of N sites, with periodic boundary conditions (i.e., a ring), where each vertex is connected to its $2k$ nearest neighbors. The vertices are then visited one after the other; each link connecting a vertex to one of its k nearest neighbors in the clockwise sense is left in place with probability $1 - p$, and with probability p it is reconnected to a randomly chosen other vertex. Long-range connections are therefore introduced. Note that, even for $p = 1$, the network keeps some memory of the procedure and is not locally equivalent to a random network; each vertex has indeed at least k neighbors. An important consequence is that we have no isolated vertices, and the graph usually has only one component (a random graph usually has many components of various sizes) (Barrat and Weigt 2000).

The small-world literature is remarkable with its diverse range of outcome variables that have been studied, contexts that have been explored, and levels of analysis that have been treated while at the same time being parsimonious in its explanatory variables. Some reviews of small-world networks have concentrated on the derivations of the methods and techniques used in small-world analysis (Newman 2000). Other reviews have examined the possibility of using complex networks as a new model for interdisciplinary research on diverse types of interconnected systems (Strogatz 2001; Amaral and Ottino 2004) or have explored how the links between small-world networks, scale-free networks, community structure, and network models of dynamic processes, such as the spread of diseases and social contagion, are creating a new science of networks (Watts 2004). Uzzi et al. (2007) review the literature on small-world networks in social science and management.

9.3 Research Design

This chapter abstracts the relationship among knowledge agents as an organization network. In order to clear the change of knowledge level in the process of knowledge sharing, four hypotheses are formulated: the knowledge of what we study belongs to the same type; different organization members have different knowledge levels; each member can share knowledge with others; and the knowledge in an organization or among members is changing all the time. Based on those hypotheses, we construct a model for knowledge sharing process (see Fig. 9.1).

The network node represents an organization member, and the line represents a connection of members. There are N members in an organization. Individual members are expressed as nodes and connection relations as edges. Thus, we use $G(V, E)$ to represent the organization network topology, V is the set of nodes of individuals within the organization $V = \{V_1, V_2, \ldots, V_i, \ldots, V_n\}$, and E is the set of relationships between nodes. Each edge in E relates to a pair of nodes in V.

9.3.1 Variable Description

In the small-world network model of knowledge sharing, the knowledge level $U_i(t)$ that belongs to the characteristics of nodes means the knowledge level of nodes V_i at time t. Moreover, the vectors of knowledge sharing are $U(t) = \{U_1(t), U_2(t), \ldots, U_i(t), \ldots, U_n(t)\}$.

1. Willingness for knowledge sharing α represents the willingness to impart knowledge to other members. It decides the basic knowledge enlargement of knowledge sharing, $\alpha \in (0, 1)$. Here, $\alpha = 0$ is the node with zero willingness for knowledge sharing; $\alpha = 1$ is the node with complete willingness for knowledge sharing.

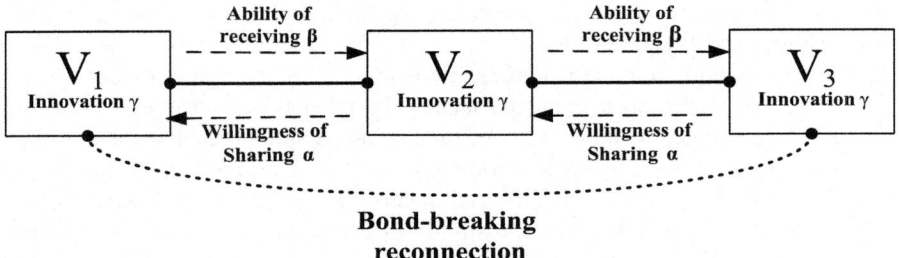

Fig. 9.1 Knowledge sharing process

2. Ability to receive knowledge β represents the ability of other members to transform sharing knowledge into self-knowledge. The value plays a key role in the final added value of knowledge, $\beta \in (0, 1)$. Here, $\beta = 0$ is the node that does not have the ability to study and receive knowledge. When $\beta = 1$, the node is able to completely grasp the shared knowledge of other nodes.
3. Knowledge innovation coefficient γ represents the ability to innovate new knowledge based on the received knowledge in the late period of knowledge sharing process. A greater ability to increase knowledge innovation implies an enhancement of the synergistic effect. This is quite important for organizations. We assume that the knowledge innovation coefficient is $\gamma \in (0, 0.002)$ in this passage.

9.3.2   Knowledge Sharing Processes

In the WS small-world network model, a line connection stands for the link between node members. Each link happens at a p bond-broking reconnection with other new nodes. There is a knowledge exchange running through it. As we know, different node members have different knowledge levels, and each node interplays with its neighbor node directly. Thus, the node shares knowledge with neighbor nodes as well as receives knowledge. The knowledge level tends to be higher among neighbors, and new knowledge is created continuously. All knowledge levels for the node members keep growing along with time.

At time t, the knowledge level of node V_i is $U_i(t)$. At time $t + 1$, this level is

$$U_i(t+1) = \begin{cases} \left[U_i(t) + \sum \alpha\beta \left(U_j(t) - U_i(t) \right) \right](1 + \gamma) & U_j(t) > U_i(t) \\ U_i(t) & U_j(t) \le U_i(t) \end{cases} \quad (9.1)$$

In the knowledge sharing model that we build, every node's knowledge level at time $t + 1$ depends on its neighbor nodes' knowledge level at time t. From formula (9.1), we see that the knowledge level of node V_i consists of three parts:

1. The level of basic knowledge at time t is $U_i(t)$.
2. The sum of knowledge that is transferred from the nodes with higher knowledge stock than node V_i to node V_i at time t is $\sum \alpha\beta(U_j(t) - U_i(t))$.
3. Knowledge creation by new knowledge is $\gamma[U_i(t) + \sum \alpha\beta(U_j(t) - U_i(t))]$.

The average knowledge level of the whole network is

$$\bar{U}(t) = \frac{1}{N} \sum_i U_i(t). \tag{9.2}$$

The variance of the knowledge level is

$$\sigma^2(t) = \frac{\sum\limits_i U_i(t)^2}{N} - \left[\frac{\sum\limits_i U_i(t)}{N}\right]^2. \tag{9.3}$$

The differences in the both degree and trend of knowledge levels for node members are two important indices when studying knowledge sharing. With a higher difference in the degree of knowledge level, members with less knowledge stock can study knowledge better and quicker, but there may exists monopoly of knowledge, because core knowledge reside with just a few members. On the other hand, with a lower difference in the degree of knowledge level, members can collaborate with each other through similar decision-making but less knowledge innovation. In the process of team knowledge sharing, the differences in the degree of individuals' knowledge level will change over time. The relative gap of the knowledge level between a node member and an organization is represented by the dispersion coefficient $\sigma(t)/\bar{U}(t)$.

9.3.3 Simulation

For clarity we note that $N = 50$ and $K = 4$ in the schematic examples shown here. The knowledge level of members can be generated randomly, and they belong to $[0, 1]$ and obey the uniform distribution. A normalized map of the accumulation coefficient and the shortest path length variation along with the change of p are subsequently generated (see Fig. 9.2). Here, $L(0)$ is the average shortest path in the rule network; $C(0)$ is the accumulation coefficient in the rule network; with normalization processing, $L(p)$ is the average shortest path about p in the small-world network; and $C(p)$ is the accumulation coefficient about p in the small-world network. As can be seen from Fig. 9.2, this network model conforms to the WS network model's characteristics—that is, the average shortest path declines rapidly, while the accumulation coefficient declines slowly.

The willingness for knowledge sharing α generates a random matrix $A_{n \times n}$ on the MATLAB software platform; A_{ij} stands for the transfer coefficient of knowledge sharing from node V_j to V_i, which satisfies $0 < A_{ij} < 1$. Similarly, the ability to receive knowledge β generates a random matrix $B_{n \times n}$ on the MATLAB software platform;

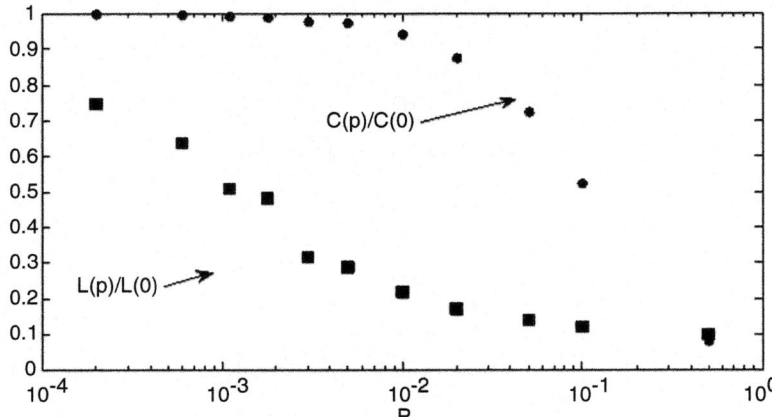

Fig. 9.2 Normalized map of accumulation coefficient and shortest path length variation along with the change of p in a small-world network

B_{ij} stands for the receiving coefficient of knowledge sharing from node V_j to V_i, which satisfies $0 < B_{ij} < 1$. Knowledge innovation coefficient γ generates a random matrix $R_{1 \times n}$ on the MATLAB software platform; R_i stands for the innovation coefficient of knowledge sharing about node V_i, which satisfies $0 < R_i < 1$. On the extraction of 0–1 matrix $\lambda_{n \times n}$, characterizing the relationship between organization members, we know that nodes V_i and V_j have no connection when $\lambda_{ij} = 0$ and that nodes V_i and V_j do have a connection when $\lambda_{ij} = 1$. Matrix $\lambda_{n \times n}$ is a diagonal symmetric matrix. The edge weight matrix $V_{n \times n}$ is simulated by $V_{n \times n} = A_{n \times n} * B_{n \times n} * \lambda_{n \times n}$. The greater the value V_{ij} is, the closer the relationship is between individuals.

We calculate the level of knowledge, the level of average knowledge, and the variance of knowledge level of an organization network according to formula (9.1), formula (9.2), and formula (9.3). From the calculation of the knowledge level under the condition $U_j(t + 1) > U_i(t + 1)$ at time $t + 1$, we know that the knowledge level of node V_i at the next time not only depends on the adjacent nodes but also depends on the increment of knowledge transfer from the nodes that are higher than V_i. Generally, we know that the new knowledge quantity at the late period of knowledge sharing process will not be more than the knowledge quantity of the subject as a knowledge source; thus, $U_i(t + 1) = \max U_j(t)$, which satisfies $U_i(t + 1) > \max U_j(t)$.

9.4   Result

We set $p = 0.005 (N = 50, K = 4)$ on a simulation experiment when studying the changes of an organization's knowledge level upon knowledge sharing. The three curves of network nodes' knowledge level, average knowledge level, and

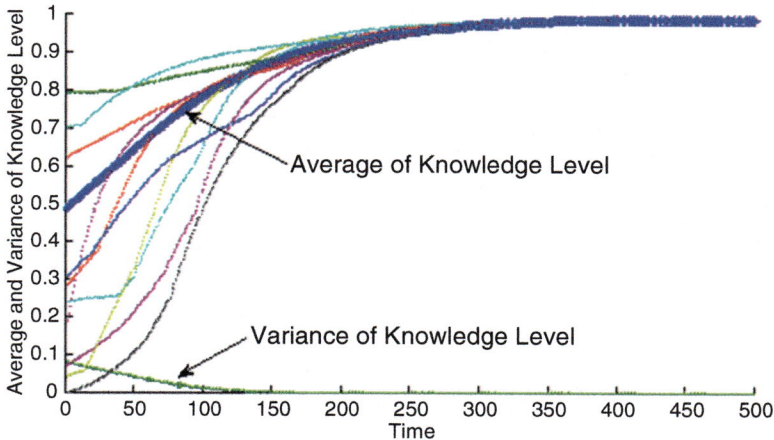

Fig. 9.3 Average knowledge level curve and variance curve

knowledge variance show changing trends with the same p and with increased simulation (this graphic just shows ten nodes randomly; see Fig. 9.3).

The simulation results illustrate that the slope of the average knowledge level curve is much larger with less than 200 times of simulation. With the increase of simulation number, the average knowledge level throughout the network grows faster. In other words, the average knowledge level curve trends to flatten from the initial stage to later stage of knowledge sharing, and the level of average knowledge is fixed at 0.978. At the same time, $\sigma^2(t)$ decreases gradually and gets closer to 0 by increasing the number of simulations.

The analysis of simulation results shows that, at the initial stage of knowledge sharing, each node has high sensitivity and degree of urgency in transferring and accepting knowledge. There is a big gap between different levels of knowledge and the highest increase of efficiency. Over a long period of knowledge sharing, the individual knowledge level turns higher, while the degrees of urgency and enthusiasm and the growth efficiency of knowledge all decline. Thus, the increase of knowledge level in a network tends to stagnate.

We note that X, Y, Z correspond to three different p, respectively, in Fig. 9.4. Their average shortest path and accumulation coefficient present significant features. Both are at a high level with small-world network characteristics of $X(p = 0.0006)$. The accumulation coefficient is at a high level, while the average shortest path is at a low level with small-world network characteristics of $Y(p = 0.005)$. Both are at a low level with small-world network characteristics of $Z(p = 0.5)$. To find how the knowledge level of an organization change in knowledge sharing process under three different combination of average shortest path and accumulation coefficient, we make 1000 simulations with different p, respectively, of $p = 0.0006$, $p = 0.005$, $p = 0.5$. The average level curve of knowledge and the dispersion coefficient curve are shown, respectively, in Figs. 9.5 and 9.6.

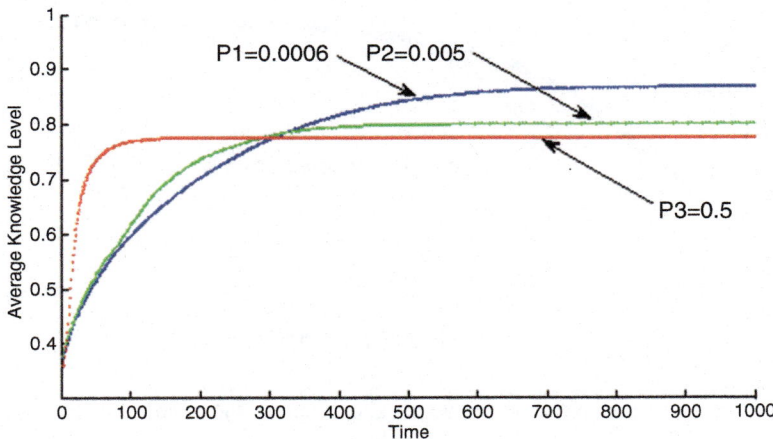

Fig. 9.4 Change of average knowledge level with different P ($K = 4$)

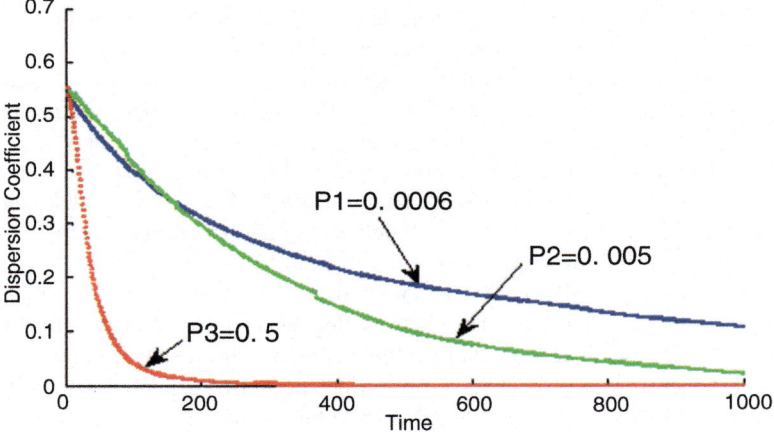

Fig. 9.5 Dispersion coefficient of knowledge with different P ($K = 4$)

As shown in Figs. 9.5 and 9.6, under the condition of P_1, the slope of the average knowledge curve is less; the knowledge level increases slowly; the dispersion coefficient is at a high level; the period of knowledge growth is longer; and the critical value of the average knowledge level appears more slowly. Organization members can get a high knowledge level through the accumulation and innovation of knowledge. Under the condition of P_3, node members can establish communication with new members constantly under a high probability of bond-breaking reconnection. The dispersion coefficient declines sharply, and the critical value of the average knowledge level appears more quickly. With less accumulation and innovation, the whole knowledge level of the organization is at a low level. Under the condition of P_3, the slope and critical value both are between curve P_1 and curve P_3.

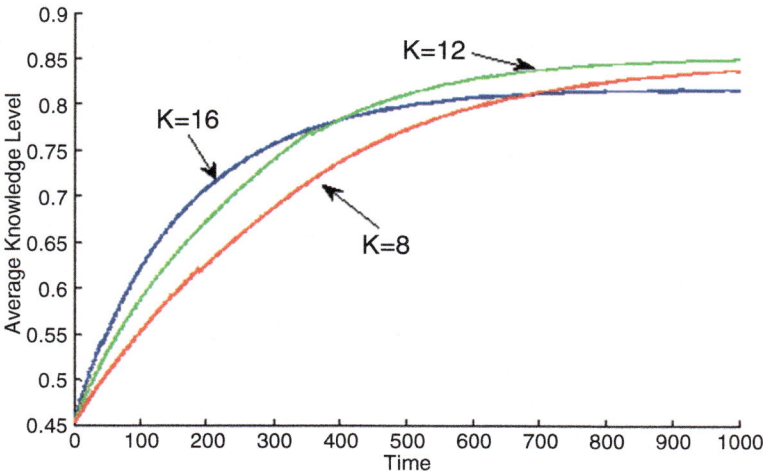

Fig. 9.6 Change of average knowledge level with different K ($p = 0.005$)

As can be seen from Fig. 9.6, the degree of the node has an effect on the rate of increasing knowledge and knowledge level. When $k = 16$, each individual node can exchange knowledge with many nodes and has a high increase rate. Nevertheless, it is bad for knowledge sharing and innovation, because of the low degrees of freedom and interference from other nodes. For $k = 8$ or $k = 12$, although the knowledge level increases slowly, it is good for knowledge sharing and innovation to have high degrees of freedom. Moreover, there are many node communications and a high knowledge level when $k = 12$.

9.5   Conclusion

Based on the study of knowledge sharing in organization members, we find that individual and team knowledge will continue to grow and achieve a higher critical level in a small-world relationship. The average knowledge of a team reaches a different level for different P, and this can promote the efficiency of interorganizational knowledge sharing by adjusting the clustering coefficient and average path length. We can enhance the efficiency of knowledge sharing with a high clustering coefficient and a low average path length while at the same time keeping the degrees of freedom and diversity factor of knowledge adequate. As a result, we get the revelation that cultivating organization members should help increase the frequency of members' communication. A reasonable common learning mechanism can be made to shorten the distance between superior organizations and inferior organizations. Lastly, the introduction of high-level knowledge workers could make an impact on the overall level of knowledge sharing.

Chapter 10
Differential Game Model of Knowledge Flow in University-Industry Collaborative Innovation

10.1 Introduction

The world is currently in the era of grand developments, reforms, and adjustments. Multi-polarization and economic globalization are deepening further, and the international business structure is changing due to fierce competition among national economies. Innovation has become the main driving force of economic social development, and intellectual innovation has become the core factor of national competitiveness. Under such circumstances, each country undertakes a strategy of further exploring human resources to realize innovative development, hence grasping the initiative of global competition.

On April 24, 2011, former President Hu Jintao gave an important speech at the conference for the 100th anniversary of the founding of Tsinghua University, indicating that China would actively promote collaborative innovation. By depending on the innovations of systems and mechanisms and policy projects, China will encourage universities, scientific research institutes, and enterprises to carry out in-depth cooperation, establish strategic alliances of collaborative innovation, promote the sharing of resources, jointly execute major scientific research projects, and make practical achievements in key area.

Taking that speech as the basis, the Ministry of Education and the Ministry of Finance decided to launch "Plan 2011." "Plan 2011" is open to universities of various kinds; takes universities as the major objects of its implementation; actively attracts participation by scientific research institutes, industrial enterprises, local governments, and international innovation forces; greatly encourages universities to cooperate with universities, scientific research institutes, industrial enterprises, local governments, and foreign scientific research organizations; and explores collaborative innovation ways to meet different requirements.

University-industry collaborative innovation (UICI) is an innovative organizational model of a large-span integration that enterprises, governments, knowledge

© Springer International Publishing AG, part of Springer Nature 2018
Y. Yu et al., *Strategy and Performance of Knowledge Flow*,
International Series in Operations Research & Management Science 271,
https://doi.org/10.1007/978-3-319-77926-3_10

production institutions (universities and research institutions), intermediaries, and users carry out in order to achieve significant technological innovation. The core of collaborative innovation is knowledge collaboration, which is the transfer, absorption, digestion, sharing, integration, utilization, and recreation of knowledge among cooperative organizations. The system of collaborative innovation is in-depth cooperation and resource integration through knowledge creation subjects and technological innovation subjects, but the cooperation of each innovation subject is not a spontaneous process, because the knowledge sharing interests and starting points of each innovation subject are not the same. The result is very likely to be a zero-sum game.

Game theory has recently been applied to issues of knowledge sharing. Statistical data show that an individual's perceived payoff of sharing knowledge in a group can be characterized by a multi-person game (Samieh and Wahba 2007). Firms that have a higher degree of knowledge sharing will exhibit better business performance and a higher level of innovation than firms that do not (Shih et al. 2006). Shih et al. (2006) claim that cooperative learning in a design studio relies not only on information technology increasing communication efficiency but also on how studio participants are motivated to cooperate. Cai and Kock (2009) study the strategic interaction between players as they decide whether and how much to collaborate with each other. They show that social punishment should be large enough to enforce full cooperation in symmetric discrete-strategy e-collaboration games.

Richard and Wayne (2009) examine the result of interactions among individuals in an organization with different preferences regarding knowledge sharing, arguing that organizations should actively encourage knowledge sharing. For knowledge sharing behavior to be engendered and sustained effectively among participants accessing a common knowledge base, Alton (2003) points out that the participation rate has to exceed a minimum threshold. Samaddar and Kadiyala (2006) use the game-theoretic framework to model the collaboration for knowledge creation as a Stackelberg leader-follower game. They identify the importance of maintaining an optimal ratio between the leader's and follower's marginal gains for the formation and continuation of the collaboration. Bandyopadhyay and Pathak (2007) model the interaction between two employees serving in different firms who have to share their knowledge to work effectively as a team. The result shows that top management should enforce cooperation among employees so that better payoffs can be achieved when the degree of complementarity of knowledge among them is high enough. Koessler (2004) provides a model for the study of direct, public, and strategic knowledge sharing in Bayesian games. Li and Jhang-Li (2010) apply game theory to analyze the incentives of knowledge sharing activities in various types of communities of practice (COPs), characterized by individual profiles and decision structures. Cress and Martin (2006) analyze knowledge exchange with shared databases based on a game-theoretical perspective.

Some studies in the literatures have examined knowledge flow from different backgrounds, but all of them use a static model to study the knowledge flow strategy of different knowledge subjects. However, due to the continuous upgrading of knowledge, the knowledge update cycle is shortening itself. Thus, in the process of UICI, the mutual communication and sharing of knowledge between enterprises and universities are not a once-and-for-all process. In order to gain long-lasting core competitiveness, enterprises must carry out continuous knowledge sharing and innovation, which means that research on the flow of knowledge between enterprises and universities in the process of UICI should be set under a dynamic framework instead of a static one in real situations. Therefore, it is of great theoretical and practical significance to examine the knowledge flow between enterprises and universities in UICI.

This chapter uses differential game theory to study knowledge sharing between enterprises and universities in UICI and to analyze the Nash noncooperative game, the Stackelberg leader-follower game, and the balanced knowledge flow strategy of different knowledge subjects under a cooperative game, in order to explore the optimal strategy of knowledge flow in UICI under a dynamic framework. This study is limited to a simple collaborative innovation system between an enterprise and a university (Yao et al. 2011, 2015).

10.2 Basic Theory of Differential Game

In this section, we supply a brief instruction about the basic theory of differential game, which is derived from Jørgensen and Zaccour (2004). A differential game is essentially a game in extensive form, being played in continuous time. For the analysis of the game, it has proven to be expedient to look at a normal form representation of it, such as through techniques of the optimal control theory (typically, the maximum principle and Hamilton-Jacobi-Bellman equations of dynamic programming). In a noncooperative game, given the other players' choice of strategies, each player solves her own individual one-person dynamic decision problem; that is, she solves an optimal control problem. The simultaneous solution of these control problems leads to the characterization of the game's equilibrium. In cooperative differential games, a Pareto optimal solution can be identified through optimal control methods, by constructing a joint payoff functional for the players.

Denote time by t and suppose that the players agree to play the game on the time interval $[0, T]$. The horizon date T can be fixed in advance, as some finite number, or it can be variable. In the latter case, it can be finite, to be determined optimally as an outcome of the game, or it can be infinite. In applied differential games, the modeler's choice of T is often quite arbitrary—although in principle the choice should be motivated by the institutional setting of the game at hand.

To characterize the state of a dynamic system at any particular instant of time, one introduces an n-vector of state variables $x(t) = (x_1(t), \ldots, x_n(t))$. The state vector represents the payoff-relevant history of the game at time t. The pair $(t, x(t))$ is sometimes referred to as the position of the system. The state $x(t)$ is constrained to lie in a set $X \subseteq R^n$, where X is called the state space. The initial value of the state vector is fixed and equals $x_0 \in X$.

The action taken by player $i \in \{1, \ldots, N\}$ at time t is denoted $u_i(t)$ and is a vector with $m_i \geq 1$ components. We call $u_i(t)$ the control variable of player i. The choice of a control must respect the constraint $u_i(t) \in U_i(t, x(t))$[1]. The set U_i is called the control space of player i.

The characteristic feature of a differential game is that the evolution over time of the state vector is described by a system of differential equations. Most often, these are ordinary differential equations, but there is also a theory for games with stochastic differential equations (typically, equations with white noise or piecewise deterministic equations), as well as differential equations with delays and partial differential equations. The focus here, and in the rest of the book, will be on ordinary differential equations. Hence, the state of the game evolves according to a system of n ordinary differential equations:

$$\dot{x}(t) = \frac{dx}{dt}(t) = f(t, x(t), u_1(t), \ldots, u_N(t)), x(0) = x_0. \tag{10.1}$$

The equations in (10.1) are called the state equations (system dynamics, evolution equations, equations of motion) and show that, in general, the rate of change of the state vector depends on the system's position $(t, x(t))$ and the choice of controls of all N players. Any player can influence the motion of the system but is also aware that the opponents have the same opportunity. When the system is in position $(t, x(t))$ and the players select their controls $u_1(t), \ldots, u_N(t)$, player i receives the payoff rate $g_i(t, x(t), u_1(t), \ldots, u_N(t))$.

The payoff can be a utility, revenue, profit, or cost. In total, player i receives the present-value payoff:

$$J_i(u_1(\cdot), \ldots, u_N(\cdot)) = \int_0^T e^{-\rho_i t} g_i(t, x(t), u_1(t), \ldots, u_N(t)) dt$$
$$+ e^{-\rho_i T} S_i(X(t)), \tag{10.2}$$

where $\rho_i = const. \geq 0$ is the discount rate of player i. If $\rho_i = 0$, then player i is perfectly farsighted and does not discount future payoffs at all. For $\rho_i \to \infty$, the player becomes increasingly myopic. The term $S_i(x(T))$ in (10.2) is a salvage value that is included to take into account that time is truncated at $t = T$. This means that events after time T have no influence on the decision problem of player i. In the case of an infinite horizon ($T = \infty$), the salvage value makes no sense and is omitted.

Player i wishes to maximize her payoff functional given by (10.2) by choosing an optimal control path $u_i(\cdot)$ for $t \in [0, T]$. The payoff functional consists of a stream of instantaneous payoffs, accumulated over the horizon $[0, T]$, and a terminal payoff at horizon date T. Note that the payoff of player i depends not only on her own control path but also on the control paths of the $N - 1$ opponents. This demonstrates a fundamental feature of game theory, viz., the strategic interdependence among players that prevails in any (interesting) game.

When setting up a differential game, one needs to specify what information is available to a player when she decides her action and, in particular, upon which information the choice of action at time t is based. At any instant of time, player i must select a value of her control variable $u_i(t)$. Suppose that she selects this value according to a strategy, henceforth denoted by φ_i. A strategy is a decision rule that selects an action as a function of some information. The assumption is that the choice of the decision rule is made at time $t = 0$ and the player commits to using the decision rule in the game that is about to be played.

We consider here a Markovian (or feedback) strategy, which selects the control action according to the rule $u_i(t) = \varphi_i(t, x(t))$. This means that player i observes the position $(t, x(t))$ of the system and then chooses her action as prescribed by the decision rule φ_i. In games played over infinite time horizons and where the fundamentals of the game (functions f and g_i) do not depend explicitly on time, it is common to confine one's interest to stationary strategies: $u_i(t) = \varphi_i(x(t))$. The reason is that at any instant of time, the players face essentially the same game for the remaining part of the time horizon.

An open-loop strategy is a degenerate Markovian strategy. With an open-loop strategy, control action is selected according to the decision rule $u_i(t) = \varphi_i(t)^2$. An open-loop strategy is a function of time only and can be applied if the player cannot observe the state vector or if she chooses to disregard the state information when taking her actions. Using an open-loop strategy essentially means that the player commits at time zero to a fixed time path for her control actions; that is, her choice of control at each instant of time is predetermined; obviously, a Markovian strategy gives more flexibility since it involves less commitment.

Recently, the number of differential games' applications in MS/OR has grown quite considerably, such as advertising strategies (Liu et al. 2012), research and development strategies (Lambertini and Mantovani 2010), pollution control (Huang et al. 2016), etc.

10.3 Model

In order to simplify the analysis, this study assumes that the UICI system consists of a university and an enterprise. In the process of UICI, the amount of knowledge shared by the university is $X(t)$, and the amount of knowledge shared by the enterprise is $Y(t)$. The innovation subsidy provided by the enterprise to the university is $\beta(t)$.

Taking into account the cost convexity of knowledge flow and making it easier to calculate, the costs of both sides' knowledge flow are then

$$C_u(X(t), t) = \frac{1}{2} c_u(t) X(t)^2 \tag{10.3}$$

$$C_e(Y(t), t) = \frac{1}{2} c_e(t) Y(t)^2, \tag{10.4}$$

where $c_u(t)$ and $c_e(t)$ are the knowledge flow cost coefficients of the university and the enterprise, respectively. Here, $C_u(X(t), t)$ and $C_e(Y(t), t)$ are the knowledge flow costs of the university and the enterprise, respectively.

In the process of collaborative innovation, the university and the enterprise internalize the knowledge through the sharing of the knowledge of the knowledge subject and then creating new knowledge. The accumulated variable $K(t)$ represents the amount of knowledge created in the process of UICI.

We suppose that the amount of newly created knowledge changes with time to satisfy the following differential equation:

$$\begin{cases} \dfrac{dK(t)}{dt} = \dot{K}(t) = r_u(t)X(t) + r_e(t)Y(t) - \delta K(t) \\ \qquad K(0) = K_0 \geq 0 \end{cases} \qquad (10.5)$$

Here, $r_u(t)$ is the coefficient of the university's knowledge innovation ability, $r_e(t)$ is the coefficient of the enterprise's knowledge innovation ability, and $\delta > 0$ is the knowledge depreciation rate in the knowledge innovation process. Constant updating of knowledge leads to the depreciation and elimination of knowledge. The total income of knowledge flow in the process of UICI is

$$\pi(t) = \lambda_u(t)X(t) + \lambda_e(t)Y(t) + \mu K(t), \qquad (10.6)$$

where $\lambda_u(t)$ and $\lambda_e(t)$ are the marginal revenue coefficients, respectively, and μ is the influence coefficient of knowledge innovation on knowledge flow income.

Assume that the total income of the university and enterprise's knowledge flow is distributed between the two participants. The enterprise gets $\alpha(t) \in (0, 1)$, and the university gets $1 - \alpha(t)$. The distribution ratio is given in advance. We assume that the university and the enterprise have the same positive discount rate ρ. Both sides aim to seek knowledge flow strategies that maximize their profits in an infinite time zone.

The objective function of the university is

$$J_u = \int_0^\infty e^{-\rho t} \left\{ \begin{array}{l} (1 - \alpha(t))[\lambda_u X(t) + \lambda_e Y(t) + \mu K(t)] \\ -\dfrac{1}{2}(1 - \beta(t))c_u(t)X(t)^2 \end{array} \right\} dt. \qquad (10.7)$$

The objective function of the enterprise is

$$J_e = \int_0^\infty e^{-\rho t} \left\{ \begin{array}{l} \alpha(t)[\lambda_u X(t) + \lambda_e Y(t) + \mu K(t)] \\ -\dfrac{1}{2}c_e(t)Y(t)^2 - \dfrac{1}{2}\beta(t)c_u(t)X(t)^2 \end{array} \right\} dt. \qquad (10.8)$$

Equations (10.5) to (10.8) define a two-person differential game with three control variables $X(t) \geq 0$, $Y(t) \geq 0$, and $\beta(t) \in [0, 1]$ and a state variable $K(t) \geq 0$. The feedback strategy means that the decision-making is the function of the current state variable, i.e., the amount of knowledge innovation and time. The strategies of the university and the enterprise's knowledge flow are represented by $X(K(t), t)$ and Y

$(K(t), t)$, respectively. Because of the difficulty of solving the analytic solution under dynamic parameters, it is assumed that all the parameters $c_u(t)$, $c_e(t)$, $\lambda_u(t)$, $\lambda_e(t)$, and $\alpha(t)$ in the model are time-independent constants. The game that the participants face is the same at any time in the infinite time zone. Thus, the strategies can be constrained as static strategies. The university and the enterprise's knowledge flow strategies are represented by $X(K(t))$ and $Y(K(t))$, of which the equilibrium is a static feedback equilibrium. For simplicity, the symbol of time t would be omitted in the following.

10.3.1 Nash Noncooperative Game

When the university and the enterprise carry out a Nash noncooperative game, both sides will simultaneously and independently select their own optimal knowledge flow strategies to maximize their own profits. The combination of the optimal knowledge flow strategies of the two participants in the game is thus the static feedback Nash equilibrium.

Theorem 10.1 In the case of the Nash noncooperative game, the static feedback Nash equilibrium strategies of the university and the enterprise are, respectively:

$$X^N = \frac{(1-\alpha)[\lambda_u(\rho+\delta) + r_u\mu]}{(\rho+\delta)c_u} \tag{10.9}$$

$$Y^N = \frac{\alpha[\lambda_e(\rho+\delta) + r_e\mu]}{(\rho+\delta)c_e}. \tag{10.10}$$

Proof
We assume that there exists a continuous bounded differential profit function $V_i(K)$, $i \in (u, e)$ by using the sufficient conditions of a static feedback Nash equilibrium. For all $K \geq 0$, the following Hamilton-Jacobi-Bellman equation is satisfied:

$$\rho V_u(K) = \max_X \left\{ \begin{array}{l} (1-\alpha)[\lambda_u X + \lambda_e Y + \mu K] \\ -\frac{1}{2}(1-\beta)c_u X^2 + V_u'(K)(r_u X + r_e Y - \delta K) \end{array} \right\} \tag{10.11}$$

$$\rho V_e(K) = \max_Y \left\{ \begin{array}{l} \alpha[\lambda_u X + \lambda_e Y + \mu K] - \frac{1}{2}c_e Y^2 \\ -\frac{1}{2}\beta c_u X^2 + V_e'(K)(r_u X + r_e Y - \delta K) \end{array} \right\}. \tag{10.12}$$

From above, in order to maximize its own profits, a rational enterprise will be reluctant to provide any knowledge sharing subsidies, which means $\beta^* = 0$. Both sides will simultaneously and independently determine their own optimal knowledge flow strategies. Solving the first-order partial derivatives for Eqs. (10.11) and (10.12), respectively, and making them equal to zero bring about

$$X = \frac{(1-\alpha)\lambda_u + r_u V_u'(K)}{c_u} \tag{10.13}$$

$$Y = \frac{\alpha\lambda_e + r_e V_e'(K)}{c_e}. \tag{10.14}$$

Substituting Eqs. (10.13) and (10.14) into the HJB equation, we have

$$
\begin{aligned}
\rho V_u(K) &= (1-\alpha)[\lambda_u X + \lambda_e Y + \mu K] - \frac{1}{2}c_u X^2 \\
&+ V_u'(K)(r_u X + r_e Y - \delta K) = [(1-\alpha)\mu - \delta V_u'(K)]K \\
&+ \frac{[(1-\alpha)\lambda_u + V_u'(K)r_u]^2}{2c_u} + \frac{[(1-\alpha)\lambda_e + r_e V_u'(K)][\alpha\lambda_e + r_e V_e'(K)]}{c_e}
\end{aligned}
\tag{10.15}
$$

$$
\begin{aligned}
\rho V_e(K) &= \alpha[\lambda_u X + \lambda_e Y + \mu K] - \frac{1}{2}c_e Y^2 + V_e'(K)(r_u X + r_e Y - \delta K) = [\alpha\mu - \delta V_e'(K)]K \\
&+ \frac{[\alpha\lambda_e + r_e V_e'(K)]^2}{2c_e} + \frac{[\alpha\lambda_u + r_u V_e'(K)][(1-\alpha)\lambda_u + r_u V_u'(K)]}{c_u}
\end{aligned}
\tag{10.16}
$$

From Eqs. (10.15) and (10.16), we know that the linear optimal value function of K is the solution of the equation HJB. Let

$$V_u(K) = \eta_1 K + \eta_2 \tag{10.17}$$
$$V_e(K) = \theta_1 K + \theta_2, \tag{10.18}$$

where η_1, η_2, θ_1, and θ_2 are constants. We then have

$$V_u'(K) = {dV_u(K)}/{dK} = \eta_1 \tag{10.19}$$
$$V_e'(\pi) = {dV_e(K)}/{dK} = \theta_1. \tag{10.20}$$

Substituting the above equations into Eqs. (10.15) and (10.16), we arrive at

$$
\begin{aligned}
\rho(\eta_1 K + \eta_2) &= (1-\alpha)[\lambda_u X + \lambda_e Y + \mu K] \\
&- \frac{1}{2}c_u X^2 + V_u'(K)(r_u X + r_e Y - \delta K) = [(1-\alpha)\mu - \delta\eta_1]K \\
&+ \frac{[(1-\alpha)\lambda_u + r_u\eta_1]^2}{2c_u} + \frac{[(1-\alpha)\lambda_e + r_e\eta_1][\alpha\lambda_e + r_e\theta_1]}{c_e}
\end{aligned}
\tag{10.21}
$$

$$
\begin{aligned}
\rho(\theta_1 K + \theta_2) &= \alpha[\lambda_u X + \lambda_e Y + \mu K] - \frac{1}{2}c_e Y^2 + V_e'(K)(r_u X + r_e Y - \delta K) \\
&= [\alpha\mu - \delta\theta_1]K + \frac{[\alpha\lambda_e + r_e\theta_1]^2}{2c_e} + \frac{[\alpha\lambda_u + r_u\theta_1][(1-\alpha)\lambda_u + r_u\eta_1]}{c_u}.
\end{aligned}
\tag{10.22}
$$

Equations (10.21) and (10.22) are satisfied for all $K \geq 0$, and so the parameter values of the optimal value function are

$$\eta_1 = \frac{(1-\alpha)\mu}{\rho+\delta} \tag{10.23}$$

$$\eta_2 = \frac{[(1-\alpha)\lambda_u + r_u\eta_1]^2}{2\rho c_u} + \frac{[(1-\alpha)\lambda_e + r_e\eta_1][\alpha\lambda_e + r_e\theta_1]}{\rho c_e}$$
$$= \frac{(1-\alpha)^2[\lambda_u(\rho+\delta) + r_u\mu]^2}{2\rho(\rho+\delta)^2 c_u} + \frac{\alpha(1-\alpha)[\lambda_e(\rho+\delta) + r_e\mu]^2}{\rho(\rho+\delta)^2 c_e} \tag{10.24}$$

$$\theta_1 = \frac{\alpha\mu}{\rho+\delta} \tag{10.25}$$

$$\theta_2 = \frac{[\alpha\lambda_e + r_e\theta_1]^2}{2\rho c_e} + \frac{[\alpha\lambda_u + r_u\theta_1][(1-\alpha)\lambda_u + r_u\eta_1]}{\rho c_u}$$
$$= \frac{\alpha^2[\lambda_e(\rho+\delta) + r_e\mu]^2}{2\rho(\rho+\delta)^2 c_e} + \frac{\alpha(1-\alpha)[\lambda_u(\rho+\delta) + r_u\mu]^2}{\rho(\rho+\delta)^2 c_u}. \tag{10.26}$$

We now substitute η_1, η_2, θ_1, and θ_2 into Eqs. (10.13), (10.14), (10.17), and (10.18), respectively. The respective optimal value functions of the university and the enterprise under the condition of Nash equilibrium are

$$V_u^N(K) = \frac{(1-\alpha)\mu}{\rho+\delta}K + \frac{(1-\alpha)^2[\lambda_u(\rho+\delta) + r_u\mu]^2}{2\rho(\rho+\delta)^2 c_u}$$
$$+ \frac{\alpha(1-\alpha)[\lambda_e(\rho+\delta) + r_e\mu]^2}{\rho(\rho+\delta)^2 c_e} \tag{10.27}$$

$$V_e^N(K) = \frac{\alpha\mu}{\rho+\delta}K + \frac{\alpha^2[\lambda_e(\rho+\delta) + r_e\mu]^2}{2\rho(\rho+\delta)^2 c_e} + \frac{\alpha(1-\alpha)[\lambda_u(\rho+\delta) + r_u\mu]^2}{\rho(\rho+\delta)^2 c_u}. \tag{10.28}$$

At the same time, Theorem 10.1 is proved.

10.3.2 Stackelberg Game

We now consider that in order to encourage a university to share knowledge, the enterprise pays the cost of knowledge flow under a proportion β. The purpose is to give the university direct incentives to share knowledge in accordance with the intention of the enterprise.

We assume that the enterprise is a leader in the Stackelberg game and that the optimal strategy of it is given. The university determines its own optimal strategy. The optimal strategies for both sides are the static feedback Stackelberg equilibrium strategies.

Theorem 10.2 In the case of the enterprise being the leader in the game, the static feedback Stackelberg equilibrium strategies of the university and the enterprise are

$$X^S = \frac{(1-\alpha)\lambda_u + r_u V_u'(K)}{(1-\beta)c_u} = \frac{(\alpha+1)[\lambda_u(\rho+\delta) + r_u\mu]}{2(\rho+\delta)c_u} \tag{10.29}$$

$$Y^S = \frac{\alpha\lambda_e + r_e V_e'(K)}{c_e} = \frac{\alpha[\lambda_e(\rho+\delta) + r_e\mu]}{c_e(\rho+\delta)} \tag{10.30}$$

$$\beta = \begin{cases} \dfrac{3\alpha-1}{\alpha+1}, & \dfrac{1}{3} < \alpha \le 1 \\ 0, & \text{otherwise} \end{cases}. \tag{10.31}$$

Proof

To get the Stackelberg equilibrium of this game, we utilize the inverse induction method to solve the university's optimal control problem. The optimal profit function $V_u(K)$ must satisfy the HJB equation:

$$\rho V_u(K) = \max_X \left\{ \begin{array}{l} (1-\alpha)[\lambda_u X + \lambda_e Y + \mu K] - \frac{1}{2}(1-\beta)c_u X^2 \\ +V_u'(K)(r_u X + r_e Y - \delta K) \end{array} \right\}. \tag{10.32}$$

To maximize the right side of the above equation, we solve its first-order partial derivative of X and make it equal to zero. The solution can then be obtained:

$$X = \frac{(1-\alpha)\lambda_u + r_u V_u'(K)}{(1-\beta)c_u}. \tag{10.33}$$

At the same time, the enterprise rationally predicts that the university will choose X according to the above response functions. The HJB equation of enterprise is thus

$$\rho V_e(K) = \max_Y \left\{ \begin{array}{l} \alpha[\lambda_u X + \lambda_e Y + \mu K] - \frac{1}{2}c_e Y^2 \\ -\frac{1}{2}\beta c_u X^2 + V_e'(K)(r_u X + r_e Y - \delta K) \end{array} \right\}. \tag{10.34}$$

Substituting Eq. (10.33) into Eq. (10.34), we get

$$\rho V_e(K) = \max_Y \left\{ \begin{array}{l} \alpha\left[\lambda_u \dfrac{(1-\alpha)\lambda_u + r_u V_u'(K)}{(1-\beta)c_u} + \lambda_e Y + \mu K\right] \\ -\dfrac{1}{2}c_e Y^2 - \dfrac{1}{2}\beta c_u\left[\dfrac{(1-\alpha)\lambda_u + r_u V_u'(K)}{(1-\beta)c_u}\right]^2 \\ +V_e'(K)\left(r_u \dfrac{(1-\alpha)\lambda_u + r_u V_u'(K)}{(1-\beta)c_u} + r_e Y - \delta K\right) \end{array} \right\}. \tag{10.35}$$

To maximize the right side of Eq. (10.35), we solve the first-order conditions for Y and β as

We thus arrive at

$$Y = \frac{\alpha\lambda_e + r_e V'_e(K)}{c_e} \tag{10.36}$$

$$\beta = \frac{\lambda_u(3\alpha - 1) + 2r_u V'_e(K) - r_u V'_u(K)}{\lambda_u(\alpha + 1)c_e + r_u V'_u(K) + 2r_u V'_e(K)}. \tag{10.37}$$

Substituting Eqs. (10.33), (10.36), and (10.37) into Eqs. (10.34) and (10.35), we get

$$
\begin{aligned}
\rho V_u(K) &= (1 - \alpha)[\lambda_u X + \lambda_e Y + \mu K] - \frac{1}{2}(1 - \beta)c_u X^2 \\
&+ V'_u(K)(r_u X + r_e Y - \delta K) = \left[(1 - \alpha)\mu - \delta V'_u(K)\right]K \\
&+ \left[(1 - \alpha)\lambda_u + V'_u(K)r_u\right]X - \frac{1}{2}(1 - \beta)c_u X^2 \\
&+ \left[(1 - \alpha)\lambda_e + V'_u(K)r_e\right]Y
\end{aligned}
\tag{10.38}
$$

$$
\begin{aligned}
\rho V_e(K) &= \alpha[\lambda_u X + \lambda_e Y + \mu K] - \frac{1}{2}c_e Y^2 - \frac{1}{2}\beta c_u X^2 \\
&+ V'_e(K)(r_u X + r_e Y - \delta K) = \left[\alpha\mu - \delta V'_e(K)\right]K \\
&+ \left[\alpha\lambda_u + r_u V'_e(K)\right]X - \frac{1}{2}\beta c_u X^2 + \left[\alpha\lambda_e + r_e V'_e(K)\right]Y \\
&- -\frac{1}{2}c_e Y^2
\end{aligned}
\tag{10.39}
$$

From Eqs. (10.38) and (10.39), we know that the linear optimal value function of K is the solution of the HJB equation. We set up the following:

$$V_u(K) = \eta_1 K + \eta_2 \tag{10.40}$$
$$V_e(K) = \theta_1 K + \theta_2, \tag{10.41}$$

where η_1, η_2, θ_1, and θ_2 are constants, and next we have

$$V'_u(K) = {}^{dV_u(K)}/_{dK} = \eta_1 \tag{10.42}$$
$$V'_e(\pi) = {}^{dV_e(K)}/_{dK} = \theta_1 \tag{10.43}$$

Substituting them into Eqs. (10.38) and (10.39), we get

$$
\begin{aligned}
\rho(\eta_1 K + \eta_2) &= [(1 - \alpha)\mu - \delta\eta_1]K + \frac{[(1 - \alpha)\lambda_u + r_u\eta_1]^2}{2(1 - \beta)c_u} \\
&+ \frac{[(1 - \alpha)\lambda_e + r_e\eta_1][\alpha\lambda_e + r_e\theta_1]}{c_e}
\end{aligned}
\tag{10.44}
$$

$$\rho(\theta_1 K + \theta_2) = [\alpha\mu - \delta\theta_1]K + \frac{[\alpha\lambda_e + r_e\theta_1]^2}{2c_e} + \frac{(\alpha\lambda_u + r_u\theta_1)[(1-\alpha)\lambda_u + r_u\eta_1]}{(1-\beta)c_u}$$
$$-\frac{\beta[(1-\alpha)\lambda_u + r_u\eta_1]^2}{2(1-\beta)^2 c_u}$$

$$(10.45)$$

Equations (10.44) and (10.45) are satisfied for all $K \geq 0$. Thus, the parameter values of the optimal value functions are

$$\eta_1 = \frac{(1-\alpha)\mu}{\rho+\delta} \tag{10.46}$$

$$\eta_2 = \frac{(1-\alpha)^2[\lambda_u(\rho+\delta) + r_u\mu]^2}{2\rho(1-\beta)(\rho+\delta)^2 c_u} + \frac{\alpha(1-\alpha)[\lambda_e(\rho+\delta) + r_e\mu]^2}{\rho(\rho+\delta)^2 c_e} \tag{10.47}$$

$$\theta_1 = \frac{\alpha\mu}{\rho+\delta} \tag{10.48}$$

$$\theta_2 = \frac{\alpha^2[\lambda_e(\rho+\delta) + r_e\mu]^2}{2\rho(\rho+\delta)^2 c_e} + \frac{\alpha(1-\alpha)[\lambda_u(\rho+\delta) + r_u\mu]^2}{\rho(1-\beta)(\rho+\delta)^2 c_u}$$
$$-\frac{\beta(1-\alpha)^2[\lambda_u(\rho+\delta) + r_u\mu]^2}{2\rho(1-\beta)^2(\rho+\delta)^2 c_u} \tag{10.49}$$

Substituting η_1, η_2, θ_1, and θ_2 into the respective optimal value functions of the university and the enterprise under the condition of the Stackelberg equilibrium:

$$X^S = \frac{(1-\alpha)\lambda_u + r_u V'_u(K)}{(1-\beta)c_u} = \frac{(\alpha+1)[\lambda_u(\rho+\delta) + r_u\mu]}{2(\rho+\delta)c_u} \tag{10.50}$$

$$Y^S = \frac{\alpha\lambda_e + r_e V'_e(K)}{c_e} = \frac{\alpha[\lambda_e(\rho+\delta) + r_e\mu]}{c_e(\rho+\delta)} \tag{10.51}$$

$$\beta = \begin{cases} \frac{3\alpha-1}{\alpha+1}, & \frac{1}{3} < \alpha \leq 1 \\ 0, & \text{otherwise} \end{cases}. \tag{10.52}$$

Therefore, Theorem 10.2 is proved.

Substituting Eqs. (10.50), (10.51), and (10.52) into Eqs. (10.40) and (10.41), the respective optimal profit functions of the university and the enterprise are then

$$V_u^S(K) = \frac{(1-\alpha)\mu}{\rho+\delta}K + \frac{(1-\alpha)(\alpha+1)[\lambda_u(\rho+\delta) + r_u\mu]^2}{4\rho(\rho+\delta)^2 c_u}$$
$$+ \frac{\alpha(1-\alpha)[\lambda_e(\rho+\delta) + r_e\mu]^2}{\rho(\rho+\delta)^2 c_e} \tag{10.53}$$

$$V_e^S(K) = \frac{\alpha\mu}{\rho+\delta}K + \frac{\alpha^2[\lambda_e(\rho+\delta) + r_e\mu]^2}{2\rho(\rho+\delta)^2 c_e} + \frac{(1+\alpha)^2[\lambda_u(\rho+\delta) + r_u\mu]^2}{8\rho(\rho+\delta)^2 c_u}. \tag{10.54}$$

10.3.3   *Cooperative Game*

In the case of cooperation between the university and the enterprise, the two sides can determine the values of X and Y together with the optimal profit in the university-industry collaborative innovation system as the first principle.

Theorem 10.3 In the case of a cooperative game, the optimal knowledge flow strategies of the university and the enterprise are, respectively:

$$X^C = \frac{\lambda_u(\rho + \delta) + r_u\mu}{c_u(\rho + \delta)} \tag{10.55}$$

$$Y^C = \frac{\lambda_e(\rho + \delta) + r_e\mu}{c_e(\rho + \delta)} \tag{10.56}$$

Proof
When the relationship between the university and enterprise transitions from non-cooperation to cooperation, the two sides decide on the optimal values of X and Y together. The goal is to maximize the profit of the entire UICI system, which is

$$J = J_u + J_e = \int_0^\infty e^{-\rho t} \left\{ \begin{array}{l} [\lambda_u X(t) + \lambda_e Y(t) + \mu K(t)] \\ -\frac{1}{2}c_u(t)X(t)^2 - \frac{1}{2}c_e(t)Y(t)^2 \end{array} \right\} dt \tag{10.57}$$

The optimal profit function $V(K)$ must satisfy the following HJB equation:

$$\rho V(K) = \max_{X,Y} \left\{ \begin{array}{l} [\lambda_u X + \lambda_e Y + \mu K] - \frac{1}{2}c_u X^2 \\ -\frac{1}{2}c_e Y^2 + V'(K)(r_u X + r_e Y - \delta K) \end{array} \right\}. \tag{10.58}$$

Solving the first-order conditions of X and Y, respectively, in the above equation, we get

$$X = \frac{\lambda_u + r_u V'(K)}{c_u} \tag{10.59}$$

$$Y = \frac{\lambda_e + r_e V'(K)}{c_e}. \tag{10.60}$$

We next substitute Eqs. (10.59) and (10.60) into Eq. (10.58). We can get

$$\begin{aligned}
\rho V(K) &= [\lambda_u X + \lambda_e Y + \mu K] - \frac{1}{2}c_u X^2 - \frac{1}{2}c_e Y^2 + V'(K)(r_u X + r_e Y - \delta K) \\
&= [\mu - \delta V'(K)]K + \frac{[\lambda_u + r_u V'(K)]^2}{2c_u} + \frac{[\lambda_e + r_e V'(K)]^2}{2c_e}
\end{aligned} \tag{10.61}$$

From Eq. (10.62), we know that the linear optimal value function of K is the solution to the HJB equation. We now let

$$V(K) = \varpi_1 K + \varpi_2. \tag{10.62}$$

Here, ϖ_1 and ϖ_2 are constants, and thus:

$$V(K) = {}^{dV(K)}\!/_{dK} = \varpi_1. \tag{10.63}$$

Substituting this into Eq. (10.61) results in

$$
\begin{aligned}
\rho(\varpi_1 K + \varpi_2) &= [\lambda_u X + \lambda_e Y + \mu K] - \frac{1}{2} c_u X^2 - \frac{1}{2} c_e Y^2 \\
&\quad + V'(K)(r_u X + r_e Y - \delta K) \\
&= [\mu - \delta \varpi_1] K + \frac{[\lambda_u + r_u \varpi_1]^2}{2 c_u} + \frac{[\lambda_e + r_e \varpi_1]^2}{2 c_e}
\end{aligned}
\tag{10.64}
$$

Equation (10.64) is now satisfied for all $K \geq 0$, and hence the parameter values of the optimal profit functions are

$$\varpi_1 = \frac{\mu}{\rho + \delta} \tag{10.65}$$

$$\varpi_2 = \frac{[\lambda_u(\rho + \delta) + r_u \mu]^2}{2\rho(\rho + \delta)^2 c_u} + \frac{[\lambda_e(\rho + \delta) + r_e \mu]^2}{2\rho(\rho + \delta)^2 c_e} \tag{10.66}$$

We next substitute ϖ_1 and ϖ_2 into Eqs. (10.59), (10.60), and (10.62). We see that the respective optimal value functions of the university and the enterprise under the condition of the cooperation game are

$$X^C = \frac{\lambda_u(\rho + \delta) + r_u \mu}{c_u(\rho + \delta)} \tag{10.67}$$

$$Y^C = \frac{\lambda_e(\rho + \delta) + r_e \mu}{c_e(\rho + \delta)} \tag{10.68}$$

Therefore, Theorem 10.3 is proved, and we can simultaneously get the knowledge flow optimal profit function in the entire UICI system:

$$
\begin{aligned}
V^C(K) &= \varpi_1 K + \varpi_2 \\
&= \frac{\mu}{\rho + \delta} K + \frac{[\lambda_u(\rho + \delta) + r_u \mu]^2}{2\rho(\rho + \delta)^2 c_u} + \frac{[\lambda_e(\rho + \delta) + r_e \mu]^2}{2\rho(\rho + \delta)^2 c_e}
\end{aligned}
\tag{10.69}
$$

10.3.4 Model Comparison

Theorem 10.4 Under the condition that the enterprise provides support on knowledge sharing, the university shares more knowledge. In the case of cooperation, the university and the enterprise provide more knowledge than the other two situations, which means $X^C \geq X^S > X^N$ and $Y^C \geq Y^S = Y^N$.

Proof

We know from Theorems 10.1 and 10.2 that the enterprise has the same knowledge flow strategies in the two situations, while the university has different results in the knowledge flow strategies.

From Eqs. (10.9) and (10.29), we know

$$
\begin{aligned}
X^C - X^N &= \frac{\lambda_u(\rho + \delta) + r_u\mu}{(\rho + \delta)c_u} - \frac{(\alpha + 1)[\lambda_u(\rho + \delta) + r_u\mu]}{2(\rho + \delta)c_u} \\
&= \frac{(1 - \alpha)[\lambda_u(\rho + \delta) + r_u\mu]}{2(\rho + \delta)c_u}
\end{aligned}
\tag{10.70}
$$

$$
\begin{aligned}
X^S - X^N &= \frac{(\alpha + 1)[\lambda_u(\rho + \delta) + r_u\mu]}{2(\rho + \delta)c_u} - \frac{(1 - \alpha)[\lambda_u(\rho + \delta) + r_u\mu]}{(\rho + \delta)c_u} \\
&= \frac{(3\alpha - 1)[\lambda_u(\rho + \delta) + r_u\mu]}{2(\rho + \delta)c_u}
\end{aligned}
\tag{10.71}
$$

$$
\begin{aligned}
Y^C - Y^S &= \frac{\lambda_e(\rho + \delta) + r_e\mu}{c_e(\rho + \delta)} - \frac{\alpha[\lambda_e(\rho + \delta) + r_e\mu]}{(\rho + \delta)c_e} \\
&= \frac{(1 - \alpha)[\lambda_e(\rho + \delta) + r_e\mu]}{(\rho + \delta)c_e}
\end{aligned}
\tag{10.72}
$$

Under the condition of cooperation, from Eq. (10.31), we know $1/3 < \alpha \leq 1$. Thus, $X^S - X^N > 0$, $X^C - X^N \geq 0$, and $Y^C - Y^S \geq 0$. Theorem 10.4 is thus proved. It is noted that $X^S - X^N = \beta X^S$. This equation means that compared to the situation without knowledge flow subsidies, the university increases the amount of knowledge it shares. The proportion of the increase is equal to the proportion of the subsidies that the enterprise provides. Providing subsidies on knowledge sharing is an incentive mechanism through which universities can share more knowledge than without subsidies.

Theorem 10.5 For any $K \geq 0$, under the condition that the enterprise provides subsidies on knowledge sharing, the optimal flow of the knowledge flow of the university is higher than that without subsidies. In the same way, the optimal profit of the knowledge flow of the enterprise is higher than that without providing subsidies to the university, which means $V_u^S(K) > V_u^N(K)$ and $V_e^S(K) > V_e^N(K)$.

Proof

From Eqs. (10.27), (10.28), (10.53), and (10.54), we know that

$$\Delta V_u(K) = V_u^S(K) - V_u^N(K) = \frac{(1-\alpha)(3\alpha-1)[\lambda_u(\rho+\delta)+r_u\mu]^2}{4\rho(\rho+\delta)^2 c_u} \tag{10.73}$$

$$\Delta V_u(K) = V_e^S(K) - V_e^N(K) = \frac{(3\alpha-1)^2[\lambda_u(\rho+\delta)+r_u\mu]^2}{\rho(\rho+\delta)^2 c_u} \tag{10.74}$$

Under the condition of cooperation, from Eq. (10.31), we know $1/3 < \alpha \leq 1$. Thus, $V_u^S(K) - V_u^N(K) > 0$ and $V_e^S(K) - V_e^N(K) \geq 0$. Theorem 10.5 is thus proved.

It is noted that when $1/3 < \alpha < 1/2$, $\Delta V_u(K) > \Delta V_e(K)$, which means the increase of the university's knowledge flow profit is higher than the increase of that of the enterprise. When $1/2 < \alpha < 1$, $\Delta V_u(K) < \Delta V_e(K)$, which means the increase of the university's knowledge flow profit is lower than the increase of that of the enterprise.

Theorem 10.6 In the case of a cooperation game, the knowledge flow profit of the entire UICI system is higher than the profit of the entire system in the case of the Stackelberg leader-follower game. The profit of the entire system in the case of the Stackelberg leader-follower game is higher than the profit of the entire system under the condition of the Nash noncooperative game, which means $V^C(K) > V^S(K) > V^N(K)$.

Proof

From Eqs. (10.53) and (10.54), the profit of the entire system under the condition of Stackelberg leader-follower game is

$$V^S(K) = V_u^S(K) + V_e^S(K) = \frac{\mu}{\rho+\delta}K + \frac{(3+2\alpha-\alpha^2)[\lambda_u(\rho+\delta)+r_u\mu]^2}{8\rho(\rho+\delta)^2 c_u}$$
$$+ \frac{(2\alpha-\alpha^2)[\lambda_e(\rho+\delta)+r_e\mu]^2}{2\rho(\rho+\delta)^2 c_e} \tag{10.75}$$

$$V^C(K) - V^S(K) = \frac{(1-\alpha)^2[\lambda_u(\rho+\delta)+r_u\mu]^2}{8\rho(\rho+\delta)^2 c_u}$$
$$+ \frac{(1-\alpha)^2[\lambda_e(\rho+\delta)+r_e\mu]^2}{2\rho(\rho+\delta)^2 c_e} \tag{10.76}$$

Under the condition of cooperation, from Eq. (10.31), we know that $1/3 < \alpha \leq 1$. Thus, $V^C(K) - V^S(K) > 0$, and then $V^C(K) > V^S(K)$.

$$V^S(K) - V^N(K) = \left(V_u^S(K) + V_e^S(K)\right) - \left(V_u^N(K) + V_e^N(K)\right)$$
$$= \left(V_u^S(K) - V_u^N(K)\right) + \left(V_e^S(K) - V_e^N(K)\right) \tag{10.77}$$

From Theorem 10.5, we know that $V_u^S(K) - V_u^N(K) > 0$ and $V_e^S(K) - V_e^N(K) \geq 0$. Thus, $V^S(K) - V^N(K) > 0$, and then $V^S(K) > V^N(K)$. Theorem 10.6 is hence proved.

10.4 Numerical Example

Under the condition of cooperation and noncooperation, the optimal knowledge flow strategies and the profits of the university and the enterprise depend on the selection of various parameters in the model. We assume that the parameter values in the model are selected separately: $\delta = 0.1$, $\rho = 0.1$, $c_e = 2$, $c_u = 1$, $r_e = 2$, $r_u = 0.8$, $\lambda_e = 3$, $\lambda_u = 2$, $\mu = 1.2$, $\alpha = 0.8$, and $K(0) = 10$.

In Fig. 10.1, with the ratio in profit distribution increasing, when $1/3 < \alpha \leq 1$, the proportion of the subsidies that the enterprise provides to the university equals zero. At this time, the participation level of the university's knowledge flow in the case of Nash unbalanced cooperation in UICI is higher than that in the case of the Stackelberg leader-follower game. When $1/3 < \alpha \leq 1$, there exist subsidies on knowledge sharing that the enterprise provides. At the same time, the participation level of the university's knowledge flow in the case of the Stackelberg leader-follower game in UICI is higher than that in the case of Nash unbalanced cooperation. In the context of the cooperative model, the university increases the amount of

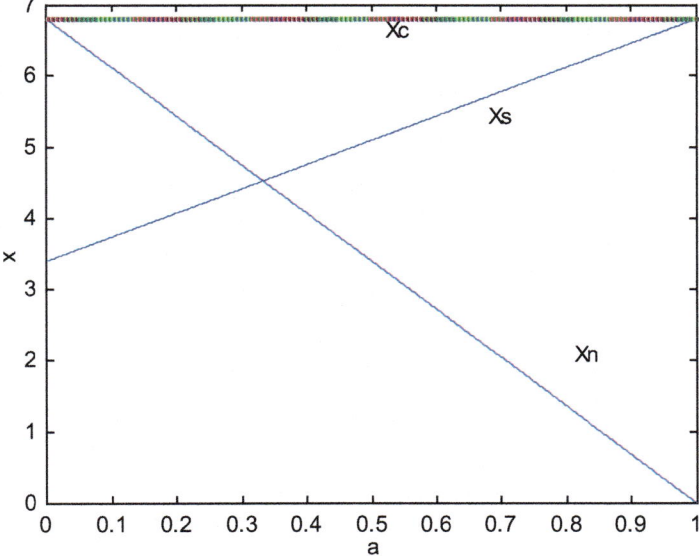

Fig. 10.1 Comparison on the strategies of knowledge flow of the university with the change of the ratio in profit distribution under different situations

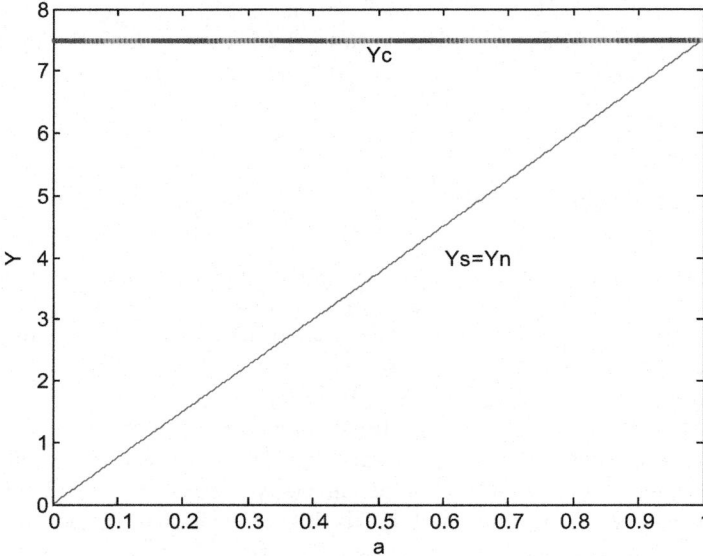

Fig. 10.2 Comparison on the strategies of knowledge flow of the enterprise with the change of the ratio in profit distribution under different situations

knowledge it shares, compared to the case where there is no knowledge sharing subsidies, which will increase in the same proportion as the proportion of the subsidies that the university provides. Providing subsidies on knowledge sharing is an incentive mechanism through which the university shares more knowledge than without subsidies. In addition, under the condition of the cooperative game, we find that the participation level of the university's knowledge flow is always higher than that under the other two situations in UICI. The "1 + 1 > 2" effect is formed through the cooperation, and thus the results of the above theorems are verified.

In Fig. 10.2, with the ratio in profit distribution increasing, no matter in the case of Nash unbalanced cooperation or Stackelberg leader-follower game, the participation level of the university's knowledge flow increases continuously in UICI, and the participation levels are the same under the two conditions. In addition, under the condition of the cooperative game, we find that the participation level of the enterprise's knowledge flow is always higher than that under the other two situations in UICI. The "1 + 1 > 2" effect is formed through the cooperation, and thus the results of the above theorems are verified.

In Fig. 10.3, with the passage of time t, under the condition of Stackelberg cooperation, the profit that the university gains through participation in the knowledge flow in UICI tends to be constant with increasing time and is always higher than that under the condition of Nash noncooperation. Thus, the results of the theorems are verified.

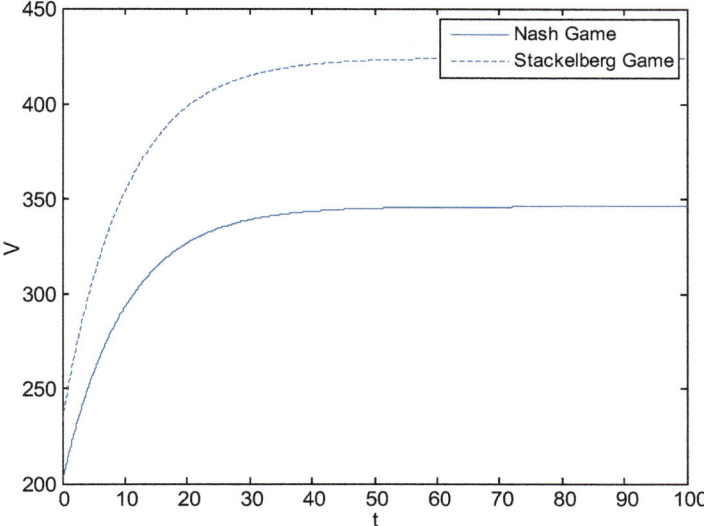

Fig. 10.3 Comparison on the profits of knowledge flow of the university under different situations

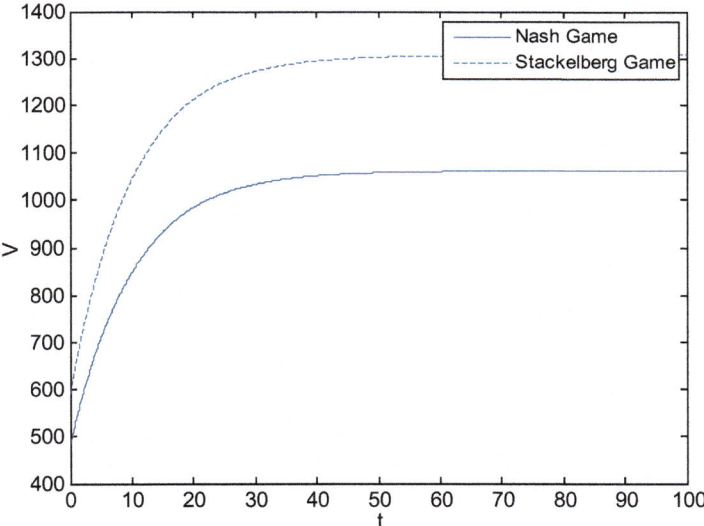

Fig. 10.4 Comparison on the profits of knowledge flow of the enterprise under different situations

In Fig. 10.4 with the passage of time t, under the condition of Stackelberg cooperation, the profit that the enterprise gains through participation in the knowledge flow in UICI tends to be constant with increasing time and is always higher than that under the condition of Nash noncooperation. Thus, the results of the theorems are verified.

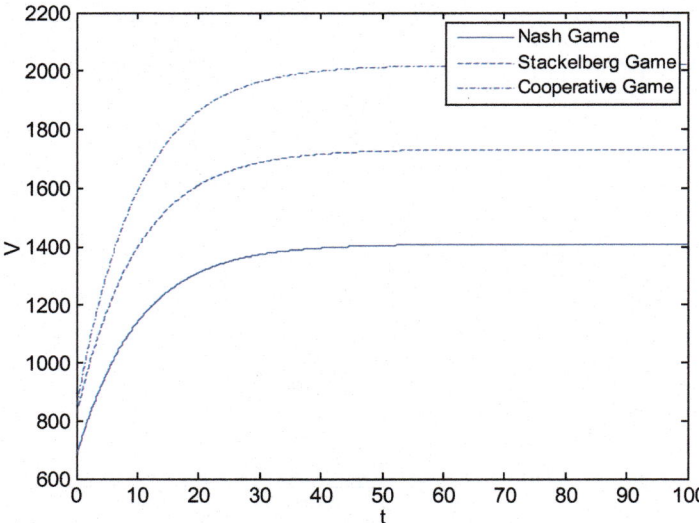

Fig. 10.5 Comparison on the total profits of knowledge flow in the process of university-industry collaborative innovation under different situations

In Fig. 10.5, with the passage of time t, under the condition of cooperative game, the total profits of knowledge flow of the university and the enterprise are higher than those under the condition of Stackelberg cooperation and Nash noncooperation. Thus, the results of the theorems are verified. At the same time, we find that the total profits of knowledge flow in UICI tend to be constant with increasing time.

10.5   Conclusion

This chapter uses the differential game theory to study the problem of knowledge flow of the university and the enterprise in UICI and establishes a stochastic differential game model. The Hamilton-Jacobi-Bellman (HJB) equation is used to obtain the respective strategies of knowledge flow of the university and the enterprise in the case of Nash noncooperative game, Stackelberg leader-follower game, and cooperative game. The three kinds of games are then compared and analyzed.

The results show that no matter in a Nash noncooperative game, Stackelberg leader-follower game, or cooperative game, the cost c of knowledge flow is higher when a less amount of knowledge is shared. A greater ability r of knowledge innovation means that greater marginal profits of knowledge flow and that the university and the enterprise will share more knowledge. The higher the degree δ of knowledge spillovers is in the process of knowledge flow, the less amount of knowledge that is shared by both knowledge subjects.

For the profits of knowledge flow for the university and the enterprise, the Stackelberg leader-follower game equilibrium strategy is strictly superior to the Nash noncooperative game. For the profits of knowledge flow in the entire UICI system, the cooperative game structure is superior to the first two noncooperative game structures. If the final scheme in profit distribution is reasonable and feasible, then the scheme satisfies the university and the enterprise's individual rational constraints (or participation constraints) simultaneously. As a result, for the profits of knowledge flow to both sides, the cooperative game is Pareto optimal.

Chapter 11
Conclusion and Further Research

This book has presented systematical research for several key issues of knowledge flow in University-Industry Collaborative Innovation (UICI) in China.

In summary, Chap. 2 constructs the model of knowledge value chain in a university and analyzes the mechanism of university knowledge value added in the process of UICI. We then measure the DEA efficiency of university knowledge value added for 31 provinces in China. Beijing and 13 other provinces have higher university knowledge value-added efficiency, and the technical efficiency of universities in Yunnan is the highest among these provinces. The university knowledge value-added efficiency in Chongqing and 13 other provinces is ineffective.

Chapter 3 illustrates the cooperation mechanism of university and industry in the collaborative innovation system. Considering the complex internal structure of the collaborative innovation system, we establish a Network DEA model with parallel decision-making units to assess the performance of UICI in China. The results suggest that the average efficiency of collaborative innovation in China is 0.7642. However, the efficiencies in some provinces are lower, e.g., Shanxi, Liaoning, Inner Mongolia, and Heilongjiang. In addition, the provinces in developed areas tend to exhibit more diminishing returns to scale. In contrast, the provinces with increasing returns to scale are mainly in the less developed areas of central and western China. Furthermore, the UICI efficiencies in the eastern, northern, and southern coastal regions are higher than those in other areas of China.

Chapter 4 addresses an empirical study that relates Big Five personality traits to knowledge flow performance in UICI. We find that researchers' consciousness has a positive influence on the performance of knowledge flow in UICI and that trust in collaborative innovation has a mediating effect on the relationship between researchers' consciousness and knowledge flow in collaborative innovation. Distributive justice and procedural justice have a positive influence on the performance of knowledge flow in collaborative innovation. Distributive justice has a significantly moderating effect on the relationship between extraversion and the performance of knowledge flow in collaborative innovation.

© Springer International Publishing AG, part of Springer Nature 2018
Y. Yu et al., *Strategy and Performance of Knowledge Flow*,
International Series in Operations Research & Management Science 271,
https://doi.org/10.1007/978-3-319-77926-3_11

Chapter 5 investigates the relations between team goal, motivation, personality, and knowledge sharing performance in Collaborative R&D teams at Chinese universities. The motivation of tacit knowledge sharing can be divided into life motivation and social motivation. R&D team members' personalities have directly positive influences on tacit knowledge sharing motivation and have indirect effects on tacit knowledge sharing performance. Furthermore, team goals have indirect positive effects on tacit knowledge sharing performance.

Chapter 6 constructs a colored Petri net model of knowledge flow based on the knowledge life cycle in order to study the asynchronization and concurrency of tacit and explicit knowledge flows, as well as their distribution and patterns in the process of UICI. The chapter employs the "telecommunications switching" technology of University of Cambridge as a case to examine the knowledge flow process in collaborative innovation.

Chapter 7 employs the evolutionary game theory based on bounded rationality to explore the best evolutionary stable strategy (ESS) in the process of UICI. Knowledge share cost, knowledge disseminative capacity, knowledge absorptive capacity, knowledge innovative capacity, and knowledge potential difference among organizations play important roles in the knowledge flow process. They also affect the knowledge agent to select the evolutionary stable strategy.

Chapter 8 divides the knowledge agents into different types according to their various behaviors in the process of knowledge sharing in collaborative innovation. Considering the bounded rationality of knowledge agents, an agent-based model is constructed to illustrate the knowledge sharing process based on the theory of cellular automaton. The NetLogo platform is employed to simulate the knowledge sharing behavior of those different types of knowledge agents in this chapter.

Chapter 9 models knowledge flow in UICI as a barter process in which agents exchange knowledge. We find that high clustering coefficients and short paths can enhance the exchange of knowledge and improve knowledge sharing efficiency in the process of collaborative innovation.

Chapter 10 applies the differential game theory to analyze the knowledge flow between an enterprise and university in UICI. The equilibrium knowledge sharing strategies of the two are explored in a Nash game, Stackelberg game, and cooperative game using the Hamilton-Jacobi-Bellman equation. This chapter finds that the optimal profits of the enterprise and university in the Stackelberg game are higher than in the Nash game under certain conditions. The overall optimal UICI knowledge sharing profit in a cooperative game is higher than those in both the Nash and Stackelberg games.

Despite significant progress having been made for the research of knowledge flow in UICI in China with this book, there are still some topics that need further explorations in the future. The complexity of innovation processes leads to increasing interactions among different actors. For the sake of clarity, simplicity, and without loss of generality, in this study we only have examined the interaction between universities and industry, neglecting the role of government and public research institutions in UICI, especially when exploring the optimal strategy with the evolutionary game and differential game theories in Chaps. 9 and 10.

Throughout recent history, governments have played an important role in technology innovation (Pavitt 1976), helping to shape technological progress (Abernathy and Chakravarthy 1979). A government is seen as a special kind of actor that is able to motivate multiple technology players with diverse interests and capacities to participate in the innovation process and to ensure that they work together efficiently (Beerepoot and Beerepoot 2007). Furthermore, public research institutions (PRIs) are also the main actor in the national innovation system and are a primary tool for governments seeking to spur research and innovation in their economies (Diez 2000; OECD 2011; Suzuki et al. 2015). PRIs remain critical for countries' innovation and economic performance through their activities in creating, discovering, using, and diffusing knowledge. Their structures, functions, and performance are diverse across countries, and their activities vary according to their mission and type. Some perform "blue sky" research, while others focus on more short-term market-oriented projects. Other roles can include education and training, technology transfer, the provision of major scientific infrastructure, and the support of public policy. Their activities can help firms to expand their capabilities and generate spillovers for the wider economy (OECD 2011). PRIs have also played a particularly important role in China's national innovation system (NIS) (OECD 2008).

It is important for policy makers to well understand the complex knowledge flow process in collaborative innovation and to develop more practicable approaches to guide the process. Therefore, a more general knowledge flow model should be established for the new relationships among government, universities, industry, and research institutes during the process of collaborative innovation. One future direction is to investigate the efficiency of different collaborative innovation network structures and to develop effective tools for identifying the influencing factors by considering innovation risk (Merton 2013) in order to find the proper trade-off between risk and revenue in the knowledge flow process.

References

Abdullateef, E. (2000). Developing knowledge and creativity: Asset tracking as a strategy centerpiece. *The Journal of Arts Management, Law, and Society, 30*(3), 174–192. https://doi.org/10.1080/10632920009597311.

Abernathy, W. J., & Chakravarthy, B. S. (1979). Government intervention and innovation in industry: A policy framework. *Sloan Management Review, 20*(3), 3–18.

Albert, R., Jeong, H., & Barabási, A.-L. (1999). Diameter of the World-Wide Web. *Nature, 401*, 130. https://doi.org/10.1038/43601.

Ali, E. A., Halit, K., Hayat, A., & Zeki, O. (2017). Knowledge sharing barriers in software development teams: A multiple case study in Turkey. *Kybernetes, 46*(4), 603–620. https://doi.org/10.1108/K-04-2016-0081.

Allee, V. (1997). *The knowledge evolution: Expanding organizational intelligence.* Newton: Butterworth-Heinemann.

Allport, G. W. (1937). *Personality: A psychological interpretation.* New York: Henry Holt and Company.

Allport, G. W. (1961). *Pattern and growth in personality.* New York: Holt, Rinehart and Winston.

Allport, G. W., & Odbert, H. S. (1936). Trait-names: A psycho-lexical study. *Psychological Monographs, 47*(1), i-171. https://doi.org/10.1037/h0093360.

Alton, C. (2003). Knowledge sharing: A game people play. *ASLIB Proceedings, 55*(3), 117–129. https://doi.org/10.1108/00012530310472615.

Amaral, L. A. N., & Ottino, J. M. (2004). Complex networks. *The European Physical Journal B, 38* (2), 147–162. https://doi.org/10.1140/epjb/e2004-00110-5.

Amaral, L. A. N., Scala, A., Barthélémy, M., & Stanley, H. E. (2000). Classes of small-world networks. *Proceedings of the National Academy of Sciences, 97*(21), 11149–11152. https://doi.org/10.1073/pnas.200327197.

Ambos, T. C., Ambos, B., Eich, K. J., & Puck, J. (2016). Imbalance and isolation: How team configurations affect global knowledge sharing. *Journal of International Management, 22*(4), 316–332. https://doi.org/10.1016/j.intman.2016.03.005.

Andersen, P., & Petersen, N. C. (1993). A procedure for ranking efficient units in data envelopment analysis. *Management Science, 39*(10), 1261–1264.

Anderson, T. R., Daim, T. U., & Lavoie, F. F. (2007). Measuring the efficiency of university technology transfer. *Technovation, 27*(5), 306–318.

Arvanitis, S., Kubli, U., & Woerter, M. (2006). University-industry knowledge and technology transfer in Switzerland: What university scientists think about co-operation with private enterprises. *Research Policy, 37*(10), 1865–1883.

Avkiran, N. K. (2001). Investigating technical and scale efficiencies of Australian universities through data envelopment analysis. *Socio-Economic Planning Sciences, 35*(1), 57–80. https://doi.org/10.1016/S0038-0121(00)00010-0.

Bandyopadhyay, S., & Pathak, P. (2007). Knowledge sharing and cooperation in outsourcing projects — A game theoretic analysis. *Decision Support Systems, 43*(2), 349–358. https://doi.org/10.1016/j.dss.2006.10.006.

Banker, R. D., Charnes, A., & Cooper, W. W. (1984). Some models for estimating technical and scale inefficiencies in data envelopment analysis. *Management Science, 30*(9), 1078–1092.

Baron, R. M., & Kenny, D. A. (1986). The moderator-mediator variable distinction in social psychological research: Conceptual, strategic, and statistical considerations. *Journal of Personality and Social Psychology, 51*(6), 1173–1182.

Barrat, A., & Weigt, M. (2000). On the properties of small-world network models. *The European Physical Journal B - Condensed Matter and Complex Systems, 13*(3), 547–560. https://doi.org/10.1007/s100510050067.

Beerepoot, M., & Beerepoot, N. (2007). Government regulation as an impetus for innovation: Evidence from energy performance regulation in the Dutch residential building sector. *Energy Policy, 35*(10), 4812–4825. https://doi.org/10.1016/j.enpol.2007.04.015.

Bell, G. G., & Zaheer, A. (2007). Geography, networks, and knowledge flow. *Organization Science, 18*(6), 955–972.

Bernard, A., & Tichkiewitch, S. (2008). *Methods and tools for effective knowledge life-cycle-management*. Berlin: Springer.

Bettis, R. A., & Hitt, M. A. (1995). The new competitive landscape. *Strategic Management Journal, 16*(S1), 7–19. https://doi.org/10.1002/smj.4250160915.

Bhargava, S. C., Kumar, A., & Mukherjee, A. (1993). A stochastic cellular automata model of innovation diffusion. *Technological Forecasting and Social Change, 44*(1), 87–97. https://doi.org/10.1016/0040-1625(93)90008-U.

Birkinshaw, J., & Sheehan, T. (2002). Managing the knowledge life cycle. *MIT Sloan Management Review, 44*(1), 75–83.

Bonaccorsi, A., & Daraio, C. (2003). A robust nonparametric approach to the analysis of scientific productivity. *Research Evaluation, 12*(1), 47–69.

Bonaccorsi, A., & Piccaluga, A. (1994). A theoretical framework for the evaluation of university-industry relationships. *R&D Management, 24*(3), 229–247.

Bower, D. J. (1993). Successful joint ventures in science parks. *Long Range Planning, 26*(6), 114–120. https://doi.org/10.1016/0024-6301(93)90213-Y.

Brenda, K., Yajiong, X., & Yongjun, L. (2016). Factors influencing knowledge sharing among global virtual teams. *Team Performance Management: An International Journal, 22*(5/6), 284–300. https://doi.org/10.1108/TPM-10-2015-0042.

Brunner, P. H., & Rechberger, H. (2004). Practical handbook of material flow analysis. *The International Journal of Life Cycle Assessment, 9*(5), 337–338.

Bui, H. T. (2017). Big five personality traits and job satisfaction. *Journal of General Management, 42*(3), 21–30. https://doi.org/10.1177/0306307016687990.

Cabrera, E. F., & Cabrera, A. (2005). Fostering knowledge sharing through people management practices. *The International Journal of Human Resource Management, 16*(5), 720–735. https://doi.org/10.1080/09585190500083020.

Cabrera, Á., Collins, W. C., & Salgado, J. F. (2006). Determinants of individual engagement in knowledge sharing. *The International Journal of Human Resource Management, 17*(2), 245–264. https://doi.org/10.1080/09585190500404614.

Cai, G., & Kock, N. (2009). An evolutionary game theoretic perspective on e-collaboration: The collaboration effort and media relativeness. *European Journal of Operational Research, 194*(3), 821–833. https://doi.org/10.1016/j.ejor.2008.01.021.

Carayol, N., & Roux, P. (2009). Knowledge flows and the geography of networks: A strategic model of small world formation. *Journal of Economic Behavior & Organization, 71*(2), 414–427. https://doi.org/10.1016/j.jebo.2009.02.005.

Carlucci, D., Marr, B., & Schiuma, G. (2004). The knowledge value chain: How intellectual capital impacts on business performance. *International Journal of Technology Management, 27*(6–7), 575–590. https://doi.org/10.1504/ijtm.2004.004903.

Casimir, G., Lee, K., & Loon, M. (2012). Knowledge sharing: Influences of trust, commitment and cost. *Journal of Knowledge Management, 16*(5), 740–753. https://doi.org/10.1108/13673271211262781.

Cattell, R. B. (1943a). The description of personality. I. Foundations of trait measurement. *Psychological Review, 50*(6), 559–594. https://doi.org/10.1037/h0057276.

Cattell, R. B. (1943b). The description of personality: Basic traits resolved into clusters. *The Journal of Abnormal and Social Psychology, 38*(4), 476–506. https://doi.org/10.1037/h0054116.

Cattell, R. B. (1945). The description of personality: Principles and findings in a factor analysis. *The American Journal of Psychology, 58*, 69–90. https://doi.org/10.2307/1417576.

Charnes, A., & Cooper, W. (1962). Programming with linear fractional functionals. *Naval Research Logistics Quarterly, 9*(3–4), 181–186. https://doi.org/10.1002/nav.3800090303.

Charnes, A., Cooper, W. W., & Rhodes, E. (1978). Measuring the efficiency of decision making units. *European Journal of Operational Research, 2*(6), 429–444.

Chen, Y., Cook, W. D., Kao, C., & Zhu, J. (2013). Network DEA pitfalls: Divisional efficiency and frontier projection under general network structures. *European Journal of Operational Research, 226*(3), 507–515. https://doi.org/10.1016/j.ejor.2012.11.021.

Cheng, J. H., Yeh, C. H., & Tu, C. W. (2008). Trust and knowledge sharing in green supply chains. *Supply Chain Management: An International Journal, 13*(4), 283–295. https://doi.org/10.1108/13598540810882170.

Chong, C. W., Teh, P.-L., & Tan, B. C. (2014). Knowledge sharing among Malaysian universities' students: Do personality traits, class room and technological factors matter? *Educational Studies, 40*(1), 1–25. https://doi.org/10.1080/03055698.2013.825577.

Cohen, W., & Levinthal, D. (1990). Absorptive capacity: A new perspective on learning and innovation. *Administrative Science Quarterly, 35*(1), 128–152. https://doi.org/10.2307/2393553.

Colquitt, J. A. (2001). On the dimensionality of organizational justice: A construct validation of a measure. *The Journal of Applied Psychology, 86*(3), 386–400.

Cook, W. D., Zhu, J., Bi, G., & Yang, F. (2010). Network DEA: Additive efficiency decomposition. *European Journal of Operational Research, 207*(2), 1122–1129. https://doi.org/10.1016/j.ejor.2010.05.006.

Cooke, P., Kaufmann, D., Levin, C., & Wilson, R. (2006). The biosciences knowledge value chain and comparative incubation models. *The Journal of Technology Transfer, 31*(1), 115–129. https://doi.org/10.1007/s10961-005-5025-3.

Cooper, W. W., Park, K. S., & Pastor, J. T. (1999). RAM: A range adjusted measure of inefficiency for use with additive models, and relations to other models and measures in DEA. *Journal of Productivity Analysis, 11*(1), 5–42. https://doi.org/10.1023/a:1007701304281.

Cooper, W. W., Seiford, L. M., & Tone, K. (2007). *Data envelopment analysis: A comprehensive text with models, applications, references and DEA-solver software.* New York: Springer US.

Cooper, W. W., Seiford, L. M., & Zhu, J. (2011). Data envelopment analysis: History, models, and interpretations. In W. W. Cooper, L. M. Seiford, & J. Zhu (Eds.), *Handbook on data envelopment analysis.* New York: Springer US.

Costa, P. T., & MacCrae, R. R. (1985). *The NEO personality inventory manual.* Odessa: Psychological Assessment Resources.

Costa, P. T., & MacCrae, R. R. (1992). *Revised NEO personality inventory (NEO PI-R) and NEO five-factor inventory (NEO-FFI): Professional manual.* Odessa: Psychological Assessment Resources.

Cowan, R., & Jonard, N. (2004). Network structure and the diffusion of knowledge. *Journal of Economic Dynamics and Control, 28*(8), 1557–1575. https://doi.org/10.1016/j.jedc.2003.04.002.

Cress, U., & Martin, S. (2006). Knowledge sharing and rewards: A game-theoretical perspective. *Knowledge Management Research & Practice, 4*(4), 283–292. https://doi.org/10.1057/pal grave.kmrp.8500112.

Cyr, S., & Choo, C. W. (2010). The individual and social dynamics of knowledge sharing: An exploratory study. *Journal of Documentation, 66*(6), 824–846. https://doi.org/10.1108/00220411011087832.

de Moor, M. H. M., Costa, P. T., Terracciano, A., Krueger, R. F., de Geus, E. J. C., Toshiko, T., et al. (2012). Meta-analysis of genome-wide association studies for personality. *Molecular Psychiatry, 17*(3), 337–349. https://doi.org/10.1038/mp.2010.128.

DeYoung, C. G., Hirsh, J. B., Shane, M. S., Papademetris, X., Rajeevan, N., & Gray, J. R. (2010). Testing predictions from personality neuroscience. *Psychological Science, 21*(6), 820–828. https://doi.org/10.1177/0956797610370159.

DiCesare, F., Harhalakis, G., Proth, J.-M., Silva, M., & Vernadat, F. (1993). *Practice of petri nets in manufacturing.* Dordrecht: Springer.

Diez, J. R. (2000). The importance of public research institutes in innovative networks-empirical results from the metropolitan innovation systems Barcelona, Stockholm and Vienna. *European Planning Studies, 8*(4), 451–463. https://doi.org/10.1080/713666418.

Ding, Z., Ng, F., & Li, J. (2014). A parallel multiple mediator model of knowledge sharing in architectural design project teams. *International Journal of Project Management, 32*(1), 54–65. https://doi.org/10.1016/j.ijproman.2013.04.004.

Drucker, P. F. (1998). *Harvard business review on knowledge management.* Boston: Harvard Business Press.

Drucker, P. F. (2006). *The practice of management (Reissue ed.).* New York: Harper Business.

Dyer, J. H., & Chu, W. (2000). The determinants of trust in supplier-automaker relationships in the U.S., Japan and Korea. *Journal of International Business Studies, 31*(2), 259–285. https://doi.org/10.1057/palgrave.jibs.8490905.

Dyer, J. H., Kale, P., & Singh, H. (2004). When to ally and when to acquire. *Harvard Business Review, 82*(7–8), 108–115.

Eustace, C. (2003). A new perspective on the knowledge value chain. *Journal of Intellectual Capital, 4*(4), 588–596.

Fare, R., & Grosskopf, S. (1985). A nonparametric cost approach to scale efficiency. *Scandinavian Journal of Economics, 87*(4), 594–604.

Färe, R., & Grosskopf, S. (1996). Productivity and intermediate products: A frontier approach. *Economics Letters, 50*(1), 65–70. https://doi.org/10.1016/0165-1765(95)00729-6.

Färe, R., & Grosskopf, S. (2000). Network DEA. *Socio-Economic Planning Sciences, 34*(1), 35–49. https://doi.org/10.1016/S0038-0121(99)00012-9.

Farrell, M. J. (1957). The measurement of productive efficiency. *Journal of the Royal Statistical Society. Series A (General), 120*(3), 253–290. https://doi.org/10.2307/2343100.

Franić, S., Borsboom, D., Dolan, C. V., & Boomsma, D. I. (2014). The big five personality traits: Psychological entities or statistical constructs? *Behavior Genetics, 44*(6), 591–604. https://doi.org/10.1007/s10519-013-9625-7.

French, J. W. (1953). *The description of personality measurements in terms of rotated factors.* Princeton: Educational Testing Service.

Fuentes, M. A., & Kuperman, M. N. (1999). Cellular automata and epidemiological models with spatial dependence. *Physica A: Statistical Mechanics and its Applications, 267*(3–4), 471–486. https://doi.org/10.1016/S0378-4371(99)00027-8.

Gagné, M. (2009). A model of knowledge-sharing motivation. *Human Resource Management, 48*(4), 571–589. https://doi.org/10.1002/hrm.20298.

Ghobadi, S. (2015). What drives knowledge sharing in software development teams: A literature review and classification framework. *Information Management, 52*(1), 82–97. https://doi.org/10.1016/j.im.2014.10.008.

Ghobadi, S., & D'Ambra, J. (2013). Modeling high-quality knowledge sharing in cross-functional software development teams. *Information Processing & Management, 49*(1), 138–157. https://doi.org/10.1016/j.ipm.2012.07.001.

Goldberg, L. R. (1981). Language and individual differences: The search for universals in personality lexicons. In L. Wheeler (Ed.), *Review of personality and social psychology.* California: Sage Publications.

Goldberg, L. R. (1982). From Ace to Zombie: Some explorations in the language of personality. In C. D. Spielberger, J. N. Butcher, & C. D. Spielberger (Eds.), *Advances in personality assessment* (Vol. 1). New York: Routledge.

Goldberg, L. R. (1990). An alternative "description of personality": The big-five factor structure. *Journal of Personality and Social Psychology, 59*(6), 1216–1229. https://doi.org/10.1037/0022-3514.59.6.1216.

Goldberg, L. R. (1992). The development of markers for the big-five factor structure. *Psychological Assessment, 4*(1), 26–42. https://doi.org/10.1037/1040-3590.4.1.26.

Grant, R. M. (1996). Toward a knowledge-based theory of the firm. *Strategic Management Journal, 17*(S2), 109–122. https://doi.org/10.1002/smj.4250171110.

Greenberg, J. (1987). A taxonomy of organizational justice theories. *Academy of Management Review, 12*(1), 9–22. https://doi.org/10.5465/amr.1987.4306437.

Greenberg, J. (1990). Organizational justice: Yesterday, today, and tomorrow. *Journal of Management, 16*(2), 399–432. https://doi.org/10.1177/014920639001600208.

Guan, J., & Chen, K. (2012). Modeling the relative efficiency of national innovation systems. *Research Policy, 41*(1), 102–115.

Guan, J., & Wang, J. (2004). Evaluation and interpretation of knowledge production efficiency. *Scientometrics, 59*(1), 131–155. https://doi.org/10.1023/B:SCIE.0000013303.25298.ae.

Guan, J., & Zuo, K. (2014). A cross-country comparison of innovation efficiency. *Scientometrics, 100*(2), 541–575.

Hagedoorn, J., Link, A. N., & Vonortas, N. S. (2000). Research partnerships1This paper has benefited from the insightful comments and suggestions of Andy Brod and Kathy Combs.1. *Research Policy, 29*(4), 567–586. https://doi.org/10.1016/S0048-7333(99)00090-6.

Harari, M. B., Jain, N. K., & Joseph, T. (2014). The five-factor model of personality and knowledge transfer in the United Arab Emirates. *International Journal of Selection and Assessment, 22*(4), 399–410. https://doi.org/10.1111/ijsa.12086.

Hau, Y. S., Kim, B., Lee, H., & Kim, Y.-G. (2013). The effects of individual motivations and social capital on employees' tacit and explicit knowledge sharing intentions. *International Journal of Information Management, 33*(2), 356–366. https://doi.org/10.1016/j.ijinfomgt.2012.10.009.

Heintze, N. (1995). Control-flow analysis and type systems. In A. Mycroft (Ed.), *Static analysis. SAS 1995. lecture notes in computer science* (Vol. 983). Berlin/Heidelberg: Springer.

Holsapple, C. W., & Singh, M. (2001). The knowledge chain model: Activities for competitiveness. *Expert Systems with Applications, 20*(1), 77–98.

Homans, G. C. (1958). Social Behavior as Exchange. *American Journal of Sociology, 63*(6), 597–606.

Hsu, B.-F., Wu, W.-L., & Yeh, R.-S. (2011). Team personality composition, affective ties and knowledge sharing: A team-level analysis. *International Journal of Technology Management, 53*(2–4), 331–351. https://doi.org/10.1504/ijtm.2011.038597.

Hu, J., Guan, Y., & Fan, X. (2010). The innovation efficiency of industry-University- Research Cooperation based on DEA. In 2010 3rd international conference on information management, innovation management and industrial engineering, 26–28 Nov. 2010 (Vol. 3, pp. 345–348), Kunming, China. https://doi.org/10.1109/ICIII.2010.403 .

Huang, C.-C. (2009). Knowledge sharing and group cohesiveness on performance: An empirical study of technology R&D teams in Taiwan. *Technovation, 29*(11), 786–797. https://doi.org/10.1016/j.technovation.2009.04.003.

Huang, X., He, P., & Zhang, W. (2016). A cooperative differential game of transboundary industrial pollution between two regions. *Journal of Cleaner Production, 120*, 43–52. https://doi.org/10.1016/j.jclepro.2015.10.095.

Hung, S.-Y., Durcikova, A., Lai, H.-M., & Lin, W.-M. (2011). The influence of intrinsic and extrinsic motivation on individuals' knowledge sharing behavior. *International Journal of Human-Computer Studies, 69*(6), 415–427. https://doi.org/10.1016/j.ijhcs.2011.02.004.

Inzelt, A. (2004). The evolution of university–industry–government relationships during transition. *Research Policy, 33*(6–7), 975–995. https://doi.org/10.1016/j.respol.2004.03.002.

Jadin, T., Gnambs, T., & Batinic, B. (2013). Personality traits and knowledge sharing in online communities. *Computers in Human Behavior, 29*(1), 210–216. https://doi.org/10.1016/j.chb.2012.08.007.

Jafari Navimipour, N., & Charband, Y. (2016). Knowledge sharing mechanisms and techniques in project teams: Literature review, classification, and current trends. *Computers in Human Behavior, 62*, 730–742. https://doi.org/10.1016/j.chb.2016.05.003.

Janssen, O., Lam, C. K., & Huang, X. (2010). Emotional exhaustion and job performance: The moderating roles of distributive justice and positive affect. *Journal of Organizational Behavior, 31*(6), 787–809. https://doi.org/10.1002/job.614.

Jensen, K. (1994). *An introduction to the theoretical aspects of coloured petri nets*. New York: Springer.

Johnes, J., & Yu, L. (2008). Measuring the research performance of Chinese higher education institutions using data envelopment analysis. *China Economic Review, 19*(4), 679–696. https://doi.org/10.1016/j.chieco.2008.08.004.

Jørgensen, S., & Zaccour, G. (2004). A brief tutorial on differential games. In S. Jørgensen & G. Zaccour (Eds.), *Differential games in marketing*. Boston: Springer.

Judge, T. A., & Zapata, C. P. (2015). The person–situation debate revisited: Effect of situation strength and trait activation on the validity of the big five personality traits in predicting job performance. *Academy of Management Journal, 58*(4), 1149–1179. https://doi.org/10.5465/amj.2010.0837.

Kalling, T. (2003). Organization-internal transfer of knowledge and the role of motivation: A qualitative case study. *Knowledge and Process Management, 10*(2), 115–126. https://doi.org/10.1002/kpm.170.

Kao, C. (2014). Efficiency decomposition in network data envelopment analysis with slacks-based measures. *Omega, 45*, 1–6. https://doi.org/10.1016/j.omega.2013.12.002.

Kari, J. (2005). Theory of cellular automata: A survey. *Theoretical Computer Science, 334*(1), 3–33. https://doi.org/10.1016/j.tcs.2004.11.021.

Kari, J. (2012). Basic concepts of cellular automata. In G. Rozenberg, T. Bäck, & J. N. Kok (Eds.), *Handbook of natural computing*. Berlin Heidelberg: Springer.

Keeling, M. J. (1999). The effects of local spatial structure on epidemiological invasions. *Proceedings of the Royal Society of London. Series B: Biological Sciences, 266*(1421), 859–867. https://doi.org/10.1098/rspb.1999.0716.

Kleinberg, J. M. (2000). Navigation in a small world. *Nature, 406*, 845. https://doi.org/10.1038/35022643.

Kleingeld, A., van Mierlo, H., & Arends, L. (2011). The effect of goal setting on group performance: A meta-analysis. *Journal of Applied Psychology, 96*(6), 1289–1304. https://doi.org/10.1037/a0024315.

Koessler, F. (2004). Strategic knowledge sharing in Bayesian games. *Games and Economic Behavior, 48*(2), 292–320. https://doi.org/10.1016/j.geb.2003.10.002.

Koschatzky, K., & Stahlecker, T. (2010). New forms of strategic research collaboration between firms and universities in the German research system. *International Journal of Technology Transfer and Commercialisation, 9*(1–2), 94–110. https://doi.org/10.1504/ijttc.2010.029427.

Kumar, N., Scheer, L., Jan-Benedict, E. M., & Steenkamp. (1995). The effects of supplier fairness on vulnerable resellers. *Journal of Marketing Research, 32*(1), 54–65. https://doi.org/10.2307/3152110.

Kwong, J. Y. Y., & Cheung, F. M. (2003). Prediction of performance facets using specific personality traits in the Chinese context. *Journal of Vocational Behavior, 63*(1), 99–110. https://doi.org/10.1016/S0001-8791(02)00021-0.

Lambertini, L., & Mantovani, A. (2010). Process and product innovation: A differential game approach to product life cycle. *International Journal of Economic Theory, 6*(2), 227–252. https://doi.org/10.1111/j.1742-7363.2010.00132.x.

Latham, G. P., & Locke, E. A. (2007). New developments in and directions for goal-setting research. *European Psychologist, 12*(4), 290–300. https://doi.org/10.1027/1016-9040.12.4.290.

Leavitt, H. J., & Bahrami, H. (1989). *Managerial psychology: Managing behavior in organizations*. Chicago: University of Chicago Press.

Lee, C. C., & Yang, J. (2000). Knowledge value chain. *Journal of Management Development, 19* (9), 783–794.

Leonard-Barton, D. (1988). Implementation as mutual adaptation of technology and organization. *Research Policy, 17*(5), 251–267. https://doi.org/10.1016/0048-7333(88)90006-6.

Leventhal, G. S. (1980). What should be done with equity theory? In K. J. Gergen, M. S. Greenberg, & R. H. Willis (Eds.), *Social exchange: Advances in theory and research* (pp. 27–55). Boston: Springer US.

Levin, D. Z., & Cross, R. (2004). The strength of weak ties you can trust: The mediating role of trust in effective knowledge transfer. *Management Science, 50*(11), 1477–1490. https://doi.org/10.1287/mnsc.1030.0136.

Lewis, H. F., & Sexton, T. R. (2004). Network DEA: Efficiency analysis of organizations with complex internal structure. *Computers & Operations Research, 31*(9), 1365–1410. https://doi.org/10.1016/S0305-0548(03)00095-9.

Leydesdorff, L., & Etzkowitz, H. (1996). Emergence of a Triple Helix of university—Industry—Government relations. *Science and Public Policy, 23*(5), 279–286. https://doi.org/10.1093/spp/23.5.279.

Leydesdorff, L., & Guoping, Z. (2001). University—Industry—Government relations in China. *Industry and Higher Education, 15*(3), 179–182. https://doi.org/10.5367/000000001101295632.

Li, Y.-M., & Jhang-Li, J.-H. (2010). Knowledge sharing in communities of practice: A game theoretic analysis. *European Journal of Operational Research, 207*(2), 1052–1064. https://doi.org/10.1016/j.ejor.2010.05.033.

Li, D., Ma, J., Tian, Z., & Zhu, H. (2015). An evolutionary game for the diffusion of rumor in complex networks. *Physica A: Statistical Mechanics and its Applications, 433*, 51–58. https://doi.org/10.1016/j.physa.2015.03.080.

Lin, M., & Li, N. (2010). Scale-free network provides an optimal pattern for knowledge transfer. *Physica A: Statistical Mechanics and its Applications, 389*(3), 473–480. https://doi.org/10.1016/j.physa.2009.10.004.

Liu, B. (2011). Study on performance of industry-university cooperation based on DEA. In 2011 international conference on business management and electronic information, 13–15 May 2011 (Vol. 4, pp. 168–171), Guangzhou, China. https://doi.org/10.1109/ICBMEI.2011.5920944

Liu, Y., & Phillips, J. S. (2011). Examining the antecedents of knowledge sharing in facilitating team innovativeness from a multilevel perspective. *International Journal of Information Management, 31*(1), 44–52. https://doi.org/10.1016/j.ijinfomgt.2010.05.002.

Liu, D., Kumar, S., & Mookerjee, V. S. (2012). Advertising strategies in electronic retailing: A differential games approach. *Information Systems Research, 23*(3-part-2), 903–917. https://doi.org/10.1287/isre.1110.0377.

Locke, E. A., Latham, G. P., Smith, K. J., Wood, R. E., & Bandura, A. (1990). *A theory of goal setting & task performance*. Englewood Cliffs: Prentice Hall College Div.

Lodi-Smith, J., & Roberts, B. W. (2007). Social investment and personality: A meta-analysis of the relationship of personality traits to investment in work, family, religion, and volunteerism. *Personality & Social Psychology Review, 11*(1), 68–86. https://doi.org/10.1177/1088868306294590.

Lu, L., & Etzkowitz, H. (2008). Strategic challenges for creating knowledge-based innovation in China: Transforming triple helix university-government-industry relations. *Journal of Technology Management in China, 3*(1), 5–11. https://doi.org/10.1108/17468770810851476.

Lundvall, B.-A. (1992). *National systems of innovation: Towards a theory of innovation and interactive learning.* London: Pinter Pub Ltd.

Luo, Y. (2007). The independent and interactive roles of procedural, distributive, and interactional justice in strategic alliances. *Academy of Management Journal, 50*(3), 644–664. https://doi.org/10.5465/amj.2007.25526452.

Ma, Z., Lee, Y., & Chen, C.-F. P. (2009). Booming or emerging? China's technological capability and international collaboration in patent activities. *Technological Forecasting and Social Change, 76*(6), 787–796. https://doi.org/10.1016/j.techfore.2008.11.003.

Maslow, A. H. (1987). *Motivation and personality* (3rd ed.). New York: Harper & Row.

Matzler, K., Renzl, B., Müller, J., Herting, S., & Mooradian, T. A. (2008). Personality traits and knowledge sharing. *Journal of Economic Psychology, 29*(3), 301–313. https://doi.org/10.1016/j.joep.2007.06.004.

Matzler, K., Renzl, B., Mooradian, T., von Krogh, G., & Mueller, J. (2011). Personality traits, affective commitment, documentation of knowledge, and knowledge sharing. *The International Journal of Human Resource Management, 22*(2), 296–310. https://doi.org/10.1080/09585192.2011.540156.

McAdams, D. P., & Olson, B. D. (2010). Personality development: Continuity and change over the life course. *Annual Review of Psychology, 61*(1), 517–542. https://doi.org/10.1146/annurev.psych.093008.100507.

McAdams, D. P., & Pals, J. L. (2006). A new big five: Fundamental principles for an integrative science of personality. *The American Psychologist, 61*(3), 204–217.

McCrae, R. R., & Costa, P. T. (1983). Joint factors in self-reports and ratings: Neuroticism, extraversion and openness to experience. *Personality and Individual Differences, 4*(3), 245–255. https://doi.org/10.1016/0191-8869(83)90146-0.

McCrae, R. R., & Costa, P. T. (2008). The five-factor theory of personality. In O. P. John, R. W. Robins, & L. A. Pervin (Eds.), *Handbook of personality: Theory and research.* New York: The Guilford Press.

McKnight, D. H., Choudhury, V., & Kacmar, C. (2002). Developing and validating trust measures for e-Commerce: An integrative typology. *Information Systems Research, 13*(3), 334–359. https://doi.org/10.1287/isre.13.3.334.81.

Merton, R. C. (2013). Innovation risk: How to make smarter decisions. *Harvard Business Review, 91*(4), 48–56.

Metcalfe, M. (2005). Knowledge sharing, complex environments and small-worlds. *Human Systems Management, 24*(3), 185–195.

Milgram, S. (1967). The small-world problem. *Psychology Today, 1*(1), 61–67.

Minbaeva, D. B. (2008). HRM practices affecting extrinsic and intrinsic motivation of knowledge receivers and their effect on intra-MNC knowledge transfer. *International Business Review, 17*(6), 703–713. https://doi.org/10.1016/j.ibusrev.2008.08.001.

Mischel, W. (2004). Toward an integrative science of the person. *Annual Review of Psychology, 55*, 1–22.

Mooradian, T., Renzl, B., & Matzler, K. (2006). Who trusts? Personality, trust and knowledge sharing. *Management Learning, 37*(4), 523–540. https://doi.org/10.1177/1350507606073424.

Moorman, C., Zaltman, G., & Deshpande, R. (1992). Relationships between providers and users of market research:The dynamics of trust within and between organizations. *Journal of Marketing Research, 29*(3), 314–328. https://doi.org/10.2307/3172742.

Mu, J., Peng, G., & Love, E. (2008). Interfirm networks, social capital, and knowledge flow. *Journal of Knowledge Management, 12*(4), 86–100. https://doi.org/10.1108/13673270810884273.

Murray, H. A. (1938). *Explorations in personality.* New York: Oxford University Press.

Nelson, R. R. (1993). *National innovation systems: A comparative analysis*. New York: Oxford University Press.

Newman, M. E. J. (2000). Models of the small world. *Journal of Statistical Physics, 101*(3), 819–841. https://doi.org/10.1023/a:1026485807148.

Nierstrasz, O. M. (1985). Message flow analysis. In D. C. Tsichritzis (Ed.), *Office automation. topics in information systems*. Berlin/ Heidelberg: Springer.

Nigg, J. T., John, O. P., Blaskey, L. G., Huang-Pollock, C. L., Willcutt, E. G., Hinshaw, S. P., et al. (2002). Big five dimensions and ADHD symptoms: Links between personality traits and clinical symptoms. *Journal of Personality and Social Psychology, 83*(2), 451–469. https://doi.org/10.1037/0022-3514.83.2.451.

Nonaka, I. (1994). A dynamic theory of organizational knowledge creation. *Organization Science, 5*(1), 14–37. https://doi.org/10.1287/orsc.5.1.14.

Nonaka, I., Toyama, R., & Hirata, T. (2008). *Managing flow - A process theory of the knowledge-based firm*. London: Palgrave Macmillan UK.

Norman, W. T. (1963). Toward an adequate taxonomy of personality attributes: Replicated factor structure in peer nomination personality ratings. *The Journal of Abnormal and Social Psychology, 66*(6), 574–583. https://doi.org/10.1037/h0040291.

Odum, E. P. (1968). Energy flow in ecosystems: A historical review. *American Zoologist, 8*(1), 11–18.

OECD. (2008). *OECD reviews of innovation policy: China*. Paris: OECD Publishing.

OECD. (2011). *Public Research Institutions: Mapping sector trends*. Paris: OECD Publishing.

Olaisen, J., & Revang, O. (2017). The dynamics of intellectual property rights for trust, knowledge sharing and innovation in project teams. *International Journal of Information Management, 37*(6), 583–589. https://doi.org/10.1016/j.ijinfomgt.2017.05.012.

O'leary-kelly, A. M., Martocchio, J. J., & Frink, D. D. (1994). A review of the influence of group goals on group performance. *Academy of Management Journal, 37*(5), 1285–1301. https://doi.org/10.2307/256673.

Ozer, D. J., & Benet-Martínez, V. (2006). Personality and the prediction of consequential outcomes. *Annual Review of Psychology, 57*, 401–421.

Pavitt, K. (1976). Government policies towards innovation: A review of empirical findings. *Omega, 4*(5), 539–558. https://doi.org/10.1016/0305-0483(76)90005-0.

Perkmann, M., & Walsh, K. (2007). University–industry relationships and open innovation: Towards a research agenda. *International Journal of Management Reviews, 9*(4), 259–280. https://doi.org/10.1111/j.1468-2370.2007.00225.x.

Picazo-Vela, S., Chou, S. Y., Melcher, A. J., & Pearson, J. M. (2010). Why provide an online review? An extended theory of planned behavior and the role of big-five personality traits. *Computers in Human Behavior, 26*(4), 685–696. https://doi.org/10.1016/j.chb.2010.01.005.

Pinjani, P., & Palvia, P. (2013). Trust and knowledge sharing in diverse global virtual teams. *Information Management, 50*(4), 144–153. https://doi.org/10.1016/j.im.2012.10.002.

Polanyi, M. (2015). *Personal knowledge: Towards a post-critical philosophy*. Chicago: University of Chicago Press.

Porter, M. E. (1996). What is strategy? *Harvard Business Review, 86*(5), 926–929.

Poyago-Theotoky, J., Beath, J., & Siegel, D. S. (2002). Universities and fundamental research: Reflections on the growth of University–Industry partnerships. *Oxford Review of Economic Policy, 18*(1), 10–21. https://doi.org/10.1093/oxrep/18.1.10.

Quigley, N. R., Tesluk, P. E., Locke, E. A., & Bartol, K. M. (2007). A multilevel investigation of the motivational mechanisms underlying knowledge sharing and performance. *Organization Science, 18*(1), 71–88. https://doi.org/10.1287/orsc.1060.0223.

Rahm, D., Kirkland, J., & Bozeman, B. (2000). *University-Industry R&D Collaboration in the United States, the United Kingdom, and Japan*. Netherlands: Springer.

Reisig, W. (1985). *Petri nets: An introduction*. New York: Springer.

Richard, J., & Wayne, W. (2009). Using agent based simulation and game theory analysis to study knowledge flow in organizations: The KMscape. *International Journal of Knowledge Management (IJKM), 5*(1), 17–28. https://doi.org/10.4018/jkm.2009010102.

Robbins, S. P., & Judge, T. A. (2014). *Organizational behavior* (16th ed.). New York: Pearson.

Rosendaal, B., & Bijlsma-Frankema, K. (2015). Knowledge sharing within teams: Enabling and constraining factors. *Knowledge Management Research & Practice, 13*(3), 235–247. https://doi.org/10.1057/kmrp.2013.45.

Rousseau, D. M., Sitkin, S. B., Burt, R. S., & Camerer, C. (1998). Not so different after all: A cross-discipline view of trust. *Academy of Management Review, 23*(3), 393–404. https://doi.org/10.5465/amr.1998.926617.

Sabel, C. F. (1993). Studied trust: Building new forms of cooperation in a volatile economy. *Human Relations, 46*(9), 1133–1170. https://doi.org/10.1177/001872679304600907.

Salimifard, K., & Wright, M. (2001). Petri net-based modelling of workflow systems: An overview. *European Journal of Operational Research, 134*(3), 664–676.

Samaddar, S., & Kadiyala, S. S. (2006). An analysis of interorganizational resource sharing decisions in collaborative knowledge creation. *European Journal of Operational Research, 170*(1), 192–210. https://doi.org/10.1016/j.ejor.2004.06.024.

Samieh, H. M., & Wahba, K. (2007). Knowledge sharing behavior from game theory and socio-psychology perspectives. In *40th annual Hawaii international conference on system sciences, 3-6 Jan. 2007 (pp. 187c–187c)*. Big Island: University of Hawaii. https://doi.org/10.1109/HICSS.2007.319.

Santoro, M. D., & Gopalakrishnan, S. (2000). The institutionalization of knowledge transfer activities within industry–university collaborative ventures. *Journal of Engineering and Technology Management, 17*(3), 299–319. https://doi.org/10.1016/S0923-4748(00)00027-8.

Santoro, M. D., & Saparito, P. A. (2003). The firm's trust in its university partner as a key mediator in advancing knowledge and new technologies. *IEEE Transactions on Engineering Management, 50*(3), 362–373. https://doi.org/10.1109/TEM.2003.817287.

Savolainen, R. (2009). Small world and information grounds as contexts of information seeking and sharing. *Library & Information Science Research, 31*(1), 38–45. https://doi.org/10.1016/j.lisr.2008.10.007.

Schmit, M. J., & Ryan, A. M. (1993). The big five in personnel selection: Factor structure in applicant and nonapplicant populations. *Journal of Applied Psychology, 78*(6), 966–974. https://doi.org/10.1037/0021-9010.78.6.966.

Seibert, S. E., & Kraimer, M. L. (2001). The five-factor model of personality and career success. *Journal of Vocational Behavior, 58*(1), 1–21. https://doi.org/10.1006/jvbe.2000.1757.

Seiford, L. M., & Thrall, R. M. (1990). Recent developments in DEA. *Journal of Econometrics, 46*(1), 7–38. https://doi.org/10.1016/0304-4076(90)90045-U.

Selten, R. (1983). Evolutionary stability in extensive two-person games. *Mathematical Social Sciences, 5*(3), 269–363. https://doi.org/10.1016/0165-4896(83)90012-4.

Shalley, C. E., Zhou, J., & Oldham, G. R. (2004). The effects of personal and contextual characteristics on creativity: Where should we go from here? *Journal of Management, 30*(6), 933–958. https://doi.org/10.1016/j.jm.2004.06.007.

Shi, Y., & Guan, J. (2016). Small-world network effects on innovation: Evidences from nanotechnology patenting. *Journal of Nanoparticle Research, 18*(11), 329. https://doi.org/10.1007/s11051-016-3637-1.

Shih, M.-H., Tsai, H.-T., Wu, C.-C., & Lu, C.-H. (2006). A holistic knowledge sharing framework in high-tech firms: Game and co-opetition perspectives. *International Journal of Technology Management, 36*(4), 354–367. https://doi.org/10.1504/ijtm.2006.010272.

Shim, J. (2010). *The relationship between workplace incivility and the intention to share knowledge: The moderating effects of collaborative climate and personality traits*. Minneapolis: University of Minnesota.

Sikhar, B., Gaurav, A., Zhang, W. J., Biswajit, M., & Tiwari, M. K. (2012). A decision framework for the analysis of green supply chain contracts: An evolutionary game approach. *Expert Systems with Applications, 39*(3), 2965–2976. https://doi.org/10.1016/j.eswa.2011.08.158.

Silva, M., & Teruel, E. (1997). Petri nets for the design and operation of manufacturing systems. *European Journal of Control, 3*(3), 182–199.

Simon, H. A. (1955). A behavioral model of rational choice. *The Quarterly Journal of Economics, 69*(1), 99–118. https://doi.org/10.2307/1884852.

Simonin, B. L. (1999). Ambiguity and the process of knowledge transfer in strategic alliances. *Strategic Management Journal, 20*(7), 595–623. https://doi.org/10.1002/(SICI)1097-0266 (199907)20:7<595::AID-SMJ47>3.0.CO;2-5.

Smith, J. M., & Price, G. R. (1973). The logic of animal conflict. *Nature, 246*(5427), 15–18.

Sorenson, O., Rivkin, J. W., & Fleming, L. (2006). Complexity, networks and knowledge flow. *Research Policy, 35*(7), 994–1017. https://doi.org/10.1016/j.respol.2006.05.002.

Srivastava, A., Bartol, K. M., & Locke, E. A. (2006). Empowering leadership in management teams: Effects on knowledge sharing, efficacy, and performance. *Academy of Management Journal, 49*(6), 1239–1251. https://doi.org/10.5465/amj.2006.23478718.

Strogatz, S. H. (2001). Exploring complex networks. *Nature, 410*(6825), 268–276. https://doi.org/10.1038/35065725.

Suzuki, J., Tsukada, N., & Goto, A. (2015). Role of Public Research Institutes in Japan's National Innovation System: Case study of AIST, RIKEN and JAXA. *Science, Technology and Society, 20*(2), 133–160. https://doi.org/10.1177/0971721815579793.

Swink, M. (2006). Building collaborative innovation capability. *Research-Technology Management, 49*(2), 37–47. https://doi.org/10.1080/08956308.2006.11657367.

Tang, C., & Naumann, S. E. (2015). Team diversity, mood, and team creativity: The role of team knowledge sharing in Chinese R&D teams. *Journal of Management & Organization, 22*(3), 420–434. https://doi.org/10.1017/jmo.2015.43.

Taylor, P. D., & Jonker, L. B. (1978). Evolutionary stable strategies and game dynamics. *Mathematical Biosciences, 40*(1), 145–156. https://doi.org/10.1016/0025-5564(78)90077-9.

Teh, P.-L., Yong, C.-C., Chong, C.-W., & Yew, S.-Y. (2011). Do the big five personality factors affect knowledge sharing behaviour? A study of Malaysian universities. *Malaysian Journal of Library & Information Science, 16*(1), 47–62.

Teigland, R., & Wasko, M. (2009). Knowledge transfer in MNCs: Examining how intrinsic motivations and knowledge sourcing impact individual centrality and performance. *Journal of International Management, 15*(1), 15–31. https://doi.org/10.1016/j.intman.2008.02.001.

Tett, R. P., & Burnett, D. D. (2003). A personality trait-based interactionist model of job performance. *Journal of Applied Psychology, 88*(3), 500–517.

Tone, K. (2001). A slacks-based measure of efficiency in data envelopment analysis. *European Journal of Operational Research, 130*(3), 498–509.

Tone, K., & Tsutsui, M. (2009). Network DEA: A slacks-based measure approach. *European Journal of Operational Research, 197*(1), 243–252.

Tupes, E. C., & Christal, R. E. (1992). Recurrent personality factors based on trait ratings. *Journal of Personality, 60*(2), 225–251.

Uzzi, B., Amaral, L. A. N., & Reed-Tsochas, F. (2007). Small-world networks and management science research: A review. *European Management Review, 4*(2), 77–91. https://doi.org/10.1057/palgrave.emr.1500078.

van der Aalst, W. M. (1998). The application of petri nets to workflow management. *Journal of circuits, systems, and computers, 8*(01), 21–66.

Vangen, S., & Huxham, C. (2003). Nurturing collaborative relations. *The Journal of Applied Behavioral Science, 39*(1), 5–31. https://doi.org/10.1177/0021886303039001001.

Vincent, T. L. (1985). Evolutionary games. *Journal of Optimization Theory and Applications, 46*(4), 605–612. https://doi.org/10.1007/bf00939163.

von Krogh, G., Nonaka, I., & Rechsteiner, L. (2012). Leadership in organizational knowledge creation: A review and framework. *Journal of Management Studies, 49*(1), 240–277. https://doi.org/10.1111/j.1467-6486.2010.00978.x.

Wang, Z. (2012). Knowledge integration in collaborative innovation and a self-organizing model. *International Journal of Information Technology & Decision Making, 11*(02), 427–440. https://doi.org/10.1142/s0219622012400093.

Wang, C. L., & Ahmed, P. K. (2005). The knowledge value chain: A pragmatic knowledge implementation network. *Handbook of Business Strategy, 6*(1), 321–326. https://doi.org/10.1108/08944310510558115.

Wang, C.-C., & Yang, Y.-J. (2007). Personality and intention to share knowledge: An empirical study of scientists in an R&D laboratory. *Social Behavior and Personality: An International Journal, 35*(10), 1427–1436. https://doi.org/10.2224/sbp.2007.35.10.1427.

Watts, D. J. (2004). The "new" science of networks. *Annual Review of Sociology, 30*(1), 243–270. https://doi.org/10.1146/annurev.soc.30.020404.104342.

Watts, D. J., & Strogatz, S. H. (1998). Collective dynamics of 'small-world' networks. *Nature, 393* (6684), 440–442.

Wei, J., Liu, L., & Francesco, C. A. (2010). A cognitive model of intra-organizational knowledge-sharing motivations in the view of cross-culture. *International Journal of Information Management, 30*(3), 220–230. https://doi.org/10.1016/j.ijinfomgt.2009.08.007.

Wilensky, U. (1999). *NetLogo.* http://ccl.northwestern.edu/netlogo/

Wolf, D. E. (1999). Cellular automata for traffic simulations. *Physica A: Statistical Mechanics and its Applications, 263*(1), 438–451. https://doi.org/10.1016/S0378-4371(98)00536-6.

Wolfram, S. (1984). Universality and complexity in cellular automata. *Physica D: Nonlinear Phenomena, 10*(1), 1–35. https://doi.org/10.1016/0167-2789(84)90245-8.

Xu, Y., & Bernard, A. (2010). Knowledge value chain: An effective tool to measure knowledge value. *International Journal of Computer Integrated Manufacturing, 23*(11), 957–967. https://doi.org/10.1080/0951192x.2010.500677.

Yao, W., Chen, J., & Si, Y. (2011). Research on the knowledge creation process of the university-industry collaboration: A case from China. *African Journal of Business Management, 5*(32), 12586–12597.

Yao, W., Han, X., & Li, Y. (2015). Cross-organizational knowledge creation theory from the perspective of I-Ching: Case study in Chinese aerospace industry. *Chinese Management Studies, 9*(4), 528–552. https://doi.org/10.1108/CMS-07-2015-0162.

Yu, Y., Hao, J.-X., Dong, X.-Y., & Khalifa, M. (2013). A multilevel model for effects of social capital and knowledge sharing in knowledge-intensive work teams. *International Journal of Information Management, 33*(5), 780–790. https://doi.org/10.1016/j.ijinfomgt.2013.05.005.

Zhao, R., Zhou, X., Han, J., & Liu, C. (2016). For the sustainable performance of the carbon reduction labeling policies under an evolutionary game simulation. *Technological Forecasting and Social Change, 112*, 262–274. https://doi.org/10.1016/j.techfore.2016.03.008.

Zhu, J. (2009). *Quantitative models for performance evaluation and benchmarking: Data envelopment analysis with spreadsheets.* New York: Springer US.

Zhu, Y.-Q. (2016). Solving knowledge sharing disparity: The role of team identification, organizational identification, and in-group bias. *International Journal of Information Management, 36* (6), 1174–1183. https://doi.org/10.1016/j.ijinfomgt.2016.08.003.

Zhuge, H. (2002a). A knowledge flow model for peer-to-peer team knowledge sharing and management. *Expert Systems with Applications, 23*(1), 23–30. Pii s0957-4174(02)00024-62391016/s0957-4174(02)00024-6.

Zhuge, H. (2002b). A knowledge grid model and platform for global knowledge sharing. *Expert Systems with Applications, 22*(4), 313–320.

Zhuge, H. (2004). *The knowledge grid* (Vol. 2012). Hackensack: World Scientific.

Zohar, D. (1995). The justice perspective of job stress. *Journal of Organizational Behavior, 16*(5), 487–495. https://doi.org/10.1002/job.4030160508.

Index

A

Agent-based, 7, 9, 107, 156
Agreeableness, 51–56, 58, 62, 64, 66, 67

B

Big five personality, 7, 8, 49–69, 155
Bounded rationality, 7, 8, 96, 97, 102, 108, 110, 113–114, 156

C

Cellular automaton, 9, 109–120, 156
Collaborative innovation, 1–8, 11–29, 49, 64, 95–108, 133–153, 155–157
Consciousness, 55, 56, 58, 155
Constant returns to scale (CRS), 20, 46
Cooperative game, 135, 145–146, 150, 152, 153, 156
Cost of knowledge transfer, 102, 105, 141

D

Data envelopment analysis (DEA), 7, 8, 12, 14–21, 23–25, 27, 30–39, 45, 155
Decreasing returns to scale, 43, 46
Differential game, 8, 9, 133–153, 156
Distributive justice, 57, 58, 60, 63, 65–67, 155

E

Emotional stability, 51, 53, 55, 56, 58, 62
Evolutionary game, 8, 95–108, 156

Evolutionary stable strategy (ESS), 8, 97, 99, 103–108, 156
Explicit knowledge, 8, 13, 75, 89–91, 94, 109, 156
Extroversion, 54–56, 58, 62, 69

H

Hamilton-Jacobi-Bellman (HJB) equation, 135, 139, 156

I

Increasing returns to scale, 42, 46, 155

K

Knowledge absorptive capacity, 101, 106, 108, 156
Knowledge acquisition, 1, 13, 84, 85, 87
Knowledge decline, 84, 129, 130
Knowledge flow, 7, 31, 49, 83, 96, 122, 134, 155
Knowledge flow performance, 8, 49, 55–58, 60, 61, 64, 65, 68, 69, 155
Knowledge innovation capacity, 107, 108
Knowledge integration, 6, 7, 30, 84, 85, 87, 106, 115, 134
Knowledge life cycle (KLC), 7, 8, 83–94, 156
Knowledge management, 12, 14, 83, 119, 121
Knowledge potential difference, 107–108, 156

© Springer International Publishing AG, part of Springer Nature 2018
Y. Yu et al., *Strategy and Performance of Knowledge Flow*,
International Series in Operations Research & Management Science 271,
https://doi.org/10.1007/978-3-319-77926-3

Printed by Printforce, the Netherlands